Mike Sharples

Orchestrating Inquiry Learning

There is a rapidly growing interest in inquiry learning and an emerging consensus among researchers that, particularly when supported by technology, it can be a significant means for developing higher order thinking skills. Inquiry learning methods also offer learners meaningful and productive approaches to the development of their knowledge of the world, yet such methods can present significant challenges for teachers and students.

Orchestrating Inquiry Learning addresses the key challenge of how to resource and support processes of inquiry learning within and beyond the classroom. It argues that technological support, when coupled with appropriate design of activities and management of the learning environment, can enable inquiry learning experiences that are engaging, authentic and personally relevant.

This edited collection brings together, for the first time, work on inquiry learning and orchestration of learning. Drawing upon a broad range of theoretical perspectives, this book examines:

- orchestration of inquiry learning and instruction;
- trajectories of inquiry learning;
- designing for inquiry learning;
- scripting personal inquiry;
- collaborative and collective inquiry learning;
- assessment of inquiry learning;
- inquiry learning in formal and semi-formal educational contexts.

Orchestrating Inquiry Learning is essential reading for all those concerned with understanding and promoting effective inquiry learning. The book is aimed at an international audience of researchers, post-graduate students, and advanced undergraduates in education, educational technology and psychology. It will also be of interest to educational practitioners and policy makers, including teachers, educational advisors, student-teachers and their trainers.

Karen Littleton is Professor of Psychology in Education at The Open University, UK, where she directs the interdisciplinary Centre for Research in Education and Educational Technology. She is the editor of the *International Journal of Educational Research* and is the editor-in-chief for Routledge's *Psychology in Education* book series.

Eileen Scanlon is Professor and Associate Director within the Institute of Educational Technology at The Open University, UK.

Mike Sharples was at the time of writing Professor of Learning Sciences at The University of Nottingham, UK, and is now Professor of Educational Technology at The Open University, UK.

Orchestrating Inquiry Learning

Edited by Karen Littleton, Eileen Scanlon and Mike Sharples

Routledge
Taylor & Francis Group

LONDON AND NEW YORK

First published 2012
by Routledge
2 Park Square, Milton Park, Abingdon, Oxon OX14 4RN

Simultaneously published in the USA and Canada
by Routledge
711 Third Avenue, New York, NY 10017

*Routledge is an imprint of the Taylor & Francis Group, an informa
business*

British Library Cataloguing in Publication Data
A catalogue record for this book is available from the British
Library

Library of Congress Cataloging in Publication Data
Orchestrating inquiry learning / edited by Karen Littleton, Eileen
Scanlon, and Mike Sharples.
p. cm.
Includes bibliographical references and index.
1. Inquiry-based learning. I. Littleton, Karen. II. Scanlon, Eileen.
III. Sharples, Mike, 1952-
LB1027.23.O73 2012
371.3--dc23
2011030145

ISBN: 978–0–415–60112–2 (hbk)
ISBN: 978–0–415–60113–9 (pbk)
ISBN: 978–0–203–13619–5 (ebk)

Typeset in Garamond
by Fakenham Prepress Solutions, Fakenham, Norfolk NR21 8NN

Printed and bound in Great Britain by
CPI Antony Rowe, Chippenham, Wiltshire

Dedication
This book is dedicated to the memory of Phil Scott.

Contents

Contributors

Stamatina Anastopoulou, National and Kapodistrian University of Athens, Greece.

Canan Blake, The Open University, UK.

Trevor Collins, The Open University, UK.

Ton de Jong, University of Twente, The Netherlands.

Michael Filsecker, Duisburg-Essen University, Germany.

Mark Gaved, The Open University, UK.

Kai Hakkarainen, University of Turku, Finland.

Daniel T. Hickey, Indiana University, USA.

Ann Jones, The Open University, UK.

Lucinda Kerawalla, The Open University, UK.

Arianit Kurti, Linnaeus University, Sweden.

Marcia C. Linn, University of California Berkeley, USA.

Karen Littleton, The Open University, UK.

Heidy Maldonado, Stanford University, USA.

Kevin W. McElhaney, University of California Berkeley, USA.

Marcelo Milrad, Linnaeus University, Sweden.

Paul Mulholland, The Open University, UK.

Roy Pea, Stanford University, USA.

Marilena Petrou, The Open University, UK.

Eileen Scanlon, The Open University, UK.

Mike Sharples, The Open University, UK.

Pirita Seitamaa-Hakkarainen, University of Helsinki, Finland.

Daniel Spikol, Linnaeus University, Sweden.

Marjut Viilo, University of Helsinki, Finland.

Bahtijar Vogel, Linnaeus University, Sweden.

Vibeke Vold, Uni Helse, Uni Research AS, Norway.

Barbara Wasson, University of Bergen, Norway.

Acknowledgements

This book is based, in part, upon work conducted under the auspices of the 'Personal Inquiry (PI): Designing for Evidence-based Inquiry Learning across Formal and Informal Settings' project. The project (ES/E020135/1) was a collaboration between the University of Nottingham and The Open University, and was funded by the ESRC/EPSRC under their Technology Enhanced Learning Initiative.

We wish to extend our warmest thanks to Stephanie Edwards who so professionally supported us during the preparation of the manuscript and to Natalie Eggleston for help with the production of the book proposal.

Sincere thanks are also due to Bruce Roberts, James Hobbs, Hamish Baxter and the team at Routledge for their professional support, and encouragement, during the production process.

Editorial introduction: Orchestrating inquiry learning

Karen Littleton, Mike Sharples and Eileen Scanlon

There is currently increased recognition amongst researchers that inquiry learning (interpreted as the ability to plan, carry out and interpret novel investigations), particularly when supported by technology, can foster the development of higher order thinking skills and offer learners a meaningful and productive approach to the development of their knowledge of the world. Science educationalists propose that young people need to know how to 'act like scientists' if they are to understand and contribute to the major scientific debates that are shaping our world. That said, inquiry learning presents challenges for both teachers and students. For example, pupils may experience difficulties in engaging with inquiry learning, forming appropriate investigations, designing and running experiments, and interpreting data. A key challenge, then, is how to resource and support processes of inquiry learning within and beyond the classroom. Other issues include motivating young people to see their world as a site for scientific investigation, engaging them in scientific discourse, integrating inquiry learning with the teaching of science principles, and designing new tools for investigatory learning. The work being reported in this book is intended to address these challenges.

The volume brings together work on inquiry learning and orchestration of learning, where orchestration is the planning, management and guidance of learning. The contributors are working at the cutting-edge of the field, and they represent a wide range of disciplinary contexts including human-computer interaction, science learning, psychology and education. A central argument is that technological support, when coupled with appropriate design of the activities and learning environment, can enable the orchestration of inquiry learning experiences that are engaging, authentic and personally relevant. The term 'orchestration', as you will see, carries subtle differences in emphasis for each of the teams of contributing authors. That said, this metaphor captures the important sense in which the focus of attention is channelled towards a specific aspect of an ongoing activity – there being shifts between what assumes prominence and what recedes, taking into consideration the contributions of the learners.

Our authors offer characterisations of the nature of inquiry learning. They attempt to specify the conditions and pedagogic contexts within which such learning can most effectively be promoted and are working to distil the results into concrete messages for practical application. A key focus for many authors is the inquiry learning that is conducted in and framed by the concerns of formal educational settings – for example, schools and colleges. Other learning contexts are also considered, including school grounds, homes, museums and discovery centres, streets and parkland. A theme of the book is how to connect learning within and beyond the classroom.

The volume opens with a review by Eileen Scanlon, Stamatina Anastopoulou and Lucinda Kerawalla (Chapter 1). Focusing particularly on inquiry learning in science, these colleagues are especially concerned to explore: a) how contemporary research can inform the design of inquiry learning experiences, and b) the ways in which technologies can be harnessed to resource and support inquiries such that learners come to develop their knowledge and understanding of the world. Two key issues emerge from this exploration. The first concerns the efficacy and value of 'personalizing' inquiries in ways that make them meaningful to learners – a process that may incorporate elements of personal relevance, choice and learner responsibility. Seen in these terms, personal inquiry cannot simply be equated with 'personal interest', rather it is the process of grounding scientific content and process in students' existing points of view and activities that can enable them to see the intellectual relevance of their learning activities. It is evident that helping learners reframe their everyday experiences in empirical and scientific terms is a substantive challenge. The simplistic use of the 'everyday' in educational contexts is problematic – not least because it trivialises the complex processes involved in meaning-making, and falls far short of the authenticity that is essential to engage young people and support learning. It may also be the case that some inquiries are too personal to be explored within an educational context. To explore some issues of personal relevance would be to engage learners in complex processes of negotiating, re-negotiating and managing identity work – processes full of the inherent possibility of invoking 'troubled identities' in relation to one's peers. Even preparing for such an activity might pose problems, for, as Murphy (2000) notes: 'even the imaginary gaze of critical peers is a major threat to [learners'] identities and significantly affects how they learn to position themselves in subjects. Positions that can constrain future learning'. A second substantive focus concerns how educators might harness the pedagogic potential and affordances of representations of the inquiry cycle to resource the process of teaching and learning. Scanlon and her colleagues argue that representations of the inquiry cycle can constitute powerful mediating tools that frame teaching-learning interactions in ways that scaffold learners to gain meta-cognitive awareness of inquiry processes. For these authors, it is in the creative alignment and interplay of teacher, learner(s), mediating tools/technologies, and activities of which efficacious personal inquiry learning is constituted – with orchestration being the process that productively supports interventions across multiple activities and contexts occurring at multiple social levels. Orchestration is thus construed as a process that is necessarily and inherently adaptive to the emergent learning trajectory.

The significance of learning trajectories is explored in Chapter 2, by Karen Littleton and Lucinda Kerawalla, who focus specifically on the challenge educators confront in ensuring that young people have a coherent, cumulative experience of the diverse activities, ideas and settings that are implicated in the process of inquiry learning. These authors suggest that a crucial educational challenge facing teachers working on inquiry projects is how to ensure that the overall educational experience for the students is one that is genuinely *cumulative and reciprocal*, rather than simply extended in time. The work they present highlights how the affordances of the technologies in play distinctively enter into, and resource, the processes of *connection building* across phases of activity – such that from the learner's perspective, the work they are undertaking begins to develop a cumulative quality in which specific activities, and their goals, begin to form part of a greater whole – a purposeful educational 'journey' through which they come to understand the nature and processes of inquiry learning. The metaphor of 'orchestration' sits crucially at the heart of Littleton and Kerawalla's exploration, and for these authors the metaphor draws attention to the subtle interweaving of activities, ideas and resources and the ways in which a teacher may make (what are often moment-by-moment) shifts between what is fore-grounded and what is back-grounded in an ongoing inquiry. It also captures the sense in which a teacher encourages, and works with, learners' contributions in the context and pursuit of overall goals as part of a longer trajectory of meaning-making.

The necessity of working with learner's contributions is further underscored by Kevin W. McElhaney and Marcia C. Linn who, in Chapter 3, describe how their knowledge integration framework can strengthen inquiry instruction. Crucially, they argue that centring inquiry investigations on 'realistic and relevant' contexts encourages students to take advantage of their knowledge in designing experiments and in reasoning about their findings. Returning to the significance of personalisation (introduced earlier by Scanlon and colleagues) and the imperative to help learners build connections (Littleton and Kerawalla), McElhaney and Linn also underscore the efficacy of students testing *their* ideas rather than following a 'recipe' that may not *connect* to their prior conceptions or relevant everyday ideas. That said, they also caution that prevailing canonical notions of classroom science and what it entails may preclude authentic interpretations of inquiry investigations. Young people's 'interpretations of experience, the meanings they attach to their learning – will, in part, be determined by their involvement with schools and other institutions of their society ... schools have their own body of cultural knowledge, and their own ways of communicating and legitimizing knowledge' (Mercer, 1992, p.31). Learners' interactions and experiences are thus framed by, and therefore can only ever be fully understood within, their specific cultural niches. Different contexts will afford different opportunities for, and place different constraints upon, learning. According to McElhaney and Linn the implication of all this is that students need to 'let go' of their positioning as science students to assume the role of science investigators. Their work with the distinguishing task of *Airbags* exemplifies the substantial effect that subtle changes in the framing of inquiry tasks can have on student's insights. This in turn underscores that, whilst meaning is not a tangible or fixed commodity, in practice it is often assumed that educational 'tasks are given' (Murphy, 2000). The work reported in this chapter, however, reminds us that inquiry tasks are constructed through a complex process of interpretation and re-interpretation, emerging as a consequence of mediated action and interaction.

The complexity of the pedagogic challenges and the dilemmas facing teachers committed to inquiry learning are thrown into further relief by Sharples and Anastopoulou (Chapter 4). These authors underscore the delicate balance between the need to teach the fundamentals of a science topic in a well-structured way and the value of open-ended inquiry (where students may conduct investigations that yield inconclusive results, for instance). They also draw attention to the ways in which the teacher must be able to initiate and guide activities that take place beyond the classroom. Organizing inquiry learning for the home, or other sites where the teacher is not present, is a compelling pedagogic challenge, and the authors detail the work of the Personal Inquiry project designed to address this challenge through the development of a mobile toolkit specifically designed to support the orchestration of teaching activities across formal and non-formal settings. As the authors explain, the intention is 'to provide a seamless handover from teacher orchestration supported by the technology to technology guided personal inquiry'. The ways in which one can 'script' such technologically-mediated support for personal inquiry is the focus of Chapter 5.

Collins, Mullholland and Gaved (Chapter 5) argue that scripting support for personal inquiry necessarily entails an open approach that enables teachers and students to author or customise inquiries on personally relevant topics, which may span, for example, home, school and field trip contexts. Based on a theatrical metaphor, scripts characterise a set of activities which both engineer and harness differences between students' opinions or knowledge in order to foster effective learning. Crucially, students' actions and decisions can be reified through the tools they use to support their inquiry, and the chapter explores five aspects of personal inquiry that can be addressed through scripting support: personal choice; collaboration, regulatory process support, transformative process support and orchestration. The suggestion is that scripting provides a set of representations that are used for orchestration and involves the identification and co-ordination of students' activities, their learning process, and the technological support used. It is clear that scripting enables teachers to specify the overall structure of an inquiry and the options available to students. Both the activities undertaken and the students' progress through them can be shown in a scripting application. A crucial affordance here, then, is the potential of the technology to resource the linking of activities in meaningful ways which help lend cohesion and coherence to learners' experience of inquiry-based activities, especially those which extend over lengthy periods of time. The experienced and anticipated learning trajectory becomes rendered visible in ways intended to foster purposeful understanding. Given that changes to a script can be made at any time by a teacher in response to student progress, or to follow up issues of particular interest, significance or consequence, it is clear that, far from being prescriptive, scripts can support flexibly the more 'improvisational' elements of inquiry learning, where students and their teachers can explore and interrogate emerging questions and issues.

A commitment to participatory design is shared by many of the authors in the book and it is clear how researchers are increasingly undertaking work *with* teachers and other education professionals and students, rather than conducting research *on* them, thereby recognising them as people with concerns rather than treating them as objects of concern. This process of participatory design is in evidence in Chapter 6, where Roy Pea, Marcelo Milrad, Heidy Maldonado, Bahtijar Vogel, Arianit Kurti and Daniel Spikol discuss learning and technological designs for mobile science inquiry collaboratories. The chapter explores how this team moved from visions of mobile science inquiry, to co-design activities with educators, through system architecture and technical developments to the instantiation of mobile science collaboratories. Aiming to afford the seamless integration of, for example, data coming from multiple devices, Pea and colleagues' work carries important implications for enhancing the orchestration of inquiry-based learning activities. Moreover, the significance of representations as objects to think with and 'interthink' with (Mercer and Littleton 2007) is once again underscored.

The focus on collaborative inquiry that sits at the heart of Chapter 6 also assumes prominence in Chapter 7, where Marjut Viilo, Pirita Seitmaa-Hakkarainen and Kai Hakkarainen examine the practices of supporting collaborative inquiry. Their analyses of an elementary school teacher's practices and efforts to support pupils' cognitive responsibility for advancing their own collaborative-oriented inquiry process highlights how the epistemic, social, technological and cognitive infrastructure of the class are implicated in ensuring the efficacy of students' experience of inquiry. It is also evident from these authors' work that the orchestration of inquiry learning necessitates efforts that are strategically oriented at multiple levels (characterised here as the micro, macro and meso level) if serious inquiry is to be object-oriented.

At this point in the book the vexed issue of assessment is raised. The chapters presented thus far yield substantial evidence of creative and innovative approaches to the design of inquiry learning experiences. Yet assessment practices, often shaped by statutory imperatives, remain somewhat conservative and heavily reliant on individual testing methods. In Chapter 8, Daniel T. Hickey and Michael Filsecker summarise a comprehensive approach to instruction and assessment that uses situative theories of cognition, participatory views of learning and design-based methods to transform classroom assessment and educational testing. Adopting a broad view of assessment and testing, learning is aligned within embedded assessments of communal discourse to classroom assessments of individual understanding. This focus on the orchestration of assessment is taken up by Barbara Wasson, Vibeke Vold and Ton de Jong in Chapter 9. Wasson and colleagues argue that the orchestration of assessment in inquiry learning environments requires the careful design of mechanisms for both formative and summative assessment. Rooted in the learning by design literature, the work by these authors also shows the centrality of designed artifacts and emerging learning objects in both learning and assessment processes.

The volume ends with a contribution from Ann Jones, Canan Blake and Marilena Petrou, whose research addresses the issue of how to support inquiry learning in non-formal contexts. They suggest that given the increasing rise and importance of science inquiry learning in a range of less formal settings, it is imperative that we develop our understandings of how students learn in these settings, and how such learning might be supported and resourced by technologies. The Sustainability Squad investigation they report here represents an important contribution to this emerging field.

This is a book about multiplicity, plurality and complexity. The scholars who have contributed are engaged in a dynamic process of inquiry into inquiry learning. Through their work, involving committed engagement with teachers, learners and other education professionals, they are participating in an iterative research process that is producing invaluable support for theoretically-informed ways of promoting productive inquiry learning. And now the inquiry continues ...

References

Mercer, N. (1992) 'Culture, context and the construction of knowledge in the classroom', in Light, P. and Butterworth, G. (eds) *Context and Cognition: Ways of Learning and Knowing*, Hemel Hempstead, Harvester Wheatsheaf.

Murphy, P. (2000) 'Understanding the process of negotiation in social interaction', in R. Joiner, K. Littleton, D. Faulkner and D. Miell (eds) *Rethinking Collaborative Learning*, London: Free Association Press.

Chapter I

Inquiry learning reconsidered: contexts, representations and challenges

Eileen Scanlon, Stamatina Anastopoulou and Lucinda Kerawalla

Introduction

Inquiry learning is an educational approach with a long intellectual pedigree (see e.g. Dewey 1938; Bruner 1996). This chapter consists of a review of the literature on inquiry learning particularly related to inquiry learning in science subjects, exploring how this work has informed the design of inquiry learning experiences, and how inquiry-based learning supported by technology can afford learners at school a meaningful and productive approach to the development of their knowledge of the world.

The chapter considers approaches to inquiry learning, personalisation and the nature and effectiveness of different representations of the inquiry learning process. These issues are selected for consideration here because of our belief in the importance of personalisation of inquiries to make them meaningful to learners, and the importance of the representation of the processes of inquiry to overcome some of the difficulties which have been experienced in its implementation. The chapter also highlights the implications of this work for the teaching of inquiry – drawing on evidence to suggest that, when supported appropriately, learning by inquiry is a potentially effective strategy (see e.g. Chinn and Malhotra 2002).

Support for inquiry learning can be orchestrated using technological resources coupled with the appropriate design of activities and the learning environment (see e.g. Anastopoulou 2004). Orchestration is the metaphor we are using to describe the interplay between teacher, pupil, technology and activity. The chapter explores the variety of ways in which such support has been instantiated in practical terms, with the requirements for supporting personal inquiry being given particular consideration.

Approaches to inquiry learning

The consideration and reconsideration of the benefits of inquiry learning is a contemporary issue. We have used a working definition of inquiry-based learning as follows: 'inquiry-based learning involves learners asking questions about the natural or material world, collecting data to answer those questions, making discoveries and testing those discoveries rigorously' (de Jong 2006a p.532). The National Science Foundation (2008) defines inquiry as 'an approach to learning that involves a process of exploring the natural or material world, and that leads to asking questions, making discoveries, and rigorously testing those discoveries in the search for new understanding' (p. 20). There have been many empirical research studies in this field. For example, Edelson et al. (1999) has conducted a programme of research on the use of scientific visualisation technologies to support inquiry-based learning in the geosciences. Their aim was to help students develop an integrated understanding of science including a knowledge of scientific concepts, an understanding of scientific tools and media and inquiry skills. This understanding could be said to be similar to that which scientists have. Keselman (2003) describes inquiry learning as 'an educational activity in which students are placed in the position of scientists gathering knowledge about the world' (p. 898). This is not a straightforward position to put students in, as many commentators have noted. Further discussion of inquiry learning can be found in Scanlon et al., (in press).

A significant shift in the reconsideration of science curricula in the post-war years was the move to inquiry-based learning and laboratory-based experiences. Duschl and Grandy (2008) discuss the National Science Foundation (NSF)-sponsored curriculum developments of the 60s and 70s in the US, which had the aim of 'downgrading the role of the textbook in science teaching and elevate the role of investigative and laboratory experiences in science classrooms'. According to Joe Schwab (1962), first Director of Biological Sciences Curriculum Strategy, science education should be designed so that learning is 'enquiry into enquiry'. Reviewing the work of the last 50 years in the UK and US, Grandy and Duschl (2007) report on an NSF sponsored conference to reconsider the character and role of inquiry in school science which concluded that there was a need to develop an expanded notion of the scientific method, due to the importance of the role of models in the inquiry process.

These important insights raise issues to consider in a discussion of inquiry learning. For example, we might wonder what it is that children need to do to learn inquiry processes, what is the appropriate role of models in learning, what kind of models are necessary for us to consider and how best to develop a balance in learning science between learning inquiry skills and learning domain knowledge.

Recently too, there has been a fresh consideration of inquiry learning in other science-related activities. Bradley-Smith (2005) argues that the development of inquiry skills in Geography can enable students to become active global citizens by reflecting upon their own behaviours and giving them confidence to take action. In relation to Geography fieldwork, Ofsted (2008) argues that inquiry-based fieldwork 'sharpens and deepens learners' understanding of Geography and the progressive development of geographical skills, both in situ and in the lessons in school related to it' (p.34).

Anderson (2002) refers to the difficulty of making sense of the large number of empirical studies on inquiry learning, and of the number of meta-analyses conducted, due to the variety of conceptions of inquiry teaching used, but concludes that there is 'a pattern of general but not unequivocal support for inquiry teaching' (p.6). He describes the importance of preparing teachers for inquiry teaching, although it is less clear how to do so. This is in line with the view that learning by inquiry is a potentially effective strategy when supported appropriately (e.g. Chinn and Malhotra 2002; White and Frederiksen 1998). In addition to teacher preparation, other areas requiring support have also been identified. Recent work suggests that learners can find difficulties in applying the processes of hypothesis forming, experimentation and dealing with evidence and interpreting models (e.g. de Jong 2006a and b; Manlove et al. 2006). Learners often lack skills in regulating their own learning – for example, in planning, monitoring and effectively evaluating what they have learnt. In addition, Sandoval and Reiser (2004/2) report on difficulties that learners have in reconciling their ideas about the nature of science and those they need to use in inquiry learning settings. However, de Jong et al. (2006) indicate the specific difficulties that children have in engaging with inquiry learning, in addition to general meta-cognitive problems in failing to regulate their behaviour or plan effectively. In an extensive meta-review of studies on discovery learning with simulations, de Jong and van Joolingen (1998) isolate a range of difficulties that have been reported in other studies. This implies that children will need specific support in:

- designing appropriate experiments (e.g. what variables to chose, how many variables to change, how to state and test hypotheses) (de Jong and van Joolingen 1998)
- implementation of experiments (e.g. making predictions, avoiding being fixated with achieving particular results rather than testing hypotheses) (van Joolingen et al. 2005)
- interpreting results (e.g. children can misinterpret data and representations) (de Jong and Van Joolingen 1998; White and Frederiksen 2005).

Edelson et al. (1999) point out that discovery learning is not the only form of inquiry learning. They describe how a number of forms of inquiry learning have been explored including: controlled experimentation, modelling, synthesis of primary sources and exploration of quantitative data, each of which require the development of a particular set of skills. They also note that different subject domains in science have their own specific skills e.g. controlled experimentation in chemistry or psychology. Hodson (1998) argues also that it is important that students are able to engage in a wide variety of types of inquiry to improve their understanding of the nature of science. He also believes it is important that: 'worthwhile scientific activities can be conducted outdoors in the school grounds field centres, forests beaches and mountains and in museums zoos and botanic gardens' (p. 148). In these settings, students have the opportunity to work alongside scientists and to take part in community and environmental work (see chapters by Seitamaa-Hakkarainen,Viilo and Hakkarainen and Hickey and Filsecker (this volume)).

Grandy and Duschl (2007) refer to a particular challenge for learners in obtaining a perspective on scientific inquiry is how to contend with the transition from sense–perception-based science in early grade levels to theory-driven based science at later grade levels. They also note that scientists' contemporary experience of science is that it is, in practice, decreasingly about experiments and increasingly about data and data modelling. They also draw attention to the importance of promoting scientific discourse practices, a theme which is also elaborated on by Millar (2003) as of central importance as it requires the teacher to see him/herself less as a transmitter of information, reliant on a closed authoritative dialogue, and more as a facilitator of opportunities which enable discursive consideration and exploration by students of the epistemic and cognitive dimensions of science (p.3).

This is indeed a contentious statement. Sharples (2011) writes 'Many people would argue that teachers should not simply, or even largely, facilitate scientific discourse amongst students, but that they need also to communicate established scientific knowledge in a way that enables students to distinguish between scientific principles (e.g. Newton's Laws), scientific consensus (e.g. global warming, species evolution) and current scientific debate (e.g. existence of life on other planets). It's especially important to make these distinctions if children are to join debates in contemporary society'.

Challenges in inquiry learning

We have seen that there is a need to support the development of inquiry skills which can influence science teaching and learning practices so that students develop the knowledge and understanding they need to engage, as informed citizens, with science-based issues. There is a need for students to be supported to know where they are in an inquiry, and to follow a pattern of reflection on their data (e.g. selecting the useful data from the data collected, and constructing and interpreting representations, Chinn and Malhotra 2002; Kuhn and Pease 2008). There is a need for support in the selection of appropriate data to collect, and in selecting which contextual factors to consider during data collection. Researchers have studied in detail the particular challenges that inquiry learning poses with the following results.

Learners can find difficulties in applying the processes of hypothesis forming, experimentation, dealing with evidence and interpreting models (e.g. de Jong 2006; Manlove et al. 2006). Learners often lack skills in regulating their own learning – for example, in planning, monitoring and effectively evaluating what they have learnt. Thus, there is a need to support learners in managing inquiry learning. Most scientific enquiries, whether professional or by students, are collaborative (Driver et al. 2000), so learners also need support for effective collaboration (see e.g. Scardamalia 2002; Linn and Slotta 2006). Sandoval et al. (2002) suggest that many teachers, as well as their students, see science as being the discovery and collection of facts about the world, rather than as being theories that have been created by people. This is not to say that all theories are contested by the scientific community. The role of the scientific process of replication and hypothesis testing in validating theories is important here too. However it can be that experiments are seen to create answers rather than to test ideas. Often, children's participation in an activity is taken as sufficient for learning to take place, and teachers may not understand why children 'do not understand' by the end of it. Despite the considerable advances made by the conceptual change research traditions (see e.g. Driver et al. 2000; Zimmermann 2007), students' views are often still not seen as something to work from – they are either right or wrong, and little effort is made to understand why they think what they do. In these circumstances it is not surprising that teachers find inquiry teaching challenging. Sandoval et al. (2002) argue that: 'teachers' discourse needs to shift from a focus on descriptions of or implications about an activity, to an explicit analysis of the justifications behind particular activities and the evidence available for understanding them' (p.12).

In a study of 50 Key Stage 2 science lessons in UK primary schools (involving children aged 8–11 years old), Newton and Newton (2000) found that science teachers' discourse consists mainly of stating facts or asking children questions about descriptions and facts, with very little attention being paid to eliciting causal understanding, i.e. the reasons behind the facts. This is supported by Watson, Swain and Robbie (2004), whose study of science teaching in two Year 8 (12–13 years) science classes revealed that both the teachers and the children treated scientific inquiry as a set of routinized procedures to be completed in order to write a report. Consequently, children were unable to describe the aims of their inquiry, and unable to explain their findings. The lessons were not seen as an opportunity for discussion and decision-making. The authors suggested that the teachers lacked the pedagogical skills to stimulate and manage discussion. There is now developing a body of work that aims to develop such pedagogical skills (see, for example, Dawes et al. 2004).

Furtak (2005) illustrates that a significant challenge to teachers in inquiry learning environments is their ability to know how to deflect direct requests for domain knowledge from their pupils. She suggests that scientific inquiry is difficult to teach due to lack of lesson time, teachers' weak understanding of the nature of science, inappropriate curricula, and lack of pedagogical skills (Roehrig 2004; Tobin, Tippins, and Gallard 1994; Welch, Klopfer, Aikenhead, and Robinson 1981). Furtak points out also that the answers to most of the children's' inquiries are already known (i.e. the teacher knows the outcomes, and most children know that the teacher knows). She describes the classroom inquiry process in terms of 'guided scientific inquiry teaching', as opposed to the genuine open-ended scientific inquiry carried out by professional scientists. She argues that this can give rise to the 'teacher's dilemma', identified by Edwards and Mercer (1987), and described as the teacher 'hav[ing] to inculcate knowledge while apparently eliciting it' (p. 126). Furtak carried out a study with three teachers who videoed their own lessons over several weeks. She interviewed the teachers and analysed the video footage. She found that there were several ways in which these teachers dealt with their dilemma:

1 giving false 'don't knows' in response to queries;
2 telling students that they would not know the 'answer' for several weeks and that they were to spend time trying to work it out. All attempts were valued and respected. The pupils were advised what to focus on, without telling them precisely how;
3 quickly correcting or stopping themselves from giving an answer that was on the tip of their tongue;
4 pretending to be a humorous 'evil scientist' that will not tell them the answers;
5 explaining they will learn more if they work it out for themselves;
6 reflecting the questions back to the pupils.

Some of the teachers, particularly those with limited experience of inquiry learning, found this challenging and felt guilty that they could not answer their pupils' questions. This can make adherence to inquiry learning methods challenging. Interestingly, Millar (2002) argues that practical work in classrooms should not be criticised for being unlike that carried out by professional scientists. He argues that practical experimentation is about communicating the known rather than exploring the unknown. The focus of practical work should be on communicating ideas such as scientific models and methods, and is an opportunity for students to use scientific language and to learn how to see the world from a scientific perspective (see Scott 2009 for an account of talk in science classrooms).

Sandoval (2005) argues that simply engaging children in inquiry in schools in insufficient to change most students' ideas about the nature of science. He suggests that there is a mismatch between their inquiry practices and their expressed epistemological beliefs (which he describes as 'hopelessly naïve', p. 635). He argues that more attention should be paid to evaluating children's epistemologies by, for example, asking them to justify decisions that they make.

The aim of the Twenty First Century Science project pilot study was to evaluate a more flexible model of the science curriculum at Key Stage 4 (students aged 15–16) in England. It involved a three year study of work in 78 schools evaluating the reorganisation of the science curriculum into a central Core Science GCSE module based around Science Explanations and Ideas about Science prior to the introduction of Science in the 21st Century in 2008. The pilot was essentially a formative evaluation and the results were to be fed into the development of materials. Some of the studies were conducted in terms of the comparison of outcomes with students following the more traditional GCSE curriculum. In terms of learners' understanding, Scott et al. (2007) report that children involved in the pilot demonstrated a general improvement in most areas of 'Ideas about Science', but that they made a statistically significant improvement, compared to the comparison group, only in the area of 'data and its limitations'. Donnelly (2007), in his overview of all the pilot studies on the project, concludes that this lack of improvement is unlikely to be linked to teachers' reports that they found teaching 'Ideas about Science' difficult and demanding, and that most of their teaching was directed towards promoting conceptual understanding.

However, the hope was that this new curriculum can be effective in improving students' overall enthusiasm for science.

The role of technology in supporting inquiry learning

One way in which support for teachers and learners with the challenges of inquiry learning can be provided is by the judicious use of technology-enhanced learning.

Often the discourse about the power of technology in education is seen to be one of technological determinism on the one hand, and of scepticism on the other. For example, Cuban (2001) is an effective advocate of the importance of remaining sceptical about the inevitability of the technological influence on the future of schooling, but other commentators see technology as central to a transformation of schooling (see e.g. Sawyer's (2006) commentary on the importance of collaborative teaching and learning and computer networking). A number of commentators have commented on the broad notion of transformation. Alongside this there has been a body of work looking in detail at the specific support for inquiry learning which can be delivered by the judicious and thoughtful use of technology.

In Scanlon, Anastopoulou, Kerawalla and Mulholland (in press) we have recorded our agreement with Edelson et al. (1999) that: 'all of the fundamental properties of computing technologies can offer benefits for inquiry learning, such as the ability to store and manipulate large quantities of information, to present and permit interaction with information in a variety of visual and audio formats, to perform complex computations, to support communication and expression, and the ability to respond rapidly and individually to users. The question that arises is how these technological affordances can be integrated to enhance science teaching and learning practices so that students develop the knowledge and understanding they need to engage, as informed citizens, with science-based issues'. These properties are also important as they allow us to orchestrate inquiry learning activities.

There is a considerable history of the use of technologies to support inquiry learning with school children. Technologies that have been developed specifically to support inquiry learning have been focusing on:

- Tools for modelling phenomena and processes from the real world (e.g., Co-Lab, van Joolingen et al. 2005; SCI-WISE (ThinkerTools), Shimoda et al. 2002; SimQuest, van Joolingen et al.1997);
- Visualising and analysing quantitative data (e.g., GLOBE, Wormstead et al. 2002);
- Exchanging data and ideas across distances (e.g., GLOBE, Wormstead et al. 2002);
- Structuring and supporting discussion (e.g., WISE-SenseMaker, Bell and Linn 2000; Weinberger and Fischer 2006);
- Providing access to information in the form of digital collections and libraries (e.g., Knowledge-Integration Environment, Linn et al. 2003).

This list is based on one first presented in Edelson et al. (1999) with the addition of some more recent examples of studies, such as the GLOBE project (Wormstead et al. 2002). Global Learning and Observations to Benefit the Environment (GLOBE) is a unique program that enables school children to learn about the environment by taking scientific measurements of their natural surroundings. GLOBE is a worldwide network of students, teachers and scientists working together to study and understand the global environment. It is a student–teacher–scientist partnership in which students, with the support of their teachers, participate in and contribute to the research of scientists (Wormstead et al. 2002). GLOBE students make a core set of environmental observations at or near their schools, and report their data and communicate with scientists via GLOBE's web site (http://www.globe.gov), which enables them to share evidence with peers. The WorldWatcher project, (Edelson et al.1999; Edelson and Reiser 2006) involved visualising rich information.

There is another line of work surrounding engagement in informed debate. This is supported by technologies that incorporate data collection tools, different types of data visualisations (depending on the subject matter) and argumentation support tools. WISE provides an internet-based platform for middle and high school science activities where students work collaboratively on inquiry projects, making use of resources drawn from the Web. The technology serves to present content, as well as to scaffold students and teachers as they use this content collaboratively in designing, debating or critiquing inquiry topics. The Web-based Inquiry Science Environment (WISE) was a result of the experiences gained from two projects: Computer as Learning Partner (CLP, Linn and Hsi 2000) and Knowledge Integration Environment (KIE, Linn, Bell and Hsi 1998).

Probably the highest profile attempts to support inquiry learning with technology involve modelling and simulation environments. These allow multiple explorations of single or multiple variables (e.g., Co-Lab, van Joolingen et al. 2005). Within the Co-Lab (van Joolingen et al. 2005) environments, on which students work in small groups in a shared workspace, exploring 'phenomena' in the form of simulations and/or remote laboratories, to create their own models of these phenomena. In collaborative discovery learning environments, groups of students examine scientific phenomena and express their shared understanding through engaging in three analytically distinct processes – namely, inquiry, modelling and collaboration. In Co-Lab, these processes are not as distinct since collaboration runs as a continuous thread through the learning experience, affecting the way in which inquiry and modelling are performed and should be supported. Furthermore, modelling is integral to the inquiry process. Learners express their initial understanding of scientific phenomena in a model sketch, which is then used to predict and explain what will occur in the phenomena to be modelled. By testing these hypotheses with the simulation or the remote laboratory, learners gain knowledge they can use to refine or extend their model.

The dynamic website entitled the Web of Inquiry incorporates two previous prototype systems that were developed and tested within middle school science classrooms. The SCI-WISE system was a stand-alone multimedia program using modifiable 'advisors' (software agents) that allowed students to modify and select advice while working on science inquiry projects in an online workbook (Shimoda, White, and Frederiksen 2002). The main modules in the Web of Inquiry are a suite of advisors and advisor editor, a project template builder, a project workspace, a set of inquiry tools and a project assessment workspace (Shimoda 2006).

The design and use of SCI-WISE (Social and Cognitive Improvement within an Inquiry Support Environment, among other meanings) builds on earlier work on the Thinker Tools Inquiry Curriculum. They approach collaborative inquiry and reflective learning as the product of a social system of interacting agents, who each have expertise in accomplishing particular high-level goals (for information on Web of Inquiry SCI-WISE, see Shimoda 2006; for ThinkerTools, see White and Frederiksen 1998).

Recent developments

Two further projects investigating the role of technological support for inquiry learning are 'Science Created by You' and 'LET's GO' (Wasson et al.; Pea et al. 2011 (this volume)).

Science Created by You (SCY) is a EU-funded project producing a system for constructive and productive learning of science and technology, aiming at students between 12 and 18 years old, using a flexible and adaptive pedagogical approach to learning based on 'emerging learning objects' (ELOs) that are created by learners. Emerging learning objects, the construction of artefacts that emerge from the learning process, is one of the central ideas in SCY. Emerging Learning Objects are re-usable and sharable products of learning activities created by learners. The assumption behind Emerging Learning Objects is that learners create artefacts in partly unanticipated ways in phases of individual and small group work (e.g. Hoppe 2007). In the SCY project, students engage in inquiry learning activities supported by computer tools such as simulations and modelling software (de Jong, van Joolingen, and Weinberger 2009). In SCY-Lab, the SCY learning environment, students work on missions and meet challenges, collaboratively and individually supported by learning material, tools and scaffolds (for more information, see http://www.scy-net.eu).

These 'missions' are guided by a general socio–scientific question (for example 'how can we produce healthier milk?'). Fulfilling the mission requires a combination of knowledge from different domains (e.g. physics and mathematics, or biology and engineering) and several types of learning actions that can be characterised as productive (e.g. experiment, game, share, explain, design). Students encounter multiple resources, they collaborate with varying groups of peers, and they use changing sets of tools and scaffolds (e.g., to design a plan, to state a hypothesis, etc). The configuration of SCY-Lab is adaptive to the actual learning situation, advising students on appropriate learning actions, resources, tools and scaffolds, or peer learners that can support the learning process.

The SCY approach is enabled by the architecture of SCY-Lab that supports the creation, manipulation and sharing of ELOs (models, data sets, designs, plans, etc). In SCY Lab, students start with a research question and perform activities to answer that question. Students create models – for example, in relation to the milk question above, they might design nutrition schemes for cows, design and conduct experiments with virtual cows, and collect data 'in the field'. The work then provides the basis for writing a recommendation to farmers and the dairy industry. In this process, students have access to, and exchange their learning products or Emerging Learning Objects (ELOs) with, other learners.

The LET´s GO project is working on fostering high school student learning in teams for environmental science. Its vision of 'open inquiry' is defined as the opportunity to catalyze and sustain global learning using mobile science collaboratories that provide open software tools and resources, and online participation frameworks for learner project collaboration, mobile media and data capture, analysis, reflection and publishing (Lotan 2003; Pea and Maldonado 2006). The aim is to integrate geo-location sensing, multimedia communication, information visualization and Web 2.0 mash-up technologies, and to create science learning collaboratories using interdisciplinary research teams (Vogel et al. 2010). The aim of this rich type of technological environment is to provide an experimental arena for learning about complex topics in science through the process of exploring natural phenomena – as students use sensors and software tools for conducting systematic and collaborative investigations (Novak and Gleason 2001). Pea et al., in this volume, give a description of the first trials or iterations of these mobile inquiry science collaboratories.

These two projects raise new features to consider in our review of inquiry learning. The first emphasises collaboratively produced artefacts as a shared focus for development, and the second emphasises the potential for mobile learning to influence the contexts for science inquiry. Mobile technologies are providing new opportunities for teachers and learners to engage interactively with science learning, and in particular offer the opportunity to support inquiry learning across contexts, and to support the transitions made by learners across settings. Scanlon et al. (2005 p. 5) have drawn attention to the role that both mobility and collaboration can play in science learning, and asserts that 'Mobility and portability provide a communication channel between the technological wireless network and the social, face-to-face network, and mediate the social interaction of the participants during learning situations'. In both projects, there is also a consideration of the types of inquiry which may be motivating to learners, associated with inquiries of personal or societal relevance. The US National Science Foundation (2008) argues that cyber-learning (the use of networked computing and communications technologies to support learning) 'has the potential to transform learning throughout a lifetime, enabling customised interaction with diverse learning materials on any topic...' (p. 7). The UK strategy document 'Harnessing Technology: Next Generation Learning' (Becta, 2008) argues for the need for a strategy for learners to be engaged and empowered through the use of technology for learning, arguing that personalised learning needs to be improved through providing learners with choices.

Personalising inquiry

One approach to personalizing inquiry encourages the learner to be responsible for formulating their own stimulating hypothesis to investigate, and to construct the knowledge for themselves, rather than being given the knowledge in a conventional teacher-led lesson (see Hakkarainen and Sintonen 2002).

This approach will promote investigation of how the individual and community are affected by the environment, as well as investigation of how the individual and community interact, giving the students the opportunity to reflect upon how science may impact upon their own lives, and how their own behaviours may be contributing to the phenomenon they are studying. In this way, the students' inquiries can be distinctly personal in nature.

Personal inquiries can incorporate elements of:

- personal relevance;

- choice;
- learner responsibility.

In the next section we will consider the role of technology-enhanced learning to support shifts in context and personalisation of inquiries.

Technology to support shifts in contexts and personalisation

As we have seen there are powerful technologies which have been put to the service of supporting inquiry learning in terms of data collection, data visualisation and collaborative working. One limitation is that many previous projects focus on specific topics and contexts, or patterns of collaboration. Therefore the ability of technology to flexibly support work across contexts is relatively unexplored, as is the extent to which inquiries wholly designed by students and teachers are supported, and inquiries which include the whole inquiry process. To date there appears to be a dearth of studies where a flexible toolkit has been designed to support teachers and students throughout the whole inquiry process, across a range of settings, in carrying out inquiries which they can design. This is the imperative adopted by the work of the Personal Inquiry project, which has taken the view that personalisation is a key route to improving learning by inquiry.

Personal Inquiry project

The broad aim of the project was to understand how effective inquiry learning can be enabled with technology across formal and informal settings. More specifically, the focus was on designing blended support for evidence-based inquiry learning such that pupils aged 12–15 years old can be supported to understand the inquiry learning process. Learners are guided through a process of posing inquiry questions, gathering and assessing evidence, conducting experiments and engaging in informed debate on topic themes of personal relevance within the parameters of the secondary-level UK National Curriculum. More specifically, the focus was on designing blended support for evidence-based inquiry learning. We developed an innovative 'scripted inquiry learning' approach, where young people carry out scientific explorations supported by their teachers and also a personal inquiry toolkit. This toolkit, running on an Ultra-Mobile PC, provides 'scripts' in the form of dynamic lesson plans that guide the learners through a process of gathering and assessing evidence, conducting experiments and engaging in informed debate on topic themes of relevance to the secondary-level UK National Curriculum. Project partners include schools, technology companies that develop sensing and data-logging equipment, museums, community resource centres and fieldtrip sites. The particular slant of the project was to support personal inquiry.

Another key decision in the project was recognition of the need to represent the whole inquiry process to learners, to use this representation of the process to develop their understanding of how inquiry activities are interdependent and iterative and to support their progress through an inquiry (see Scanlon et al., in press).

Representations of the inquiry learning process

Representations of the inquiry learning process have been used extensively by researchers (e.g. Huffman et al. 2006; Bruce and Bishop 2002; Llewellyn 2002; Schwartz et al.1999) However, it is not always clear from accounts of their use in the literature whether the representation of the inquiry cycle is ever used by students themselves, or by researchers themselves as a conceptual tool. Our work has explored whether a representation of the inquiry cycle itself could be a powerful representation for students to become aware of inquiry processes and useful as a mediating tool in their work (see e.g. Scanlon et al., in press).

The most well known representation of the inquiry cycle in the literature is described by White and Frederiksen (1998), and has informed the design and mode of use of the ThinkerTools simulations and curriculum activities. Activities and environments enable students to carry out a sequence of activities that correspond to the steps in the Inquiry Cycle (White, Shimoda and Frederiksen 1999).

The Inquiry Cycle engages students in a six step inquiry (Question, Hypothesise, Investigate, Analyse, Model and Evaluate) and introduces them to criteria for evaluating their reasoning. Each of the inquiry steps was presented on a separate page of their 'reflection-assessment' tool called Project Journal, which augments the inquiry by unpacking the goals and sub-goals associated with each step. It also gives general advice rather than step-by step procedures (Shimoda, White and Frederiksen 2002). The Inquiry Cycle is presented as a sequence of goals to be pursued, thereby guiding the students' research, and is repeated with each module of the curriculum (White, Shimoda and Frederiksen 1999).

In this case, however, the inquiry process is represented as proceeding in one direction – i.e. students progress by moving forward from one phase to the next, and they have a specific starting point of the inquiry[1]. Presenting inquiry learning in this way does not highlight its iterative nature, which can be either between inquiries (the result of one inquiry being the starting point of another) or within them (retracing steps and revisiting phases). When the iterative nature of inquiry is addressed, it is unidirectional and outside the technological support, embedded in the curricular activities.

---

1 The Web of Inquiry (Shimoda, 2006) is an exception which represents inquiry as a fictional island, with phases in the periphery of the island and useful social, cognitive and reflective processes in the centre.

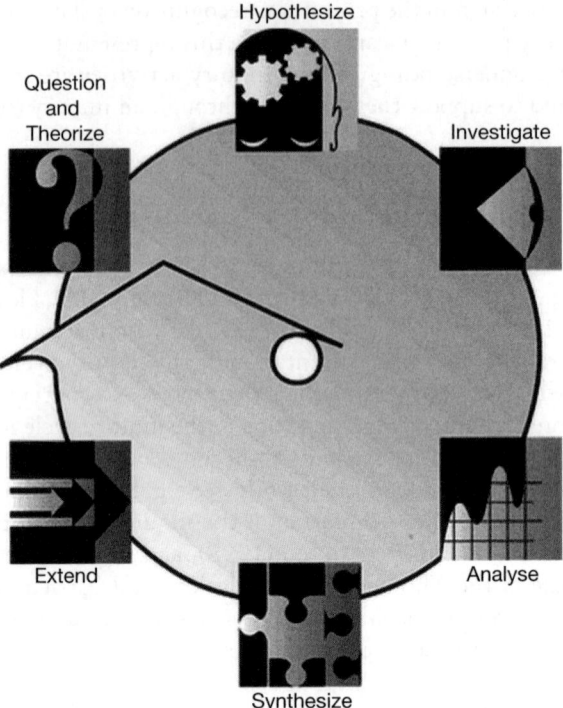

Figure 1.1 The Inquiry Cycle.

A different way of representing inquiry learning is offered by Wells (2001). His framework for dialogic inquiry divides the process of inquiry into three stages, outlines the aims and activities of each stage and the types of dialogue that could achieve the aims, so it is useful for a consideration of the activities of a class as a whole, and as a framework for teachers to use to design their activities. Well's model pays attention to the sequencing of activities in terms of scientific epistemology (research, interpret, present).

A similar approach is adopted by Weinberger, Stegmann, Fischer and Mandl (2007) who adopt a Learning by Design (LBD) approach to science learning. They discuss two interlinked iterative cycles of scripted activity in which scientific questions are answered through students building and testing models:

Cycle 1: Iterative design/redesign cycle. Understand challenge, plan design, present and share posters, construct and test, analyse and explain, present and share gallery walk.

Cycle 2: Iterative investigate and explore cycle. Clarify question, make hypothesis, design investigation, conduct investigation, analyse results, present and share poster session.

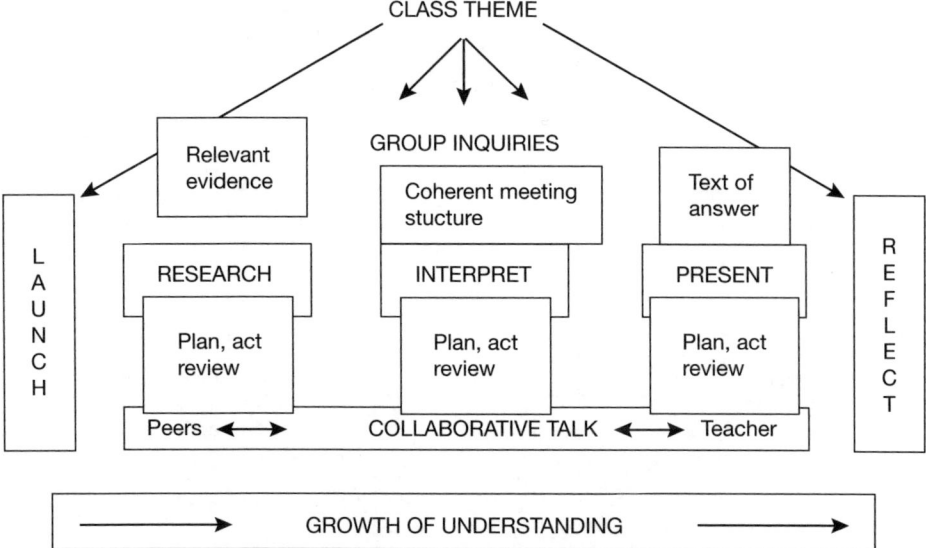

Figure 1.2 Wells' model of dialogic inquiry (adapted from book).

The authors argue that sequencing has an important impact on the discourse that occurs, as well as on how the students learn to do science. They focus on poster sessions, pin-up sessions and gallery walks to encourage explanation and transparency. For example, a poster session can be used by the teacher to interrogate understanding of the investigative process and for making the reasoning behind the procedure clear.

There are implications arising from the previous representations of the inquiry process. Firstly, there is a need to offer learners a representation that can support their progress through an inquiry

In the Personal Inquiry project, we decided that we needed a representation to inform the learner of the phases of the inquiry process which also emphasises that the phases consist of a range of activities and resources. All phases of the inquiry process need to be depicted. The representation needs to convey a sense of personal ownership, agency, responsibility and choice. The terminology used to describe each phase focuses on identifying who chose the topic, who generated the hypothesis/question and who is responsible for carrying out the inquiry (me).

If the learner is beginning a brand new inquiry, they begin by 'finding my topic'. This may be a topic of their choice within a domain introduced by the teacher, or it may be a free choice made by the learner. The representation needs to develop students' understanding of the iterative nature of the inquiry process. So, the representation does not prioritise a start and end point. The representation needs to develop students' understanding of the

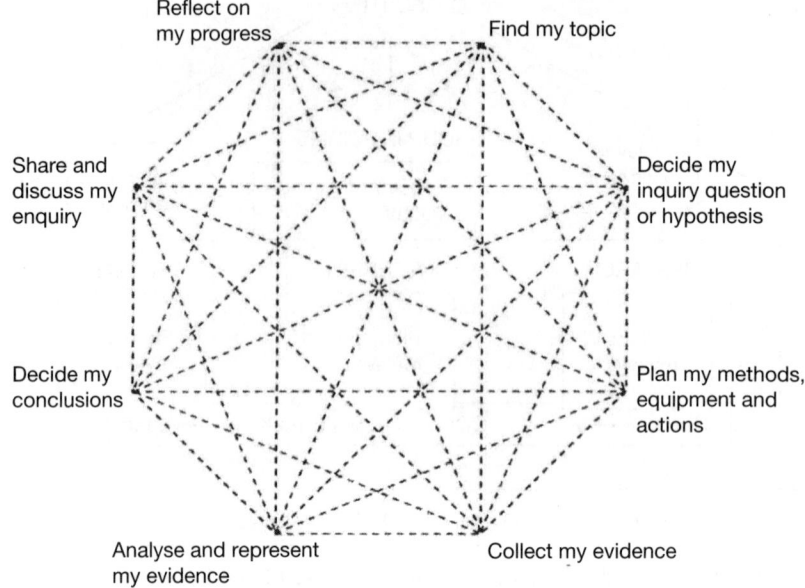

Figure 1.3 The Inquiry Cycle.

interdependencies between phases of the inquiry process. All of the phases are interlinked graphically with the other phases. The lines are dashed to imply bi-directionality. The representation needs to support students to understand that an inquiry may omit phases (e.g. by analysing secondary data).

The inquiry process is represented as a set of iterative, interdependent phases. The dashed lines between the phases graphically represent the iterative nature of the inquiry process, and show that the phases are interdependent. These phases build on previous formalizations but improve them in certain ways – e.g. White et al., had no explicit reflection phase. Also, as personal inquiry has different requirements of the phase structure, existing formulisations are not ideal – e.g. because these are real world investigations and most other formalisations are better suited to inquiries using simulations.

Within each phase we conceptualise the activities in the following ways (reproduced from Scanlon et al., in press):

- Find my topic: during this phase, the learner defines the topic of their investigation. This may be a free choice or may be from a domain selected by the teacher;
- Decide my inquiry question or hypothesis: here, the learner formulates their own hypothesis or key question;
- Plan my methods, equipment and actions: in this phase the learner

chooses the equipment, methods and actions that they will need to undertake to respond to their research question or hypothesis. This choice will be scaffolded by the teacher depending upon the ability and domain knowledge of the learner and mediated by, for example, the available equipment and data collection spaces available to the learner;

- Collect my evidence: the learners then carry out their inquiry by collecting the evidence using the methods and equipment decided upon in the previous phase;
- Analyse and represent my evidence: in this phase, the learner analyses their data using the tools available to them (e.g. Excel) and represents their data using, for example, graphs, tables, maps or diagrams;
- Respond to my question or hypothesis: the learner addresses their original research question or hypothesis and considers whether it is supported and evidenced;
- Share and discuss my inquiry: here the learner produces a representation of their whole inquiry in order to facilitate communication of their activities to others. This may be in the form of a report, a poster or a video, for example;
- Reflect on my progress: in this phase, the learner reflects in a variety of ways with the aim of evaluating their progress and understanding. They may reflect on, for example, the success of their methods, the relevance of their research question or hypothesis, or the suitability of their chosen data representations.

Significant features of this representation are that: the phases are named with a focus on emphasising the 'personal' nature of the inquiries (e.g. my conclusions) and the representation also presents inquiry learning as a series of phases (as opposed to stages implying a bounded activity that has a beginning and an end).

Consequences of personal inquiry and the representation of the inquiry learning framework for the design of technological support

As we have seen above, one way of making inquiries more personal is offering *choice* to the young people themselves. Making such choices is difficult. The Personal Inquiry project has argued that allowing young people to choose the actions undertaken during the inquiry is a positive step which increases learner motivation. The Personal Inquiry project team decided to support such student choices through the design of technological support, and especially by representing Figure 1.3 as an inquiry learning framework. But such design decisions have consequences.

One consequence of this representation is that students need to be supported in selecting the order of actions that they engage in, and to understand the constraints on and consequences of their choice of actions in terms of time, equipment necessary or resources. The tool developed in the project to support students in conducting the inquiry is nQuire. nQuire supports the students in choosing and sequencing their inquiry activities, carrying out activities and reviewing their progress round the inquiry cycle. The representation of inquiry developed in Figure 1.3 above supported the development of nQuire and is used within the software as an orienting device for students. Collins et al., (this volume) further describes nQuire and the scripting of inquiry learning.

Orchestration

As discussed earlier, the metaphor we have used to describe the ways in which teacher, tool, technology and activity have come together is that of orchestration.

This metaphor is in use widely in the technology-enhanced learning literature, and in particular Sutherland and Joubert (2009) discuss this as follows:

> Dillenbourg and Jermann (2009) discuss the potential of the word 'orchestration' as a metaphor for understanding and informing the design of technology-enhanced learning situations, and at the same time introduce the idea of the classroom as an eco-system. While scenarios describe the organisation of learning from a time, event and activity perspective, orchestration takes up the challenge of the actual implementation of all the interactions needed for a successful scenario (Niramitranon et al. 2006) It is in this sense that Fischer and Dillenbourg (2006) spoke of orchestration as the process of productively coordinating supportive interventions across multiple learning activities occurring at multiple social levels. It is also important to consider the ways in which the orchestration of a learning intervention has to adapt to the local situation, that is 'adaptive orchestration' that takes into account the needs and flow of the learning moment. (p16)

Sutherland and Joubert (2009) go on to consider the role of the teacher in these rich technology-enhanced learning environments using this orchestration metaphor. They contrast the idea of the conductor of orchestra as opposed to the instrumentalist or performer. They point out that the oft quoted transition in the teacher's role from 'the sage on the stage' to the 'guide on the side' should also be accompanied by a consideration of a transition to the conductor's role.

> The conductor would have knowledge of how music is perceived but not specialist knowledge of how to play a particular instrument. The

conductor has competence in assembling together what sounds good in terms of a collective performance. In this respect orchestration is more than guiding or facilitating, but should rather be seen as bringing together the parts to a make a 'new' whole. (p. 18)

Concluding comments

In this chapter, we have reviewed the literature on inquiry learning in science with a particular focus on what difficulties have been highlighted and how technology can support such inquiries. We have illustrated how inquiry learning frameworks have represented the underlying views on the inquiry learning process adopted in certain projects. We have discussed different approaches to inquiry learning and the ways in which technology has provided support for different parts of the inquiry learning process. The concerns of the Personal Inquiry project to deal with the complete inquiry learning process, to make use of mobile technologies to support inquiry learning across a range of contexts or learning settings, to allow for choice for learners in the inquiries they pursue and the requirements for a tool to support this person-alisation agenda for inquiries conducted across contexts have been shown to be grounded in the experiences of previous inquiry learning projects.

Our belief in the importance of the personalisation of inquiries in order to make them meaningful to learners, and of the representation of the processes of inquiry to overcome some of the difficulties which have been experienced in its implementation and to produce a list of design requirements for the development of tools combine together in our Personal Inquiry 'manifesto'.

We have introduced the notion of personal inquiry that a) supports learners to implement inquiries that are personally relevant, and b) allows teachers to orchestrate learners' activities in a more learner-centred fashion. We have drawn attention to the particular challenges for the orchestration of personal inquiry. These challenges are outlined here, but the solutions developed within the Personal Inquiry project to provide a flexible means of support are outlined in the succeeding chapters on scripting and orchestrating personal inquiry.

References

Anastopoulou, S. (2004) *Investigating Multimodal Interactions for the Design of Learning Environments: a case study in science learning*. PhD Thesis, School of Electronics, Electrical and Computing Engineering, Birmingham, UK: The University of Birmingham.

Anderson, R. (2002) 'Reforming science teaching: what research says about inquiry?', *Journal of Science Teacher Education*, 13 (1): 1–12.

Becta (2008) Harnessing Technology: Next Generation Learning 2008–14. Department for Schools, Children and Families, Coventry, UK: Becta.

Bell, P. and Linn, M. C. (2000) 'Scientific arguments as learning artifacts: designing for learning from the web with KIE', *International Journal of Science Education*, 22 (8): 797–817.

Bradley-Smith P. (2005) 'The challenges of teaching global citizenship through secondary geography'. CitizED. Available at: http://www.citized.info/pdf/commarticles/Paula_Bradley_Smith.pdf (accessed 3 January 2010).

Bruce, B. C. and Bishop, A. P. (2002) 'Using the web to support inquiry-based literacy development', *Journal of Adolescent and Adult Literacy*, 45 (8): 706–714.

Bruner, J. (1996) *The Culture of Education*, Cambridge MA: Harvard University Press.

Chinn, C. and Malhotra, B. (2002) 'Epistemologically authentic enquiry in schools: a theoretical framework for evaluating inquiry tasks', *Science Education*, 86 (2): 175–218.

Clark, D. and Slotta, J. D. (2003) 'WISE Design for Knowledge Integration', *Science Education*, 87 (4): 517–538.

Cuban, L. (2001) *Oversold and Underused: computers in the classroom*, Cambridge, MA: Harvard University Press.

Dawes, L., Mercer, N. and Wegerif, R. (2004) *Thinking Together: programme of activities for developing speaking, listening and thinking skills*, Birmingham: Imaginative Minds.

Dewey, J. (1938) *Logic: the theory of inquiry*, Holt, New York: Rinehart and Winston.

de Jong, T. (2006a) 'Computer simulations: technological advances in inquiry learning', *Science*, 312 (5773): 532–533.

de Jong, T. (2006b) 'Scaffolds for Computer Simulation-based Scientific Discovery Learning', in J. Elen and R. E. Clark (eds) *Dealing with Complexity in Learning Environments*, London: Elsevier Science Publishers.

de Jong, T. and Van Joolingen, W. (1998) 'Scientific Discovery Learning with Computer Simulations of Conceptual Domains', *Review of Educational Research*, 68 (2): 179–201

de Jong, T., Lazonder, A.W., Savelsbergh, E.R. and Manlove, S. (2005) 'Co-Lab: Research and development of an online learning environment for collaborative scientific discovery learning', *Computers in Human Behaviour*, 21: 671–688.

de Jong, A. J. M., van Joolingen, W. R., Weinberger, A. and the SCY team (2009). Learning by design. An example from the SCY-project. Proceedings of the CSCL 2009. Rhodes, Greece.

Dillenbourg, P. and Jermann, P. (2009) 'Technology for Classroom Integration', in M. Khine and I. Saleh (eds) *New Science of Learning: cognition, computers and collaboration in education..* New York: Springer.

Driver, R., Newton, P. and Osborne, J. (2000) 'Establishing the norms of scientific argument in the classroom', *Science Education*, 84: 287–312.

Donnelly, J. (2007) 'Overview of the evaluation studies', in *Twenty First Century Science Pilot Evaluation Report*. UYSEG and Nuffield Foundation. Available at: http://www.21stcenturyscience.org/data/files/c21–evaln-rpt-feb07–10101.pdf (last accessed June 2011).

Duschl, R. and Grandy, R. (eds) (2008) *Teaching Scientific Inquiry: Recommendations for Research and Implementation*. Rotterdam: Sense Publishers.

Edelson, D., Gordin, D. and Pea, R. (1999) 'Addressing the challenge of inquiry-based learning through technology and curriculum design', *Journal of the Learning Sciences*, 8 (3/4): 391–450.

Edelson, D. C. and Reiser, B. J. (2006) 'Making authentic practices accessible to learners: Design challenges and strategies', in K. Sawyer (ed), *The Cambridge Handbook of the Learning Sciences*, New York: Cambridge University Press.

Edwards, D. and Mercer, N. (1987) *Common Knowledge: the development of joint understanding in the classroom*, London: Routledge.

Fischer, F. and Dillenbourg, P. (2006) 'Challenges of orchestrating computer supported collaborative learning' Proceedings of 87th *Annual Meeting of the American Education Research Association* (AERA).

Furtak, E. (2005) 'The problem with answers: an exploration of guided scientific inquiry teaching', *Science Education*, 90 (3): 453–467.

Grandy, R. and Duschl, R. (2007) 'Reconsidering the character and role of inquiry in school science; analysis of a conference', *Science and Education*, 16 (2): 141–166.

Hakkarainen, K. and Sintonen, M. (2002) 'Interrogative Model of Inquiry and computer-supported collaborative learning', *Science and Education*, 11 (1): 25–43.

Hickey, D. and Filsecker, M. (2012) 'Participatory learning assessment for organising inquiry in educational video games and beyond', in K. Littleton, E. Scanlon and M. Sharples (eds) (2012) *Orchestrating inquiry learning*, Abingdon: Routledge.

Hodson, D. (1998) *Teaching and Learning Science: towards a personalised approach*, Milton Keynes: Open University Press.

Hoppe, H. U. (2007) 'Integrating learning processes across boundaries of media, time and group scale', *Research and Practice in Technology Enhanced Learning*, 2: 31–49.

Huffman, D., Lawrenz, F., Thomas, K. and Clarkson, L. (2006). 'Collaborative evaluation communities in urban schools: A model of evaluation capacity building for STEM education'. *New Directions for Evaluation, Special Issue: Critical Issues in STEM Evaluation*, 2006, (109): 73–85. doi: 10.1002/ev.179

Keselman, A. (2003) 'Supporting inquiry learning by promoting normative understanding of multivariable causality', *Journal of Research in Science Teaching*, 40 (9): 898–921.

Kuhn, D. and Pease, M. (2008) 'What Needs to Develop in the Development of Inquiry Skills?', *Cognition and Instruction*, 26: 512–559.

Linn, M. C. and Slotta, J. D. (2006) 'Enabling participants in online forums to learn from each other', in A. O'Donnell, C. Hmelo-Silver and G. Erkens (eds) *Collaborative Learning, Reasoning and Technology*, Mahwah, NJ: Lawrence Erlbaum.

Linn, M. C., Clark, D. and Slotta, J. D. (2003) 'WISE Design for Knowledge Integration', *Science Education*, 87 (4): 517–538.

Linn, M. C. and Hsi, S. (2000) *Computers, Teachers, Peers,* Mahwah, NJ: Erlbaum.

Linn, M. C., Bell, P. and Hsi, S. (1998) 'Using the Internet to enhance student understanding of science: The knowledge of integration environment', *Interactive Learning Environments*, 6 (1/2): 4–38.

Llewellyn, D. (2002) *Inquire Within*, Thousand Oaks, CA: Corwin Press

Lotan, R. (2003) 'Group-worthy tasks', *Educational Leadership*, 60 (6): 72–75.

Manlove, S., Lazonder, A. W. and de Jong, T. (2006) 'Regulative support for collaborative scientific inquiry learning', *Journal of Computer Assisted Learning*, 22 (6): 87–98.

McElhaney, K. and Linn, M. (2012) 'Orchestrating inquiry instruction using the knowledge integration framework', in K. Littleton, E. Scanlon and M. Sharples (eds) (2012) *Orchestrating inquiry learning*, Abingdon: Routledge.

Millar, R. (2003) *Towards Evidence-Based Practice in Science Education 3: Teaching and Learning:* research briefing no 3. Available at: http://www.tlrp.org. (accessed June 2011).

Millar, R. (2002) 'Thinking about practical work', in S. Amos and R. Boohan (eds) *Aspects of Secondary Science*, London and New York: Routledge/Falmer and the Open University.

National Science Foundation (2008) *Fostering Learning in the Networked World: the cyberlearning opportunity and challenge.* Available at http://www.nsf.gov/pubs/2008/nsf08204/nsf08204. pdf (accessed January 2009).

Newton, D. and Newton, L. (2000) 'Do teachers support causal understanding through their discourse when teaching primary science?', *British Educational Research Journal*, 25 (5): 599–613.

Niramitranon, J., Sharples, M. and Greenhalgh, C. (2006) *COML (Classroom Orchestration Modelling Language) and Scenarios Designer: toolsets to facilitate collaborative learning in a one-to-on technology classroom,* TELearn Online Archive.

Novak, A. M. and Gleason, C. I. (2001) 'Incorporating portable technology to enhance an inquiry, project-based middle school science classroom'. In R. F. Tinker and J. S. Krajcik (eds) *Portable Technologies: science learning in context.* New York: Kluwer.

OFSTED (2008). Reference no: 070044 Geography in schools – changing practice. Available at: http://www.ofsted.gov.uk/Ofsted-home/News/Press-and-media/2008/January/Geography-in-schools-changing-practice (accessed June 2011).

Pea, R., Milrad, M., Maldonado, H., Vogel, B., Kurti, A. and Spikol, D. (2012) ' Learning and technological designs for mobile science inquiry collaboratories', in K. Littleton, E. Scanlon and M. Sharples (eds) (2012) *Orchestrating inquiry learning,* Abingdon: Routledge.

Pea, R. and Maldonado, H. (2006) 'WILD for learning: interacting through new computing devices anytime, anywhere', in K. Sawyer (ed) *Cambridge Handbook of the Learning Sciences,* New York: Cambridge University Press.

Roehrig, G. H. (2004) 'Constraints experienced by beginning secondary science teachers in implementing scientific inquiry lessons', *International Journal of Science Education,* 26 (1): 3–24

Sandoval, W., Deneroff V. and Franke, M. (2002) 'Teaching, as learning, as inquiry: moving beyond activity in the analysis of teaching practice'. Presented at *Annual Meeting of the American Educational Research Association,* April 1–5, New Orleans, LA.

Sandoval, W. (2005) 'Understanding students' practical epistemologies and their influence on learning through inquiry', *Science Education,* 89 (4): 634–656.

Sandoval, W. and Reiser, B. (2004) 'Explanation driven inquiry: integrating conceptual and epistemic scaffolds for scientific enquiry', *Science Education,* 88: 345–372.

Sharples, M. (2011) Personal communication

Sawyer, K. (2006) 'Conclusion: the schools of the future', in Sawyer, K. (ed) *Cambridge Handbook of the Learning Sciences,* New York: Cambridge University Press.

Scanlon, E., Anastopoulou, S., Kerawalla, L. and Mulholland, P. (in press) 'How technology resources can be used to represent personal inquiry and support students' understanding of it across contexts', *Journal of Computer Assisted Learning.*

Scanlon, E., Jones, A. and Waycott, J. (2005) 'Mobile technologies: prospects for their use in learning in informal science settings', *Journal of Interactive Media in Education* 21 (5): 1–17.

Scardamalia, M. (2002) 'Collective cognitive responsibility for the development of knowledge', in B. Smith (ed) *Liberal Education in a knowledge society.* Chicago: Open Court

Schwartz, D. L., Brophy, S. Lin, X. and Bransford, J. D. (1999) 'Software for Engaging complex learning: examples from an Educational Psychology Course', *Educational Technology Research and Development,* 47 (2): 39–59.

Scott, P. H., Ametller, J., Mortimer, E. and Emberton, J. (2009) 'Teaching and Learning Disciplinary Knowledge: Developing the dialogic space for an answer when there isn't even a question', in K. Littleton, and C. Howe (eds) *Educational Dialogues,* Taylor & Francis, pp. 322–337

Scott, P. H., Ametller, J., Hall, K., Leach, J., Lewis, J. and Ryder J. (2007) 'Study 1 knowledge and understanding: executive summary', in *Twenty First Century Science Pilot Evaluation Report.* UYSEG and Nuffield Foundation. Available at: http://www.21stcenturyscience.org/data/files/c21–evaln-rpt-feb07–10101.pdf (accessed October 11 2010).

Shimoda, T. (2006) 'The Web of Inquiry: Technology for learning inquiry and reflective assessment'. Paper presented at the 2006 *Annual Conference of the American Educational Research Association*, San Francisco, CA.

Shimoda, T., White, B. Y. and Frederiksen J. R. (2002) 'Student goal orientation in learning inquiry skills with modifiable software advisors', *Science Education*, 86 (2): 244 – 263.

Slotta, J.D. (2004) 'The Web-based Inquiry Science Environment (WISE) Scaffolding knowledge integration in the science classroom', in M. C. Linn, E. A. Davis, and P. Bell (eds) *Internet Environments for Science Education*, Mahwah, New Jersey: Lawrence Erlbaum Associates.

Sutherland, R. and Joubert, M. (eds) (2009) D1.1: The STELLAR Vision and Strategy Statement. Available at: http://www.stellarnet.eu/repository/deliverable_repository_list/ (accessed June 2011)

Schwab, J. (1962) 'The teaching of science as inquiry', in J. Schwab and P. Braandwein (eds) *The Teaching of Science*, Cambridge, MA: Harvard University Press.

Tobin, K. G., Tippins, D. J. and Gallard, A. J. (1994) 'Research on instructional strategies for teaching science', in D. L. Gabel (ed) *Handbook of Research on Science Teaching and Learning*, New York; Macmillan.

Van Joolingen, W. R., de Jong, T., Lazonder, Ard, W., Savelsbergh, Elwin, R. and Manlove, S. (2005) 'Co-Lab: research and development of an online learning environment for collaborative scientific discovery learning', *Computers in Human Behavior*, (21), 671–688.

Van Joolingen, W. R., Weinberger, A. and the SCY team (2009) 'Learning by design. An example from the SCY-project'. Paper presented at *Issues in Scaffolding Collaborative Inquiry Science Learning* Symposium held in CSCL 2009: CSCL Practices, University of the Aegean, Rhodes, Greece.

Van Joolingen, W. R. (1998) 'Scientific Discovery Learning with Computer Simulations of Conceptual Domains', *Review of Educational Research*, 68: 179–201.

Van Joolingen, W. R. King, S. and Jong de, T. (1997) 'The SimQuest authoring system for simulation-based discovery learning', in B. du Boulay and R. Mizoguchi (eds) *Artificial Intelligence and Education: knowledge and media in learning systems*, IOS Press, Amsterdam.

Viilo, M., Seitamaa-Hakkarainen, P. and Hakkarainen, K. (2012) 'Infrastructures for technology-supported collective inquiry learning in science', in K. Littleton, E. Scanlon and M. Sharples (eds) (2012) *Orchestrating inquiry learning*, Abingdon: Routledge.

Vogel, B., Spikol, D., Kurti, A, and Milrad, M. (2010) 'Integrating Mobile, Web and Sensory Technologies to Support Inquiry-Based Science Learning', in *Proceedings of the 6th IEEE WMUTE International Conference on Wireless, Mobile and Ubiquitous Technologies in Education WMUTE 2010*, Kaohsiung, Taiwan, April 12–16th.

Wasson, B., Vold, V. amd de Jong, T. (2012) 'Orchestration of assessment: assessing emerging learning objects', in K. Littleton, E. Scanlon and M. Sharples (eds) (2012) *Orchestrating inquiry learning*, Abingdon: Routledge.

Watson, R., Swain, J. and Robbie, C. (2004), 'Students' discussions in practical scientific inquiries', *International Journal of Science Education*, 26 (1): 25–45.

Weinberger, A. and Fischer, F. (2006) 'A framework to analyse argumentative knowledge construction in computer-supported collaborative learning', *Computers and Education*, 46 (1): 71–95.

Weinberger, A., Stegmann, K. and Fischer, F. (2007) Knowledge convergence in collaborative learning: Concepts and assessment. *Learning and Instruction*, 17(4), 416–426. SSCI: 1,81

Welch, W. W., Klopfer, L. E., Aikenhead, G. S. and Robinson, J. T. (1981) 'The role of inquiry in science education: analysis and recommendations', *Science Education*, 65 (1): 33–50.

Wells, G. (2001) *Action, Talk and Text: Learning and Teaching Through Inquiry,* Teachers College

Press. Available at: http://people.ucsc.edu/~gwells/Files/Papers_Folder/ATT.theory.pdf (accessed February 2011) [Article online, based on Chapters 1 and 10 of this book].

Weinberger, A. and Fischer, F. (2006) 'A framework to analyse argumentative knowledge construction in computer-supported collaborative learning', *Computers and Education*, 46 (1): 71–95.

Weinberger, A., Stegmann, K., Fischer, F. and Mandl, H. (2007) 'Scripting argumentative knowledge construction in computer supported collaborative learning environments', in F. Fischer, H. Mandel, J. Haake and I. Kollar (eds) *Scripting Computer Supported Communication of Knowledge-Cognitive Computational and Educational Perspectives*, New York: Springer.

White, B. Y. and Frederiksen, J. R. (1998) 'Inquiry, modeling and metacognition: Making science accessible to all students', *Cognition and Instruction*, 16 (1): 3–118.

White, B. and Frederiksen, J. (2005) 'A Theoretical Framework for Fostering Metacognitive Development', *Educational Psychologist*, 40 (4): 211–223.

White, B., Shimoda, T. and Frederiksen, J. (1999) 'Enabling Students to Construct Theories of Collaborative Inquiry and Reflective Learning: Computer Support for Metacognitive Development'. *International Journal of Artificial Intelligence in Education*, 10 (2), 151–182,

Wormstead, S. J., Becker M. L. and Congalton R. G. (2002) 'Tools for successful student–teacher–scientist partnerships', *Journal of Science Education and Technology*, 11 (3): September.

Zimmerman, C. (2007) 'The development of scientific thinking skills in elementary and middle school', *Developmental Review*, 27: 172–223.

Chapter 2

Trajectories of inquiry learning

Karen Littleton and Lucinda Kerawalla

Introduction

The contributors to this volume make a compelling case for the potential, value and significance of inquiry-oriented learning and instruction. The debate then is not so much whether sciences should be taught via inquiry, but rather how to do so (see Hickey and Filsecker 2012, p. 146).

There are of course considerable challenges to be faced in supporting and resourcing inquiry learning – a process that involves learners asking questions about the natural or material world, collecting data to answer those questions, making discoveries and testing those discoveries rigorously (de Jong 2006). Pupils may, for example, experience difficulties in engaging with inquiry learning, forming appropriate investigations, designing and running experiments, and interpreting data. A key issue, then, is how to resource and support processes of inquiry learning within and beyond the classroom. Whilst recognising the multiplicity of challenges facing those of us committed to fostering inquiry-based learning, our chapter focuses on one specific challenge – namely, the need to ensure that young people have a coherent, cumulative experience of the diverse activities, ideas and settings that are implicated in the process of inquiry. The focus in this chapter is on understanding how connections are made between ideas and events over time. Specifically, we will explore how connections, between known and new (Rogoff 1990) and between everyday and scientific understandings (Mortimer and Scott 2003), are negotiated in talk and interaction between learners and learners and their teachers, and how this process is mediated by representations and technologies. In both cases the focus is on how connections are made to previous activities and interactions. A key concern is how time is harnessed as a pedagogical resource – not only in the sense that the students' understanding progressively develops over time, but also in the sense that the teacher draws upon past understandings and points to the future, in the present.

Making connections

> Learning is a process that happens gradually over time and, given this, one of the critical functions of classroom interaction is 'connection building'
>
> (Gee and Green 1998).

'Most learning does not happen suddenly: we do not one moment fail to understand something and the next moment grasp it entirely' (Barnes 1992: 123). From the pupil's perspective, then, it is vital that school-based inquiries have a connected, cohesive and cumulative quality in which activities and their goals become construed in ways that constitute a purposeful educational journey. That said, coherent knowledge and new understandings will not naturally emerge for students simply from their extended immersion in classroom life (Lemke 2001; Mercer and Littleton 2007). Rather such understandings have to be pursued actively, with teachers orchestrating tools (including language) and technologies such that activities and ideas become connected and aligned to broader pedagogic goals. The emphasis is not only on ensuring continuity (whereby the teacher explicitly makes connections between new knowledge and concepts or topics learned earlier) but also on resourcing the progressive deepening or expansion of a concept or topic to be explored and investigated (Nurkka, Viiri and Littleton submitted).

In this chapter we present extracts drawn from analyses of an extended technology-mediated scientific inquiry learning activity concerning microclimates undertaken by 11–12 year olds, as part of the Personal Inquiry project (described in Chapter 1) to both exemplify and explore how progressive 'connection building' is accomplished multimodally over time through a multiplicity of semiotic resources. Such progressive connection building is not, as we shall see, a narrow and unidirectional process. Rather, the effective co-construction of mutual, cohesive understandings makes use of multiple representations and interactions and involves revisiting and (re)negotiating ideas and understandings.

The metaphor of 'orchestration' sits at the heart of our exploration as this metaphor draws attention to the subtle interweaving of activities, ideas and resources and the ways in which a teacher may make (what are often moment-by-moment) shifts between what is foregrounded and what is backgrounded in an ongoing inquiry. It also captures the sense in which a teacher, or more knowledgeable other, encourages and works with learners' contributions in the context and pursuit of overall goals as part of a longer trajectory of meaning-making (Rasmussen 2005; Baldry and Thibault 2006).

The inquiry context and analytic approach

The analytic extracts presented in this chapter are derived from the detailed analysis of observations made as a mixed-ability, mixed-sex class of 28 students, supported by their teacher and researchers, undertook an inquiry on microclimates spanning four lessons over 2 weeks. Lesson one was classroom-based and initially involved a whole-class teaching session on the topic of microclimates. An initial design for an inquiry on microclimates was also scoped as part of this whole-class session. This required the students to design an inquiry to explore the existence and nature of microclimates within their school grounds so that they could recommend where to locate a new picnic bench. Whilst this provided an initial frame and contextualization, it was intended that the inquiry could be adapted, personalised and refined by the students themselves. Following this initial orientation to the purpose and nature of the inquiry, the students were then divided into small groups of four to five, and a netbook was given to each of the groups. Each group was then shown (by the teacher and researchers) how to use 'Activity Guide', an instantiation of nQuire – a web-based application developed to guide secondary school students in designing, conducting and evaluating their inquiries (Collins, Mulholland and Gaved 2012) (see also Chapters 1 and 5). The students were then asked to work in their groups to discuss the data they wanted to collect (a discussion that was resourced with reference to the relevant Activity Guide screen). Each of the small groups subsequently fed back their decisions in a class plenary, and the class members collectively agreed which data they were to collect. The students then worked in their small groups to discuss which locations within the school grounds they wanted to collect data from, and they then once again fed their decisions back to the whole class so that the locations from which to collect data could be agreed. Towards the end of the first lesson each of the groups worked on developing their own hypothesis. They were advised to structure their hypothesis as follows: 'I think the best place to put a picnic bench would be X because Y'. The second lesson began in the classroom, with the distribution of equipment to the groups of pupils. The whole class then moved outside into the school grounds. The students walked around their selected data collection locations as a class, supervised by their teacher, and they collected data in groups. During the third and fourth lessons, the students worked in an ICT suite. Here they focused on writing a report consisting of an introduction about microclimates, a description of their methodology, representations of their data in bar graphs and some written analysis of their findings. This report was completed as homework.

Qualitative analysis of the data involved repeated consideration of all video-recorded whole-class data and the recordings made of focal groups (who gave consent for their group-work sessions to be recorded and analysed), together with the associated transcriptions and observation notes in order to trace the ways in which connections were built, using language and other semiotic resources. We built upon the sociocultural discourse analytic approach (Mercer and Littleton 2007) to focus on the ways in which shared understanding is developed, within a social context, over time. The analysis thus necessitated an iterative process of moving backwards and forwards through time, trying to make sense of episodes and events as linked chains of interactions. The extracts we present here are drawn predominantly from detailed analyses of the first two lessons and as such they are not intended to be representative of the totality of the lessons observed, but are rather used as exemplifictions and vehicles for exploring the issues of interest outlined above. As our focus is on how ideas are chained and how knowledge is co-constructed using language and other semiotic resources, the presentation of findings and their discussion is necessarily interwoven.

Making connections between known and new: from climate to microclimate

Prior to commencing the microclimate inquiry, the students had been taught about weather (e.g. clouds, anticyclones and depressions) and climate. The teacher therefore initiated the inquiry process with a whole-class teaching session in which she mobilised and revisited the students' prior work. She made explicit reference to shared, common knowledge, previously established during earlier lessons, using this as an 'anchor' (see Littleton, Twiner and Gillen 2010), an initial starting point, upon which to build, expand and extend the students' understanding into the new realm of microclimates. She thus works to 'bridge' students' understanding from what they already know (climate) to the new (microclimate). In Extract 1, we see how the establishment of this anchor was constructed multimodally – in dialogue mediated crucially through the use of a slide deck displayed on the interactive whiteboard.

Extract 1: From weather and climate to microclimate

Teacher: So, first of all, let's quickly recap on the difference between weather and climate. So there's two different definitions that are going to come up (on the interactive whiteboard), you need to tell me which is which. X means the day to day changes in the atmosphere. What is x? Weather or climate? (students then raise their hands and give their answers as requested by the teacher)	**Weather or Climate?** • 2 definitions, which is which? • X means the day-to-day changes in the atmosphere • Y is the average X in a place. It tells us what the X is usually like.

Teacher: Very good. So (reads statements on interactive whiteboard), deserts are always dry, is this weather or climate?

Pupil: Weather.

Teacher: Deserts are always dry, is this weather or climate? Hands up. Hand up first.

Pupil: Climate.

(pupils then continue to give their answers to the remaining statements on the interactive whiteboard)

Weather or Climate?

- Deserts are always dry
- Wednesday was very wet
- I hope Saturday is sunny
- Tropical Rainforests are very humid
- The cyclone in Bangladesh was tragic
- It was very foggy on Monday
- The UK has mild winters and warm summers

Teacher: So this is what you need to write in your books. (reads from interactive whiteboard) 'A microclimate is the something state of the something close to a very something area of the earth's something. Generally, we take a something to be the climate of a small something such as a town, forest or something.' Now all the words you need are at the bottom. Fill them in and we'll go through it as a class in just a minute.

(Pupils discuss together then feedback their answers to the class. Teacher then reveals a slide with the words in the correct places which the pupils write in their exercise books)

What is a Microclimate?

A microclimate is the _____ state of the _____ close to a very ____ area of the earth's _____. Generally, we take a _____ to be the climate of a small _____ such as a town, forest or _____.

small   environment   physical   garden
surface   atmosphere   microclimate

Through focused questioning the students are asked to 'recap' what they already know about the difference between weather and climate, and then are encouraged to extend their understanding of climate to complete the missing words of a paragraph which describes a microclimate (all of the terminology is familiar except for 'microclimate'). In this way, the trajectory from previous lessons into the current lesson is contextualised for the students as being a cumulative development – building on and progressively extending prior knowledge, a process which Wells (1999) describes as the 'development of expertise through participation in activities in which ... knowledge is progressively constructed, applied and revised' (p. 138).

The concept of a microclimate is initially presented to the students as a theoretical construct, through a scientific definition (see 'What is a Microclimate' slide in Extract 1). However, the concept is gradually re-contextualised such that it is made personally relevant to the students by the teacher, as she alerts them to the fact that their own school grounds consists of different microclimates. She thus initiates the crucial process of grounding scientific content and process in students' existing points of view and activities, thereby working to enable them to see the intellectual relevance of their learning activities, helping learners to reframe their everyday experiences in empirical and scientific terms.

Throughout lesson 1, the teacher continually reminds the students that their investigation will be carried out in their school grounds and that microclimates can be found there. She repeatedly grounds the students' inquiry in the familiar. In one of her very early utterances addressed to the whole class she said 'we're going to be looking at what a microclimate is, what affects a microclimate and what the microclimates of [our] school are'. Similarly, following the activity presented in Extract 1 above, in which the students were supplying the missing words of a definition of microclimates, the teacher added that the last word could indeed in their case be "school" (i.e. 'generally we take a microclimate to be the climate of a small area such as a town, forest or school'). Personal inquiry cannot simply be equated with personal interest – rather it crucially entails personal relevance. Thus the simplistic use of the 'everyday' in classroom contexts is problematic not least because it trivialises the complex processes involved in meaning making and falls far short of the authenticity that is essential to engage young people and support learning (Murphy, 2000). As Scott, Ametller, Mortimer and Emberton (2010) suggest, grounding scientific content in students' existing points of view needs to enable a student to see the intellectual relevance of their learning activities. However, as we will go on to show later in the chapter, it can be difficult for learners to reframe their everyday experiences in empirical and scientific terms.

Making connections between known and new: from microclimate as an abstract definition, to investigating microclimates in the school grounds

Later in lesson 1 the teacher gradually dialogically transforms the familiar context of the school grounds into a site for inquiry and investigation, making purposeful shifts between scientific and everyday perspectives. Earlier in the lesson she had worked to help the students understand the definition of a microclimate. She subsequently focuses on enabling the students to understand that they can investigate microclimates in the context of their school grounds, a process that will involve them in hypothesis testing and taking salient measurements. In Extract 2, we can see how she foregrounds prospective scientific activity, building a connection to work they will undertake in the future, simultaneously introducing key scientific vocabulary and inquiry concepts (indicated in italics).

Extract 2: Re-contextualizing the school grounds as a site for inquiry

1   Teacher: Our *inquiry question* is going to be 'where shall we put the new picnic bench?' OK so we're going to be trying to find the place around school to put a new bench.

2   Pupil: MUGA (Multi-Use Games Area)

3   Teacher: First, to start off our *research* we need to come up with a *hypothesis*. Now (reads statement from IWB as in Figure 2.1a) 'a hypothesis is a suggestion or guess – suggestion or a guess – that tries to explain something but has not yet been proved'. So you're going to write a hypothesis, and then you're going to go out, and that's what you'll be doing next lesson, you'll be trying to *prove it, or disprove it.* So we're going to write our hypothesis and then we'll go out and *measure*…(T changes slide to that shown in Figure 2.1b) So for an example, you might say, the best place to put the picnic bench would be outside the canteen, *because…*

4   Pupil: there's too many there

5   Teacher: … *it is warmer.* OK, you might decide the best place to put the picnic bench would be …

6   Pupil: MUGA (Multi-Use Games Area)

7   Teacher: … by the MUGA, *because there might be more sunshine there.* OK. But you'll be working this out in your groups in a minute.

8   Pupil: In the middle of the field.

9   Teacher: So, we're going to be looking at *places to measure*, and then we'll also be looking at *what we're going to measure.*

Firstly we need to write our hypothesis	We need to decide where to measure
• A hypothesis is a suggestion or a guess that tries to explain something but has not yet been proved to be true or false.	• Use the map of Oakgrove school to think about the places where you might like to put the bench.
• We will write a hypothesis and then go and measure the weather to try to prove or disprove our hypothesis.	• You will go round the school to the places you have chosen as a group.

(a)   (b)

Figure 2.1(a) and (b) The slide deck in use

It is evident that here the teacher serves as an influential discourse guide, modelling in her own talk the use of the new scientific discourse she wishes the students to appropriate – enacting scientific ways of thinking and talking in classroom contexts (Mercer and Littleton 2007). Crucially, she models the kind of critical reasoning and thinking that is crucial to learning through inquiry, by placing an emphasis on the need to explicate the reasons that underpin the hypothesis to be tested. She does this by emphasising the word 'because' (see Extract 2: 3 and 7). Thus, as the students call out some suggested locations for the bench, the teacher elaborates on these suggestions, reformulating and recasting them through offering a possible rationale, based on the types of data that the students would be collecting. So through her talk she begins to recontextualise the school grounds as a site for future scientific inquiry and prefigures the work they will be undertaking in subsequent lessons.

Making connections between everyday and scientific: the challenge of reframing the familiar school grounds in terms of scientific variables

In the group-based session at the end of the first lesson, the students needed to decide from where in the school grounds they would collect their data. In Extract 3, a focal group of four students were sitting around a table using

Figure 2.2 Students grouped around their netbook discussing where the class should collect their data, pointing to the photographs of the lockers in nQuire.

nQuire on a netbook and were discussing where the class should undertake their data collection (see Figure 2.2).

Extract 3: Where to collect data?

1 Beth is operating the netbook. She has clicked on the 'lockers' tab (See Figure 2.3)
2 Dan: I think lockers.
3 Beth: I think lockers too because everyone hangs around there when it rains.
4 Beth: Everybody. So do you want it in the lockers?
5 Dan: Yeah, lockers. That's one.
6 Beth: So that's one. So keep that in mind, Dan.
7 Carl: But you don't get very much light. (points to photo. See Figure 2.3)
8 Beth: Yes, you do. These bits here (points to photo) you do, you get a lot of light.
9 Angela: The lights come on, don't they? (points to photo)
10 Beth: Yeah, so lockers, keep that in mind.
11 Carl: So lockers are one.
   (Beth clicks on 'football pitch' tab)
12 Beth: Erm... football pitch. I think football pitch ...
13 Dan: Yeah, football pitch.
14 Beth: ... because of the boys. Yeah around here (points to photo).
15 Dan: Yeah.
16 Beth: So keep football pitch in mind.
17 Angela: Yeah, it's not very sheltered is it?
18 Dan: Lockers, football pitch.
   (a few seconds later)
19 Beth: Yeah. Car park. Yeah, 'cause how about if somebody's waiting for their mums, they sit on the floor most of the time.
20 Beth: Yeah, yeah, yeah.
21 Carl: So car park.

What is evident is that photographs of key school locations, presented in nQuire, provided an important multimodal focal resource and common representational reference point that mediated the students' classroom-based discussions. Key considerations, such as whether a location was in light or shade, could be discussed with reference to specific features of individual photographic resources. What is also significant is that both everyday and scientific frames of reference were interwoven and juxtaposed in the students' discussions regarding the choice of locations. Thus, they wanted the picnic bench to be near the lockers so people could sit on it when it was raining and because it is light there (they have previously discussed the possibility of 'light levels' as being one of the types of data the class collects). They also thought the picnic bench would be well positioned near the football pitch as the boys who play football could use it, but Angela argues that it is not very sheltered there (they have previously discussed wind speed and wind direction as potential measures). Similarly, they think the car park would be a possible location as it would be somewhere to sit whilst waiting to be collected by parents at the end of the day. In the case of the lockers and football pitch, suggestions are justified with reference to an everyday and an empirical rationale. However, the car park is suggested solely on the basis of an everyday argument. It was this argument which they subsequently decided to use to construct their initial hypothesis. So one can see here the very real challenge the students faced in disambiguating their everyday knowledge regarding the use of physical space around the school and the empirically rooted inquiry question regarding the appropriate siting of a picnic bench given the microclimatic conditions in the school grounds. Given their orientation to everyday reasoning, later in the same lesson the teacher encouraged the students to reframe their hypothesis. They found this challenging and needed prompting with examples before they understood that their hypothesis needed to be based on empirical measures and not on needing 'somewhere to sit'. In terms of the development of the students' learning trajectory throughout this lesson, the process of re-contextualizing

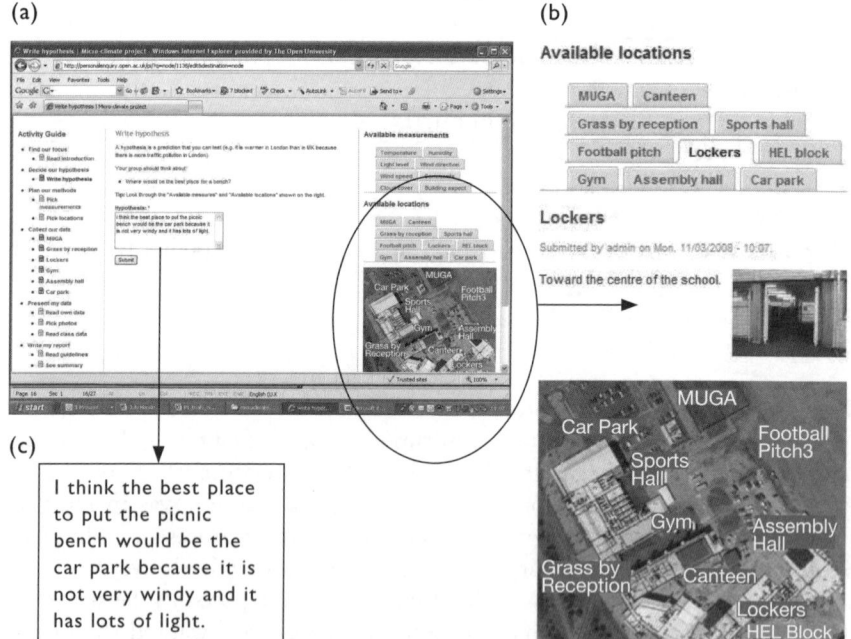

Figure 2.3 Screen shot of the hypothesis entry screen in nQuire (a) with the content of the 'lockers' information tab enlarged in (b) and the hypothesis text later created by the group enlarged in (c).

and reconceptualising the everyday and familiar context of the school grounds as a site for scientific inquiry proved to be a challenge for the students. This indicates that teachers cannot rely upon mobilising prior understandings and experiences as a pedagogic strategy. Rather, they also need to pay close attention to how *bridging* (between the everyday and the scientific) can be resourced and supported. Whilst the students used the photographs in nQuire as a crucial, valuable resource to help navigate this bridging process, they were continually juxtaposing empirical and everyday perspectives, and found it difficult to acknowledge that there was indeed a difference between the two.

Making connections between the everyday and the scientific: collecting scientific data from familiar (but newly 'empiricised') school grounds

Some of the ways in which instructors encourage students to make purposeful shifts between the everyday and the scientific are exemplified in Extract 4. Here a second group of students are collecting data from different locations in the school grounds. They are engaged in an activity that necessitates them characterising the school grounds in a new, scientific way – namely, in terms of measurable variables.

Extract 4: It is windy

1 Researcher: What are you doing for your temperature?
2 Tina: I'm taking that.
3 Researcher: Hold it up. Otherwise you get it right by you.
4 Tina: (holds sensor up high. On the right of photo opposite) 8.4.
5 Clare (typing, centre of photo): What's the light level? Put it up!
6 Tina: 2700.
7 Clare: What do you say cloud cover is? I can't see no clear sky.
8 Matt (left of photo): Seven still.

9 Tina: Eight. 10 Researcher: You decide amongst yourselves. 11 Clare: Seven. Right and now I need to do a comment. I need to sit on something that's d[ry] (goes to a dry area nearby).	
12 Researcher (out of shot): So what do you think's special about the environment here? 13 Clare (sitting on the ground): Like there's not a lot of, like the buildings are in the way of the sun so ... 14 Researcher: What do you think guys about ... 15 Matt: It's windy.	
16 Researcher: It's windy. Why do you think it's windy? 17 Ben (left in photo): It's windy because it's quite open. 18 Researcher: Quite open, yeah. When you were out here, just coming through, do you think the buildings have any effect? 19 Ben: No. 20 Researcher: So the buildings would block it in some direction. 21 Ben: It depends which way the wind is coming from (gestures wind directions, as in photo). 22 Researcher: Yeah, does it always come in different directions here, or does it always come in one direction when you're out here? 23 Ben: (inaudible but gesturing a wind direction)	

In lines 12–23 in particular, the researcher, through prompts and open questioning, works to support the students, encouraging them to look at the buildings around them and to think about how they might impact the wind speed. In terms of the orchestration of inquiry, he is working to help the students make an important shift in terms of what is foregrounded for consideration and discussion. He encourages them to think of causal explanations as to why a specific location is windy and to draw upon their prior experiences in doing so. In lines 18 and 22, he asks them to think back to when they have been in this location before (when they were 'just coming through') and whether the wind always blows in the same direction as it was blowing during their data collection activity. At first, Ben (line 19) asserts that he does not think that the buildings have an effect on the wind speed, but the researcher encourages him to revisit this assumption. Ben begins to think about how they might do so and then uses gesture to mediate an explanation to his friend Tina regarding the typical wind direction and how the buildings may affect this. This short extract evidences how the students are beginning to characterise and explore this familiar school environment in new ways: in terms of wind speed, wind direction, and how the buildings (their classrooms) may affect these variables. The emergent dialogue constitutes the cumulation of all the new understandings which have been 'progressively constructed, applied and revised' (Wells ibid) across the previous lesson, and this lesson.

Making connections between known and new: the role of nQuire in supporting a coherent learning experience

Our analyses of the inquiry-based teaching-learning interactions have thus far underscored how, through a complex series of multimodally mediated recaps, elicitations and reformulations and careful lines of questioning, the teachers and researchers supporting students' inquiries continually work to create cohesion and continuity from what might otherwise be seen by learners as no more than a series of disparate events. They strive to help students build bridges, between established and new understandings, whilst developing 'common knowledge' and new shared understandings (Edwards and Mercer 1989). In doing so it is evident that a range of discursive, physical and technological resources are orchestrated to revisit, reframe and (re)contextualize the class' shared experiences and knowledge (of climate, weather and the school grounds) in ways that render these salient and relevant to the new topic of microclimates. It is also apparent that bridging between familiar and new ideas is a complex pedagogic achievement – something to be actively resourced, supported and accomplished rather than simply assumed. It is here that we would suggest that the nQuire toolkit that runs on an ultra-mobile netbook has a distinctive role to play. This is because the toolkit has been designed in ways that mean that facets of students' everyday knowledge become recast and reframed in ways that recontextualise and situate it in the context of a scientific inquiry – in this case within a scientific investigation of microclimates.

We have already explored how the use of photographic images of familiar locations embedded in nQuire can resource detailed discussions in respect of scoping and planning the data collection phase of an inquiry. However, this is not the only relevant affordance of nQuire. Our observations indicate, for example, that the teacher harnessed the functionality of nQuire in ways that encouraged students to capture their unfolding and shared understanding of the aim of their inquiry. In lesson 1, for instance, the teacher encouraged the students working in groups to record their hypothesis and key methodological choices by entering them into nQuire. The recording of the hypothesis and methodology choices in nQuire represented the culmination of a process of dialogic negotiation and created a textual record that bridged between lesson 1 and lesson 2. The outdoor activities to be undertaken in the following lesson would build upon the classroom-based activities in the current lesson, thus creating a coherent and cumulative learning experience that contributed to meeting the longer term goal of addressing the hypothesis. In this way, nQuire supported the students in building connections between past, current and future activities across the contexts of the classroom and the school grounds. As nQuire is web-based, the group's inquiry had at this stage become mobile across contexts; the hypothesis and methodology referred to plans to carry out an inquiry outside the classroom. Similarly, the net book could be physically carried outside in the next lesson and used to access nQuire in the field (for a detailed discussion, see Kerawalla et al., in press). nQuire thus distinctively entered into and resourced the processes of *connection building* across phases of activity. From the learner's perspective, the work they were undertaking began to develop a cumulative quality in which specific activities, and their goals, began to form part of a greater whole – a purposeful educational 'journey' through which they came to understand the nature and processes of the inquiry learning cycle. Consider as a further example, the students' use of the qualitative free text 'Comments' boxes that were aligned with the numerical and categorical data entry boxes.

The 'Comments' boxes were designed to enable students to capture, during the data collection phase of their work, important contextual information that would assist them in the interpretation of their data during analysis. Initially the students could use these boxes to 'record' data. Subsequently, however, as they moved towards the individual reporting of their investigation, they could also rework, refine, continually edit and save the text within the boxes. In doing so, the text can become an ongoing work in progress. It can be an iteratively-refined aide memoire and repository for capturing emerging ideas and thinking, over time, in respect of the interpretation of data and key findings. So the initial contextual information recorded in the comments boxes provides an 'anchor' from which to build knowledge and under-standing. This process of reworking using the comments boxes can support students in making connections across different phases of the inquiry cycle – work undertaken as part of the data collection phase can become connected to and can resource further work in respect of interpretation and reporting.

So rather than moving through a sequence of prepared screens, with the associated dangers of fragmenting and compartmentalising learning, the students' iterative use and re-use of the comments boxes can constitute a kind of 'narrative trail', somewhat akin to the workings of a problem, which can be saved, remaining visible to the learner, their former group-mates and the teacher who might then offer reflections, reactions and comment. The material is thus available for working on in the present, using material generated in the recent past and in anticipation of future use.

When it comes to attempts to engage in sustained, cumulative knowledge building, spoken discourse has some particular limitations, and as Wells suggests: 'Chief among these is the evanescence of the understandings achieved in speech' (1999, p. 115). Recognising this, teachers often encourage children to either collectively or individually construct texts or representations which capture something of what has been said or discussed. Wells has suggested that such texts can serve as 'improvable objects', and by this he means that such an object 'provides the focus for progressive discourse and simultaneously embodies the progress made' (p. 115). All forms of meaning making which give permanence to, or capture something from, the ephemerality that is talk have the potential to serve as improvable objects. In each case, 'it is the material permanence of the form in which the semiotic artefact is embodied that enables it to support the recursive reflection and revision that is so important a characteristic of knowledge building' (p. 116). The creation of brief but highly salient textual comments within nQuire, clearly served as such improvable objects as the texts generated as part of this process typically became valuable resources for iterative reflection, revisiting and re-versioning over time.

Concluding remarks

As Gee has argued: 'It is the connections or associations that people make among their experiences that are crucial to learning, thinking and problem-solving' (2003, p. 73). Given this, we chose to explore and underscore the significance of the processes of connection-building for inquiry learning. In doing so, we have highlighted both the complexity and the necessity of building correspondences between ideas and experiences – both within and between lessons. The analytic extracts presented here show how, in the context of inquiry-based learning experiences, instructors work multimodally to support learners in developing trajectories of meaning making through the orchestration of diverse resources. The metaphor of orchestration is an apposite one – capturing the sense in which instructors' work to harness pupils' knowledge, experience and contributions and weave together (and connect over time) ideas, themes and sub-themes in pursuit of overall pedagogic goals. Orchestration happens in the subtle interweaving, backgrounding and foregrounding of multifaceted guided activities. Our work also indicates that the affordances of an ICT-mediated inquiry toolkit, in the hands of a teacher skilled in the pursuit of inquiry, can be of considerable use in this orchestration, enabling coherent connection building to be successfully pursued.

References

Baldry, A. and Thibault, P. J. (2006) *Multimodal Transcription and Text Analysis*, London: Equinox.

Barnes, D. (1992) 'The role of talk in learning', in K. Norman (ed) *Thinking Voices: the work of the national oracy project*, London: Hodder and Stoughton.

Collins, T., Mulholland, P. and Gaved, M. (2012) 'Scripting personal inquiry', in K. Littleton, E. Scanlon and M. Sharples (eds) *Orchestrating Inquiry Learning*, Abingdon: Routledge.

de Jong, T. (2006) 'Computer simulations – Technological advances in inquiry learning'. *Science*, 312 (5773): 532–533.

Edwards, D. and Mercer, N. (1987) *Common Knowledge: the development of understanding in the classroom*, London: Methuen/Routledge.

Gee, J. P. and Green, J. (1998) 'Discourse analysis, learning and social practice: a methodological study', *Review of Research in Education* 23: 119–169.

Gee, J. P. (2003) *What Video Games Have to Teach Us About Learning and Literacy*, New York: Palgrave Macmillan.

Hickey, D. and Filsecker, M. (2012) 'Participatory learning assessment for organising inquiry in educational videogames and beyond' in K. Littleton, E. Scanlon and M. Sharples (eds) *Orchestrating Inquiry Learning*, Abingdon: Routledge.

Kerawalla, L., Littleton, K., Scanlon, E., Jones, A., Gaved, M., Collins, T., Mulholland, P., Blake, C., Clough, G., Conole, G. and Petrou, M. (in press) 'Technical support for the construction of personal inquiry learning trajectories across contexts', *Interactive Learning Environments*.

Lemke, J. (2001). The long and the short of it: Comments on multiple timescale studies of human activity. *Journal of the Learning Sciences*, 10 (1&2), 17–26.

Littleton, K. Twiner, A. and Gillen, J. (2010) 'Instruction as orchestration: multimodal connection building with the interactive whiteboard', *Pedagogies: an international Journal*, 5(2): 130–141.

Mercer, N. and Littleton, K. (2007) *Dialogue and the Development of Children's Thinking, a socio-cultural approach*, Abingdon: Routledge.

Mortimer, E. F. and Scott, P. H. (2003) *Meaning Making in Science Classrooms*, Milton Keynes: Open University Press.

Murphy, P. (2000) 'Understanding the process of negotiation in social interaction', in R. Joiner, K. Littleton, D. Faulkner and D. Miell (eds) *Rethinking Collaborative Learning*, London: Free Association Press.

Nurkka, N., Viiri, J. and Littleton, K. (submitted) 'The nature, purpose and rhythm of classroom discourse in a cumulative, purposeful frame in science teaching, *Pedagogies: an international Journal*.

Rasmussen, I. (2005) *Project Work and ICT: Studying Learning as Participation Trajectories*, Doctoral Thesis, Faculty of Education, University of Oslo: Norway.

Scott, P., Ametller, J., Mortimer, E. and Emberton, J. (2010) 'Teaching and Learning Disciplinary Knowledge: developing the dialogic space for an answer when there isn't even a question', in K. Littleton and C. Howe (eds) *Educational Dialogues: understanding and promoting productive interaction*, Abingdon: Routledge.

Rogoff, B. (1990) *Apprenticeship in Thinking: cognitive development in social context,* Oxford: Oxford University Press.

Wells, G. (1999) *Dialogic Inquiry*, Cambridge: Cambridge University Press.

Chapter 3

Orchestrating inquiry instruction using the knowledge integration framework

Kevin W. McElhaney and Marcia C. Linn

Introduction

This chapter describes how the knowledge integration framework (Linn and Eylon 2006) can strengthen inquiry instruction. Using the Web-based Inquiry Science Environment (WISE) we designed instruction featuring scientific experimentation to help students gain an epistemologically normative view of inquiry and to support students' understanding of everyday science. We draw on studies using the *Airbags: Too Fast, Too Furious?* unit. The unit helps physics students integrate their understanding of motion and graphs during an investigation of the safety of airbags in car collisions. We report on a series of studies that illustrate how to improve virtual experimentation and at the same time ensure that students gain valuable inquiry skills.

Goals

In this chapter, we describe research that broadens students' views of classroom science. Studies show that students typically sequester their understanding of classroom science from their explorations of science in everyday life (Zimmerman et al. 2010). We draw on research about students' social (Barton 1998) and academic identities (Brown 2006) as well as their experiences in local communities (Corburn 2005) to inform design of inquiry activities. We seek ways to help students integrate their views of science from experiences in diverse settings.

We use the knowledge integration perspective (Linn and Eylon 2006; Linn and Eylon in press) based on over 25 years of research on inquiry science to guide our efforts to make experimentation meaningful and relevant within inquiry investigations. We draw on the views of Lehrer, Schauble, and Petrosino (2001) who argue that the history of experimentation within the authentic inquiry practices of argumentation, representation, and modeling 'imbues the dry bones of experimentation with meaning and significance' (p. 275). We explore ways to engage students in authentic investigations that promote the integration of scientific ideas about the domain, the methods of investigation and everyday experience. We illustrate ways that inquiry instruction can take advantage of real-world scientific issues to help students test their own ideas, build on everyday experiences, and achieve complex scientific insights.

Rationale

Experimentation is a critical aspect of professional scientific inquiry (Kuhn 1970; Latour and Woolgar 1986; Thagard 1992) and a desired component of school science (National Research Council 2007). Professional views of experimentation are diverse and include, in addition to controlled laboratory experiments, quasi-experiments (Campbell and Stanley 1966; Campbell et al. 1963), natural experiments (Freedman 2005), and design experiments (Brown 1992; Collins et al. 2004), among others. In choosing an experimentation approach, professional scientists must weigh the benefits of different methods and decide which ones align best with the context of inquiry and provide the most valuable insights about the investigation. While scientists' views of the appropriateness of these experimentation approaches may differ, their views regarding the general purpose of experiments are more uniform. Scientists conduct experiments about a wide range of questions using a plethora of methods that often require considerable creativity and cannot be reduced to a set of steps.

Typical school science instruction does little to communicate the nuances of authentic experimentation and their relationships to the context of investigation (National Research Council 2006). Students often follow recipe-like procedures that lead to predetermined outcomes rather than conducting their own investigations. Teachers instruct their students to vary one variable at a time without providing a clear rationale for this procedure. These typical classroom practices can discourage authentic student conceptions of scientific experimentation.

School science standards may also promote procedural views of experimentation. For instance, the California Department of Education (2000) states for middle school, 'Distinguish between variable and controlled parameters in a test' (p. 29) and for high school, 'Identify possible reasons for inconsistent results, such as sources of error or uncontrolled conditions,' and 'Recognise the issues of statistical variability and the need for controlled tests.' (p. 52). Though these standards address important aspects of experimentation, they focus on the validity of controlled experiments rather than on whether they answer an important question or advance understanding. These standards may encourage teachers to focus on the procedural mastery of controlling variables rather than on the nature of scientific investigation. Experimentation tasks that ask students to apply specific strategies misrepresent the nature of scientific inquiry and may preclude robust understanding of scientific experimentation. To develop authentic views of scientific experimentation, students need to explore uncertain situations and test their own conjectures. When students design experiments that test their own ideas and answer relevant questions about the world they can gain insight into science inquiry.

Role of domain knowledge in designing and interpreting experiments

The role of domain knowledge in scientific experimentation has become progressively more central to research on scientific reasoning. Early research addressed children's ability to isolate variables in experimentation contexts where domain knowledge played little or no role in making inferences. For instance, Inhelder and Piaget (1958) designed a task (later adapted by Kuhn and Phelps (1982) and others) that asked subjects to determine what combination of colorless fluids would yield a specific reaction outcome. Siegler and Liebert (1975) examined the ways subjects determined how an electric train runs on the basis of four binary switches (though in actuality, a researcher operated the train using a secret switch to ensure that subjects would test all 16 combinations). These studies examined experimentation as domain-general logical inference. In these situations, subjects could make valid inferences only by isolating variables to logically eliminate possibilities.

Research on experimentation in more knowledge-rich contexts has revealed the important role of domain-specific knowledge in how students conduct experiments. Studies in realistic contexts illustrate how designing and interpreting experiments involves a much more complex and nuanced set of factors than simply the ability to logically confirm or disconfirm hypotheses using controlled experiments. For example, studies show that children are more likely to test plausible rather than implausible hypotheses (Klahr et al. 1993; Tschirgi 1980), focus on variables they believe to be causal (Kanari and Millar 2004), and use experiments to achieve specific outcomes rather than test hypotheses (Schauble 1996). Though learners' ideas about the investigation context may lead them toward invalid experimental designs or inferences, students may also use ideas productively, such as by narrowing the range of testable values or eliminating implausible explanations. Tschirgi (1980) argued that children's tendency to use 'invalid' strategies when determining the ingredients needed to bake a good cake is reasonable, given real-life goals of reproducing positive results (good cakes) and eliminating negative ones (bad cakes). Koslowski (1996) also argued that using prior knowledge to generate and interpret evidence is a good strategy, particularly when understanding mechanisms informs the interpretation of outcomes. These studies indicate that learners' alternative strategies sometimes stem from efforts to refine their understanding of the situation, such as by narrowing the set of investigation questions or exploring the nature of the variables.

Other research shows the extent to which learners' prior understanding of the domain may affect their learning outcomes. Linn, Clement, and Pulos

(1983) compared the students' reasoning in laboratory tasks and naturalistic tasks involving the effects of system variables on an outcome. The study found that part of the variance in performance on these tasks was associated with task content knowledge. Schauble (1996) examined experimentation by children and adults in two science domains. The study revealed that subjects who conducted valid experiments often reached invalid conclusions informed by their prior knowledge of the system, and that subjects' knowledge sometimes informed their experimentation strategies. These findings show how domain knowledge contributes to scientific reasoning. Knowledge of the domain can facilitate learning from experimentation but might also mislead.

The findings point to experimentation as an important way to extend learners' understanding of a domain, as well as to strengthen appreciation of the diverse methods scientists have devised to advance knowledge. Incorporating experimentation activities within inquiry investigations provides learners with opportunities to test their own ideas about the domain and use the outcomes of experimentation to generalise knowledge to new contexts.

Controlled experiments vs. informative experiments

Today researchers still conduct studies that minimise domain knowledge and focus on promoting mastery of the control-of-variables strategy (CVS) in science classrooms (Chen and Klahr 1999; Klahr and Nigam 2004). The studies present students with stand-alone experimentation tasks where the role of students' prior domain knowledge is negligible and students' under-standing of the outcomes is inconsequential for subsequent tasks. These classroom tasks present experimentation to students as a procedure to be followed rather than a component of authentic science inquiry and treat the strategy itself, rather than insights about the context, as the relevant learning outcome. The implications of these studies for promoting valid experimen-tation in contexts where domain knowledge plays an important role are therefore unclear.

Characterising experiments as either controlled or uncontrolled may not capture the complexity of the insights students make during the course of experimentation. This chapter presents research that extends studies on students' mastery of CVS by examining a complex, realistic experimentation context. In this task, different controlled experiments for the same variable illustrate different types of variable relationships and not all controlled exper-iments are equally informative. In this way we make a distinction between *controlled* experiments and *informative* experiments.

Experimenting in realistic contexts requires learners to consider a wide range of ideas to design informative experiments. Learners need to integrate everyday ideas they have about the topic, formal knowledge about the science domain, and knowledge about strategies for experimentation in order to investigate complex questions. They need to focus their inquiry on the most salient issues. To make sensible decisions about experimental designs that test the multitude of ideas they hold, students need more than procedural guidance (such as domain general instruction of controlling variables). They need methods for sorting out their disciplinary knowledge and identifying compelling questions in order to learn how to conduct informative experiments. We draw from the knowledge integration perspective on learning (Linn and Eylon 2006) to suggest compelling ways that instructional designers can incorporate experimentation within rich, realistic, and relevant inquiry investigations.

Using the Knowledge Integration Pattern to Design Authentic Experimentation Activities

The knowledge integration (KI) perspective describes learning as occurring when students articulate their everyday ideas and intuitions then add new, normative ideas about science to their repertoire of ideas. Instruction then prompts students to bump these ideas up against one another, giving them opportunities to distinguish and evaluate ideas and resolve conflicts. These activities can help students monitor their own understanding so that they can identify and repair gaps in their knowledge. In this way, new knowledge is anchored to prior educational and personal experiences. The KI perspective informs the knowledge integration pattern, an approach to designing instruction that takes advantage of the variation in students' ideas to help learners achieve integrated understanding of science. The KI pattern guides students through four knowledge integration processes to help make the ideas in their repertoire cohere (Linn and Eylon 2006). Here we outline the four processes and discuss how they can help students integrate ideas from experiments.

Elicit ideas

First, instruction should *elicit ideas* that students have about the topic of study. Learners' initial ideas may reflect everyday experiences with the context of investigation and beliefs about the nature of science and experimentation as well as ideas students have from formal instruction. Eliciting ideas takes advantage of the variety of ideas that learners have about the investigation context and sets the stage for experiments to add new ideas that extend or conflict with students' prior ideas. Eliciting ideas near the beginning of an investigation can also motivate the need for experiments and encourage students to design informative experiments that provide relevant insights about the investigation.

The need to elicit students' ideas about the topic illustrates the value of connecting experiments to relevant contexts. Relevant socio–scientific issues can tap the productive ideas students have about everyday science and provide students with a basis for making informed conjectures. Real world problems allow the investigation to center on compelling driving questions (Krajcik et al. 1999), which make the design and interpretation of experiments consequential to the investigation. Relevant investigation contexts also reflect authentic practice of science inquiry and illustrate that experiments are a means to answering scientific questions rather than ends in themselves.

Add ideas

Next, instruction should *add normative ideas* to students' repertoires. Typical experimentation activities add ideas by illustrating monotonic (and often linear) relationships between system variables and outcomes. These relationships often illustrate key concepts in the scientific domain, such as how plants respond to sunlight or how frictional force relates to the mass of an object. These ideas are just a subset of the ideas that experiments can add for students.

In realistic experimentation contexts, aspects of experimentation may be less straightforward than in typical tasks. For instance, variables may exhibit non-linear or piecewise relationships to outcomes in situations where threshold values govern outcomes, or variables may interact. Experimentation can thus add ideas about the multitude of ways variables can vary with outcomes. Furthermore, a virtual experimentation environment may take advantage of scientific representations such as graphs or molecular models to add ideas about scientific representations.

Complex experimentation tasks may require scaffolding instruction in order for students to be successful. Inquiry investigations can add the ideas about the domain students need in order to design and interpret informative experiments. This approach makes scientific knowledge consequential for the experimentation task and motivates the need for new ideas.

Distinguish ideas

Third, instruction should encourage learners to *distinguish their ideas*. Experimentation by its very nature concerns distinguishing outcomes for one set of conditions from another – this is the main purpose of experiments. In typical experimentation tasks, students distinguish between the effects of different values of the same variable, illustrating covariation relationships. Instruction may also prompt students to distinguish observed outcomes from their expectations and to explain discrepancies. In a sense, distinctions comprise the essence of experimentation as a method of scientific inquiry.

Guiding students toward conducting valid, controlled experiments does not ensure that students will adequately distinguish ideas. Our studies suggest that even students who conduct valid controlled comparisons may not attend to the distinctions that serve as evidence in support of their views or that lead to relevant insights about the investigation. In a vignette later in this chapter, we illustrate how students' attention to the logistics of isolating variables can preclude them from considering the nature of the variables.

Designing tasks around realistic scientific contexts provides students with more opportunities to distinguish key ideas. For instance, important considerations in many variable systems are the magnitude and pattern of each variable's effect on outcomes. Inquiry questions that highlight the unique nature of each variable can prompt students to distinguish the variables from each other using these criteria. Driving inquiry questions that address the overall investigation goals rather than specific system variables can force students to connect variables to investigation goals for themselves. This activity can help students further distinguish the nature of the individual variables.

Sort out and refine ideas

Finally, instruction must allow students to *sort out and refine their ideas* in order to identify and repair gaps in their own understanding. Typical experimentation tasks may ask students to summarise their experimental results but neglect to provide opportunities to apply or generalise the findings. Summary may not compel students to evaluate the knowledge they build from conducting experiments, possibly leaving gaps in understanding. Inquiry instruction should make the findings from experiments consequential so that students recognise when their knowledge is insufficient to address the inquiry goals. Students can then revisit their experiments or conduct additional trials to strengthen connections among their ideas.

Realistic investigation contexts allow knowledge students gain from experiments to be consequential. Consequential tasks require students to bring multiple sources of evidence together, such as domain knowledge, observations and outcomes from experiments, research from the World Wide Web, ideas from peers, and everyday conceptions of science. These activities can take many forms, such as constructing an argument (as in a debate or persuasive essay), designing an artifact, or critiquing the arguments, designs and viewpoints of others.

In summary, realistic experimentation activities have the potential to help students' link scientific ideas to their everyday ideas about science. Realistic experimentation tasks embedded within inquiry investigations provide an alternative to typical laboratory experiments in their emphasis on the nature and purpose of experimentation and the role of experimentation in addressing relevant, real-world problems.

Investigating a realistic problem: *Airbags: Too Fast, Too Furious?*

Airbags is a week-long computer-based inquiry module designed for high school physics classes. *Airbags* has two primary learning goals. First, students examine the relationship between the nature of one-dimensional motion and the characteristics of position-time and velocity-time graphs. Second, *Airbags* aims to help students understand the dynamics of airbag deployment and the risks for injury from an airbag in a head-on collision. In *Airbags*, students investigate factors that lead to a high risk for injury to the driver from an airbag. The design of *Airbags* aims to integrate these two learning goals by prompting students to use graphs to further their understanding of collision events.

In this section, we describe the activity sequence of *Airbags* and illustrate how it takes advantage of the relevant context of airbag safety and the KI pattern to make the experimentation activity meaningful, relevant, and consequential.

Activity I: Orient and Elicit Ideas

Activity 1 introduces students to the investigation context, elicits their ideas about how airbags work and why they might present dangers in certain circumstances. A screenshot of the first activity of *Airbags* appears in Figure 3.1. The activity presents students with different types of evidence, such as a slow motion video of a head-on crash test, a full-speed video of an airbag deploying, and fatality statistics from accidents involving airbags. Students articulate their initial ideas in response to prompts concerning how airbags are designed to work, why they must deploy at such high speed, and the conditions in which they might be dangerous. The activity encourages students to view the crash test video multiple times to familiarise them with the sequence of events that occur during a head-on collision. The prompts guide students toward developing the primary criterion for determining whether the driver was injured by the airbag – encountering an airbag that has not finished inflating. The subsequent activities build on these ideas by introducing the motion characteristics as variables and the safety of the driver as the outcome in experimental trials.

The early steps in *Airbags* were successful in motivating the topic for study. We designed *Airbags* for students at or near legal driving age in the United States, making automobile safety a particularly relevant topic for many students. Furthermore, the motion and forces that students experience as either drivers or passengers in cars from day to day provide students with a kinesthetic understanding that can be extended to this investigation. The dramatic videos depicting crash tests and the real-time airbag deployment video contributed to capturing students' interest, as did

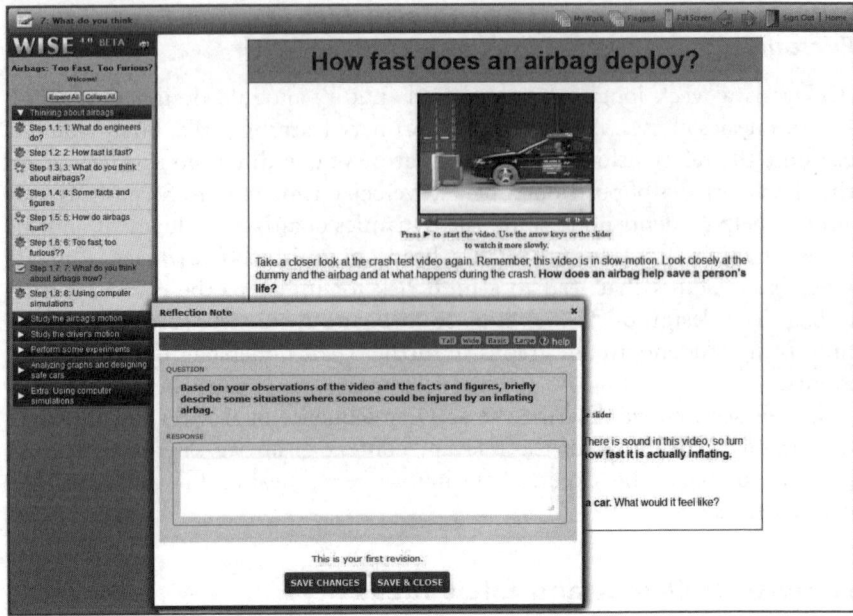

Figure 3.1 Screenshot of an evidence step and an embedded prompt in Activity 1 of *Airbags*.

examples of visualizations that professional engineers use to study the safety of automobiles. The impact of these videos was likely enhanced for students who had driving experience. Many students noted that they thought about the *Airbags* module when they drove their car during the week in which they used the module in their classrooms. The topic of car safety thus resonated with these students at a personal level.

The value of the compelling investigation context goes beyond capturing students' interest. The videos and fatality statistics prompted students to consider the speed of the airbag deployment as a trade-off between protecting and injuring the driver, depending on the conditions of the collision. Class discussions helped engage students in debating the design features of cars and airbags in light of this trade-off. The limited information students had to debate this issue at the beginning helped make the use of physics to analyse the situation consequential.

An early embedded prompt asked students to interpret the fatality statistics, which showed women to be at greater risk for death from impact with airbags. In our most recent study with *Airbags*, 60% percent of students' responses attributed the gender difference to irrelevant factors such as driving skill or inattention (due to applying make-up, for example). Class discussions revealed many students' awareness about greater insurance premiums for men compared to women and that this evidence conflicted with their initial interpretations. This discrepancy provided motivation for students to design experiments that would generate evidence for alternative explanations. Responses to assessments near the end of the module showed students greatly improved their understanding of the gender disparity. We discuss these improvements below.

Activities 2 and 3: Add and distinguish ideas about motion and graphs

Activities 2 and 3 focus on helping students add and distinguish the ideas about motion and graphs that are needed to conduct and interpret their informative experiments. These activities add ideas about kinematics that help students understand the nuances of motion of the airbag and the driver during the collision and how graphs represent this motion. *Airbags* prompts students to rewatch the crash test video while focusing on the motion of the airbag (for Activity 2) or the driver (for Activity 3). Students observe a simple animation of this motion (Figure 3.2 (a) and (b)), use a drawing tool

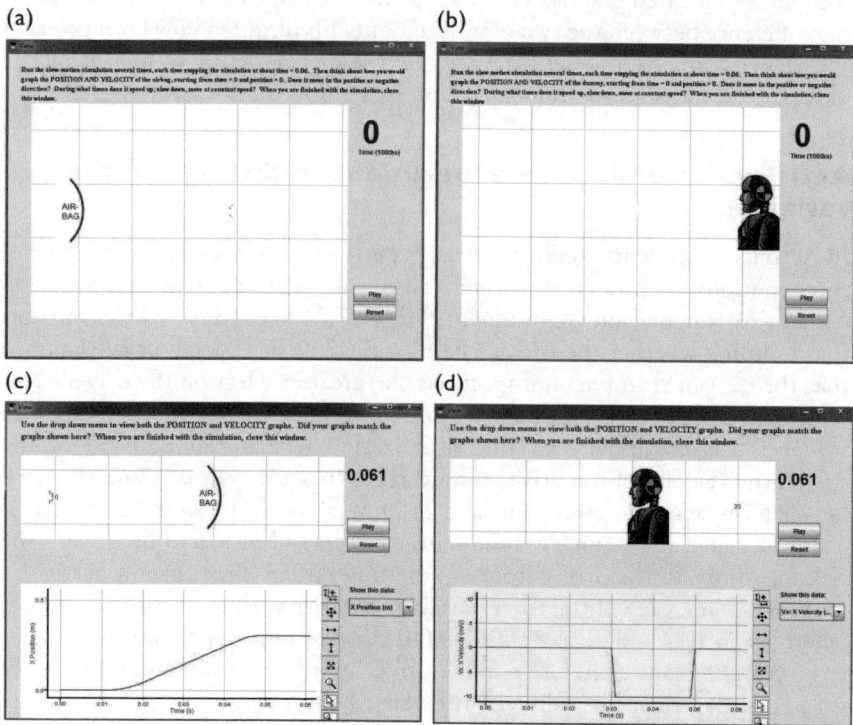

Figure 3.2 Scaffolding visualizations in Activities 2 and 3 of *Airbags*. Students observe an animation of motion [(a) and (b)], predict the appearance of graphs, then observe computer-generated position or velocity graphs simultaneously with the motion [(c) and (d)].

to sketch position and velocity graphs of the observed motion, then observe the animation concurrently with dynamically generated position and velocity graphs (Figure 3.2 (c) and (d)). The visualizations add ideas about the nature of the motion of the airbag and the driver, and how different features of the graphs represent different characteristics of motion.

After using the visualizations, *Airbags* prompts students to distinguish between the computer-generated graph and their own graph, among different parts of the graph from each other, and between graphs of motion in opposite directions. These prompts call students' attention to the difference between their initial ideas and new normative ideas about graphs and highlight distinctions among positive, negative, and zero velocity and acceleration. We observed a common interaction that students had with their teachers during the third activity as they sketched their prediction of the position and velocity graphs of the driver's motion. After having struggled with the graphs of the airbag's motion in the previous activity, many students drew accurate graphs of the driver's motion that neglected only to represent the correct direction of motion (opposite to that of the airbag). When these students observed the computer-generated graphs (which were inverted versions of their own graph), the difference between the two graphs not only highlighted how both position and velocity graphs represent the direction of motion, but also reinforced the idea that the value of the velocity graph is the slope of the position graph.

Activity 4: Conduct an experiment to distinguish the variables

In Activity 4, students conduct virtual experiments to investigate the effect of three motion variables on the driver's risk of injury from an airbag. Students use an experimentation environment (Figure 3.3) to conduct a series of trials that examine whether the driver's height, the collision speed, or the amount that the car can crumple on impact has the greatest effect on the driver's risk of injury. Each of these questions maps on to one of three motion variables students can manipulate in the visualization (the initial position of the driver, the velocity of the driver toward the airbag after impact, and the time between impact and driver's initial motion relative to the steering wheel).

In the experimentation environment, two types of relationships govern the risk for injury to the driver from an inflating airbag. First, over a particular range of values, each of the three variables covaries with the time that elapses before the driver and airbag collide. Tall drivers, low speed collisions, and a large crumple zone therefore make a driver more likely to encounter a fully inflated airbag than short drivers, high speed collisions, and a small crumple zone. Second, two threshold values (for position and time) determine situations where the likelihood of injury is invariant: (1) short drivers who sit within an airbag's zone of deployment will *never* encounter a fully inflated airbag, and (2) for sufficiently tall drivers, if the duration of the crumple zone

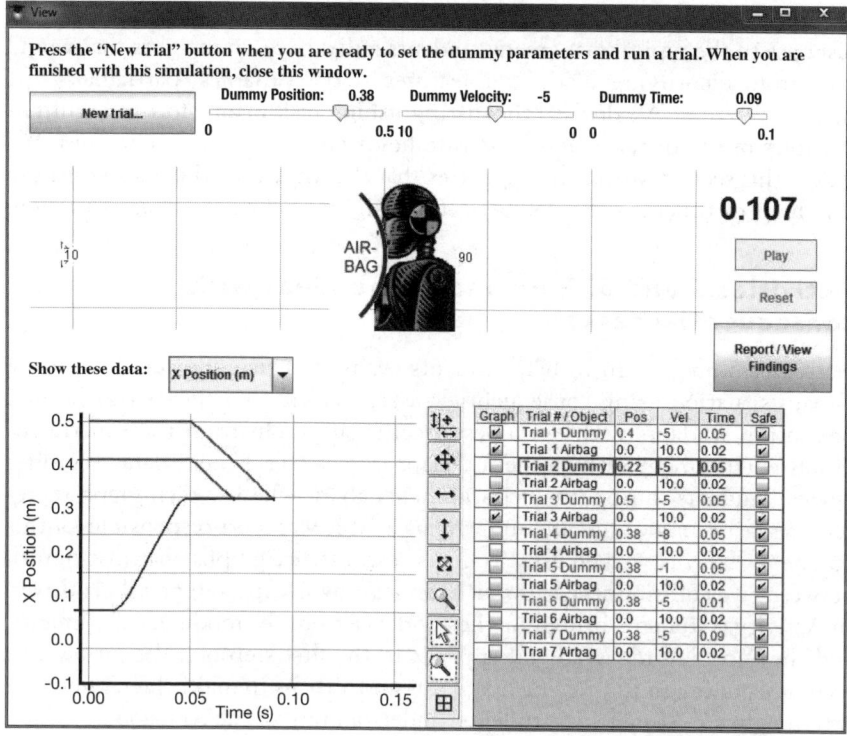

Figure 3.3 Experimentation environment in Activity 4 of *Airbags*. At the top, students select and investigation question, specify variable values, and observe the animation for each trial. In the lower left, students can view a position or velocity graph of the airbag's and driver's motion. In the lower right, students can see their trial history, which they can use to sort trial outcomes and compare the graphs of multiple trials.

exceeds the deployment time for the airbag, drivers will *always* encounter a fully inflated airbag.

The combination of covariation-based and threshold-based relationships between variables and outcomes produces piecewise, rather than simple linear, functions that describe conditions that produce safe outcomes. These complex relationships force students to combine knowledge of the collision events, motion parameters, and graph interpretation in order to achieve a sophisticated understanding of the situation. The ability of students to design informative experiments therefore depends upon more than their propensity to control variables in an arbitrary manner.

The inquiry question of determining the variable that has the greatest effect on the outcome is a distinguishing task. We also studied versions of *Airbags* that presented students with a more typical task of examining the effect of the individual variables on the outcomes. We found that in response to the typical task, many students failed to reach insights that would arise from identifying distinctive features of the variables, particularly the threshold values. We devised the distinguishing task in an effort to highlight the roles of the distance and time thresholds on the collision outcomes. We follow this section with three vignettes that illustrate how the distinguishing task helped students reach sophisticated insights about the airbags situation.

Activities 5 and 6: Sort and refine ideas with consequential tasks

Activities 5 and 6 aim to help students evaluate their understanding of the airbags situation using consequential tasks. Activity 5 achieves this by first presenting students with examples of collision graphs from the experimentation environment as hypothetical data from a 'black box' data recording device. Students must construct arguments about whether each graph represents a safe or unsafe outcome and which variable was most responsible for this outcome. Activity 5 then asks students to construct graphs that distinguish between two collision scenarios, such as those involving a tall or a short driver. In Activity 6 students bring together evidence from the module, experiments, and the World Wide Web and apply it to the first step of a design task: to recommend design improvements to cars and airbags to make them safer. The activity aims to strengthen students' understanding of the collision dynamics by applying their understanding of factors that lead to injuries from airbags. Arguments and design tasks require students to determine whether their current state of understanding is sufficient to address the broad goals of the inquiry investigations. If their level of understanding proves to be inadequate to construct a cogent argument or to inform the initial design effort, students may be compelled to revisit previous evidence to refine their understanding.

We observed students reaching insights from discussions with their working partner in efforts to reach consensus on arguments and design considerations. These discussions were likely enhanced at least in part by the design of the prompts. Rather than simply asking students to explain an observation or phenomenon, the prompts provided students with just two or three choices and asked them to defend just one of the views. For instance, some prompts asked students to explain why a graph illustrated a safe or an unsafe outcome. Other prompts asked students to choose the collision factor that was most responsible for the outcome. Requiring each dyad to take a particular position helped students recognise when they were in disagreement with their partner and required them to achieve consensus. Students often asked us to resolve disagreements between group members as they attempted to generate a unified response to these prompts. In these situations, we would ask each student to summarise their own point of view and engage them in a mini-debate. Sometimes we would instruct students to revisit evidence, such as the videos or their experimental results, to better support their views.

As we noted earlier, 60% of students attributed increased risk for women to irrelevant factors. In a similar argumentation prompt after the experimentation activity, *Airbags* presents a scenario that asks students to explain whether a short, stocky man or tall, thin woman is at greater risk for an airbag injury. On this item, the percentage of students who use irrelevant evidence to support their view fell to just 11%, while the percentage of students who correctly identified the driver's distance from the steering wheel as the determining factor in this scenario was 73%. The ability of the *Airbags* investigation as a whole to shift students' views from uninformed to those based on evidence illustrates the importance of giving students opportunities to refine their understanding of the everyday application of science.

Three Vignettes: Using Experiments to Highlight Key Distinctions

Here we present three vignettes that illustrate how an experimentation task that emphasises distinctions among the variables helped students consider the nature of the variables in the Airbags situation. These vignettes focus on the ways that the distinguishing inquiry task helped students reach insights that a typical experimentation task of examining individual variables might not have allowed them to make. All students names used in these vignettes are pseudonyms.

Vignette 1: 'Let's go to the next question.'

We first discuss Brett and Eric, who studied the version of *Airbags* that presented the typical task of examining the variables individually. Brett and Eric were enrolled in a science and mathematics program that had high standards for admission and that served the strongest students in their metropolitan area. Students in this program are concurrently enrolled in calculus and nearly always attend four-year colleges. Brett and Eric had the following exchange while conducting a controlled comparison for the position variable:

E: ...Short or tall. And now we have to move the guy back, 'cause he's taller. So we gotta keep everything except position. So move him back some. Like right there.

B: He's going to be safe, obviously.

E: He might not, let's just check. [They run a new trial.] Yeah. So mark that as safe. OK, put the graphs for the previous two. [They compare the graphs of the two trials]

B: They're both safe.

E: Yeah. So let's go to the next question.

This exchange illustrates two ways that their controlled test, though 'valid' in the strict sense of varying only one of the variables, failed to be especially informative. First, because the first of these trials produced a 'safe' outcome, Brett knew in advance that the outcome of the subsequent trial, which they conducted with the driver at a greater distance from the airbag, would also be 'safe.' However, rather than choosing a set of values that would provide them with new insights, they simply completed the test they had initially planned. Second, because both of these trials produced 'safe' outcomes, they failed to provide any evidence for their ultimate conclusion – that short drivers are at greater risk for injury.

This example illustrates why controlled experiments are not necessarily informative. Further tests aiming to illustrate conditions that led to an 'unsafe' outcome might have better informed their understanding and possibly highlighted the role of the distance threshold in determining collision outcomes. However, their variable choices and the brevity of their discussion about the results suggest they are focused more on the perceived requirement of isolating variables than on gaining insight about the situation.

A subsequent conversation during their next set of controlled trials sheds more light on their experimentation approach:

E: ...since we're doing, like, experiments, we can only change one of them, we can't change multiple ones.
B: Yeah.
E: 'Cause like in real life, there would be a combination of all three.

Eric appears to believe he is prohibited from doing anything other than isolating individual variables, even though at no point does *Airbags* instruct students on how to design experiments. Furthermore, the distinction he makes between their task and 'real life' indicates he believed these other strategies would be permissible in other contexts. Though Eric did not elaborate on what he meant by 'a combination of all three', his comments suggest he views the task of isolating variables as being a requirement of classroom science, and that in an authentic setting the investigation would require a more complex approach.

Brett and Eric provide an interesting example of students who are able to articulate the complexity of the problem in front of them but appear consciously to ignore this complexity. Their decision raises issues about the conflicting goals of classroom science and authentic inquiry. The contrived nature of Brett's and Eric's investigation approach suggests that the typical task of examining individual variables failed to jar them into a mindset that prioritised deepening their knowledge about the investigation over doing what was expected of them as high-achieving science students. Brett and Eric might have benefited from engaging in the distinguishing task, which they might have perceived as more challenging, authentic, and realistic.

Vignette 2: 'We're kind of figuring it out as we're looking at this.'

Joann and Linda were enrolled in the same selective science and math program as Brett and Eric. Joann and Linda studied the version of *Airbags* that presented the distinguishing task of determining the variable with the greatest effect on the collision outcome. Like Brett and Eric (and many other students), they began their investigation of the variables by planning an approach that would isolate each variable at three distinct values of the other variables:

L: I don't know. Maybe we just test ummm, like, test the position at, like, three different points. That's just so – that's just so many tests, never mind....

At this point they use their first three trials to isolate the position variable and test its full range but are soon discouraged by the sheer length of their proposed approach (27 trials in all). After choosing intermediate values for their fourth trial and discussing the outcome, their discussion about the 'effect' of the car crumpling empowers them to abandon their default isolation of variables strategy:

J: See we keep – we kept all that the same, but the farther away it was, the safer. Keeping the velocity and time on track. Because I would imagine let's say you had – it was closer, and it goes right there, and you had the dummy time at like 1 full second, that would give it more time to inflate. So then the dummy wouldn't start moving until 7.5.

L: Right, OK.

J: So it's an extra half – time ... or whatever ... And if you decrease the velocity, they can move slower, which I'm assuming is a slow crash, like slow impact crash.

L: OK.

J: Then it all falls back to what we said originally, the crash, the speed of the crash dictates if position and dummy time, you know, the crumpling of the car would have an effect.

L: Yeah. I don't understand why we have to do different tests for each three different sections [investigation questions]. You know? You click on them and be like whatever trials for this, kind of. 'Cause it looks like we're kind of figuring it out as we're looking at this.

This excerpt sheds light on their rationale for changing their approach. Joann summarises the results of their initial controlled trials using the typical covariation approach ('the farther away it was, the safer'). However, their view of the inquiry task appeared to change when they recognised that a simple covariation-based explanation was insufficient to address their inquiry questions. Their discussion turned to the trade-offs between variables (e.g. reducing the position but increasing the time) and their pre-experimentation hypothesis (that the speed 'dictates' the effects of the other variables). At this point they began conducting trials in a more spontaneous way in an effort simply to 'figure it out.'

The stark differences between these first two vignettes illustrate how asking students to distinguish the variables might have changed their entire conceptions of the task. For Brett and Eric, the typical isolation of variables task appeared to provoke a 'schoolish' response. They viewed the task as a simple covariation problem (a common class of problem in school science), and as a result they prioritised a valid control of variables design over gaining insight. In the process, they sequestered their classroom inquiry investigation from the real life practice of authentic science. Their analysis never went beyond a superficial characterization of the variables. The investigation questions in the typical task did not challenge Brett and Eric to deepen their understanding of the situation.

In contrast, Joann's and Linda's task of distinguishing the variables ultimately led them to incorporate a wider range of strategies to elucidate variation patterns. They conducted trials with the intention of understanding the relationships between variables and outcomes and the mechanisms that governed these relationships. Their questions encouraged them to consider the nature of the variables and to determine the unique contributions of each variable toward the outcome. This approach reflects an authentic, rather than a 'schoolish', view of the inquiry task.

Vignette 3: 'Why are they the same?'

Christine and David were enrolled in a physics class (at a different school from the students in the previous vignettes) comprised of students having wide-ranging science and mathematics ability. As with Joann and Linda, *Airbags* presented Christine and David with the distinguishing task. In this vignette, Christine and David conduct a controlled comparison for the velocity variable. Because they have set the position variable to a value within the airbag's deployment range, they achieve identical outcomes where the airbag injures the driver. As they compare the graphs from these identical outcomes, they have the following exchange:

D: Um, wait, go back to the other graph? Isn't that kind of like the same?

C: Yeah. Yeah. So...

D: Mm.

C: Why are they the same?

D: All right. Faster speed equals less safe.

Christine and David have distinctly different responses to the outcome of Trial 5. Christine appears to be interested in what causes the results. David, however, seeks evidence for covariation between speed and risk for injury, despite observing two identical outcomes. His statement 'faster speed equals less safe,' while it reflects the conventional wisdom that drivers are more at risk for injury in high speed collisions, completely ignores the evidence they generated in their experiment. Their next trial breaks David's grasp on the conventional wisdom:

C: ... It still looks the same!
D: Well that's like the airbag hitting *him* [verbal emphasis]. So he's like, driving driving driving driving driving, and the airbag's coming, psh, and it's hitting him. And then it will be like stopped, and he didn't go into it, it just kind of blew into his face, so that means that he'd be...not good.
C: Yeah, but I mean like, it still looks the same as if it was going slower. Still the same effect, the position doesn't change so that person stays the same height obviously.
D: I think I kind of get it, like. Like, um, our hypothesis was, you know, for this, the height made a difference, like the taller you are, then the safer you're going to be, and the smaller you are, the not safer you're going to be. And we thought it was really the speed that was going to affect it, but, whether you're going slower or faster, the airbag coming out and hitting you [gestures hand toward face], you know –
C: The same.
D: It's gonna be the same.
C: Oh OK, I get you.
D: So really, the speed doesn't affect it.... right now, it's more the height.

This vignette illustrates a couple of important ways that the distinguishing task and the realistic nature of the *Airbags* investigation led Christine and David to reach insights they likely would not have reached using a more typical experimentation task. First, David's detailed narrative accounts of the dynamics of the interaction between airbag and driver illustrate the degree to which their everyday understanding of the situation informed their interpretation of the experiments. Without this realistic context, they would have great difficulty making sense of the identical outcomes they observed for their controlled comparison. The *Airbags* context not only gave them information they could use to explain the results, but also gave their conclusions personal meaning.

Second, Christine and David were able to reach an important insight concerning the relative effects of the driver's height and collision speed in determining the safety of the driver. Distinguishing the variables led them to incorporate the unique nature of each variable into their explanation of the results. Throughout their experimentation sequence, David attempted to characterise variable relationships using statements of the form 'more x equals more y.' This tendency toward interpreting all outcomes in this way likely stemmed at least in part from school science's emphasis on covariation relationships. The complex nature of the variable relationships in the *Airbags* task produced an unexpected outcome, forcing them to reconcile their 'schoolish' expectations of covariation with their conflicting observations. Their insight reflects their efforts to make sense of the results in the context of everyday life rather than characterise them according to rules that did not apply to the situation.

Implications for Inquiry Instruction

The knowledge integration framework suggests ways for instruction to help students develop authentic views of experimentation within inquiry investigations. Centering investigations on realistic, relevant contexts encourages students to take advantage of their knowledge in designing experiments and in reasoning about their findings. This way, students can design experiments that test their ideas rather than merely follow a recipe that may not connect to their prior conceptions or relevant everyday ideas.

Our findings illustrate that some students have developed a formulaic approach to controlling variables, possibly from prior instruction. These students appear to miss subtleties in the investigative context and lack a propensity to make sense of their investigations. School science may condition students to focus on valid procedures at the expense of understanding the scientific implications of their experiments. As mentioned at the onset, this might stem from standards that endorse a specific view of experimentation and that equate valid experimentation with controlled tests. Another reason may be that students lack opportunities during typical instruction to conduct experiments in meaningful contexts.

Our studies illustrate a major challenge of inquiry instruction: the need for students to take on the role of scientific investigator and (to some extent) let go of their role as a science student. As Brett and Eric demonstrate in our first vignette, the students' classroom goals (such as earning a good grade or minimising effort) can interfere with making meaningful insights about realistic investigations. Designers of inquiry instruction should be mindful of ways in which students' beliefs about classroom science can preclude authentic interpretations of inquiry investigations. The success of students engaged with the distinguishing task of *Airbags* illustrates the substantial effect that subtle changes in framing of inquiry tasks can have on students' insights. In *Airbags*, presenting students with a set of uncommon investigation questions appeared to jar some students out of their roles as science students and encourage them to make more authentic inquiry choices.

The distinguishing task was not equally effective for all students who studied *Airbags*. For students who found the distinguishing task too difficult, a more direct method of scaffolding might have been more helpful. For example, we might have explicitly asked students to identify values of position, velocity, and time values that were particularly important to determining the outcomes, then prompted them to distinguish the variables on this basis. Using logging technologies currently available in WISE and other learning environments, this direct guidance might be provided if students conduct experiments in a way that does not provide evidence for these distinctions between the variables. Identifying the best forms of guidance for experimentation, as well as employing guidance that is adaptive to the nature of students' inquiry moves, are important avenues for future research on technology-enhanced inquiry instruction.

Finally, our studies emphasise the importance of conducting research on inquiry in classroom contexts. Uncovering the ways students' beliefs about classroom science affect their interpretation of inquiry tasks is not possible with laboratory studies. We illustrate that the extent to which students are conditioned to think about scientific investigations and their goals as science students can profoundly influence learning outcomes from inquiry investigations, even those about relevant everyday contexts. Research should continue to examine how students' beliefs about classroom science can affect the effectiveness of inquiry instruction. We hope that further research on inquiry learning will continue to challenge the norms of typical science instruction and bridge the gap that exists between classroom and professional views of science. These research efforts have the potential to benefit students not only within the classroom, but also as lifelong learners.

References

Barton, A. (1998) 'Teaching science with homeless children: Pedagogy, representation, and identity', *Journal of Research in Science Teaching*, 35 (4): 379–394.

Brown, A. (1992) 'Design experiments: Theoretical and methodological challenges in creating complex interventions in classroom settings', *Journal of the Learning Sciences*, 2 (2) : 141–178.

Brown, B. (2006) 'It isn't no slang that can be said about this stuff'; Language, identity, and appropriating science discourse', *Journal of Research in Science Teaching*, 43 (1): 96–126.

Campbell, D. and Stanley, J. (1966) *Experimental and Quasi-experimental Designs for Research*, Chicago: Rand McNally.

Campbell, D., Stanley, J. and Gage, N. (1963) *Experimental and Quasi-Experimental Designs for Research*, Chicago: Rand McNally.

Chen, Z. and Klahr, D. (1999) 'All other things being equal: Acquisition and transfer of the control of variables strategy', *Child Development*, 70 (5): 1098–1120.

Collins, A., Joseph, D. and Bielaczyc, K. (2004). 'Design research: Theoretical and methodological issues', *Journal of the Learning Sciences*, 13 (1): 15–42.

Corburn, J. (2005) *Street Science: community knowledge and environmental health justice*, Cambridge, MA: MIT Press.

Freedman, D. (2005) *Statistical Models: theory and practice*, Cambridge: Cambridge University Press.

Inhelder, B. and Piaget, J. (1958) *The Growth of Logical Thinking*, New York: Basic Books.

Kanari, Z., and Millar, R. (2004) 'Reasoning from data: How students collect and interpret data in science investigations', *Journal of Research in Science Teaching*, 41 (7): 748–769.

Klahr, D., Fay, A. and Dunbar, K. (1993) 'Heuristics for scientific experimentation: A developmental study', *Cognitive Psychology*, 25 (1): 111–146.

Klahr, D. and Nigam, M. (2004) 'The equivalence of learning paths in early science instruction', *Psychological Science*, 15 (10): 661–667.

Koslowski, B. (1996) *Theory and evidence: the development of scientific reasoning*, Cambridge, MA: MIT Press.

Krajcik, J., Blumenfeld, P., Marx, R. and Soloway, E. (1999) 'Instructional, curricular, and technological supports for inquiry in science classrooms', in J. Minstrell and E. van. Zee (eds.), *Inquiry into inquiry: science learning and teaching*. Washington, D.C: AAAS Press.

Kuhn, D. and Phelps, E. (1982) 'The development of problem-solving strategies.' *Advances in Child Development and Behavior*, 17: 1–44.

Kuhn, T. (1970) *The Structure of Scientific Revolutions*, Chicago: University of Chicago Press.

Latour, B. and Woolgar, S. (1986) *Laboratory Life: the construction of scientific facts*, Princeton, NJ: Princeton University Press.

Lehrer, R., Schauble, L. and Petrosino, A. (2001) 'Reconsidering the role of experiment in science education', *Designing for science; Implications from everyday, classroom, and professional settings*, 251–278.

Linn, M., Clement, C. and Pulos, S. (1983) 'Is It Formal If It's Not Physics? (The Influence of Laboratory and Naturalistic Content on Formal Reasoning)', *Journal of Research in Science Teaching*, 20 (8): 755–770.

Linn, M. and Eylon, B. (2006) 'Science Education: Integrating Views of Learning and Instruction', in P. A. Alexander and P. H. Winne (ed), *Handbook of Educational Psychology*, Mahwah, NJ: Lawrence Erlbaum Associates

Linn, M. and Eylon, B. (in press). *Science Learning and Instruction: taking advantage of technology to promote knowledge integration*, New York: Routledge.

National Research Council. (2006) *America's Lab Report; investigations in high school science*, Washington, D.C: The National Academies Press.

National Research Council. (2007) *Taking Science to School: learning and teaching science in grades K-8*, Washington, D.C: The National Academies Press.

Schauble, L. (1996) 'The development of scientific reasoning in knowledge-rich contexts', *Developmental Psychology*, 32 (1): 102–119.

Siegler, R. and Liebert, R. (1975) 'Acquisition of formal scientific reasoning by 10–and 13–year-olds: designing a factorial experiment', *Developmental Psychology*, 11 (3): 401–402.

Thagard, P. (1992) *Conceptual Revolutions*, Princeton, NJ: Princeton University Press.

Tschirgi, J. (1980) 'Sensible reasoning; A hypothesis about hypotheses', *Child Development*, 51 (1): 1–10.

Zimmerman, H., Reeve, S. and Bell, P. (2010) 'Family sense-making practices in science center conversations', *Science Education*, 94 (3): 478–505.

Chapter 4

Designing orchestration for inquiry learning

Mike Sharples and Stamatina Anastopoulou

For so long teaching has been regarded as a human task that it is novel to suggest that a machine should take over the role of contact with the students, and leave a teacher to do the planning and preparation of the lesson. But it does seem to work, and in a world that is short of teachers there is every reason to develop it as far as possible.

(Dodd, Sime and Kay 1968).

Background

From the earliest years of computer-based instruction there has been an ambition for computers to act as tutors, delivering personalised teaching to pupils while human teachers are promoted to learning managers (Dodd, Sime and Kay 1968). For many reasons the vision has never become a reality. Designing and implementing adaptive computer-based tutoring is a skilled and time-consuming task, one that requires the software developers to have a deep knowledge of the domain, the differences in knowledge and misconceptions of learners, and the structure and progress of the lessons, in a form that can be implemented as a tutorial computer programme. By contrast, most teachers are rather good at maintaining personal contact with students, guiding each of them through programmes of study suited to their needs and abilities. The irony is that rather than reducing the work of teachers, modern technology-mediated classrooms are requiring them to take on the dual roles of educator and learning manager.

As learning becomes more mechanised, through lesson plans, web-based resources, and re-usable learning objects, so teachers become conductors of an orchestra of students equipped with their learning instruments. The term 'orchestration' has been used by educational researchers to refer to the design and classroom management of a sequence of activities for individuals and groups to enable effective learning (e.g. Forman and Ansell 2002), and has been adopted by researchers in computer supported collaborative work to describe the management by a teacher, in real time, of a class of learners supported by interactive technology (Dillenburg and Jermann 2007;

Dillenbourg, Jarvela and Fischer 2009). It should be noted that 'orchestration' in education covers both the musical sense of the word, as the prior arrangement of a performance, and the alternative meaning, of dynamic management of people and activities to achieve some productive and harmonious result. To avoid confusion, where it is important to distinguish the two meanings, we shall refer to them as 'orchestration design' and 'dynamic orchestration'.

Orchestration design has overlaps with contemporary research into learning design (Goodyear and Retalis 2010), where the aim is to develop a suite of design patterns for capturing and communicating successful teaching practices. Dynamic orchestration of learning has been explored in relation to improvisational classroom teaching (Sawyer 2004) and in computer-based tutoring (Mitrovic and Koedinger 2009). Some computer-based tutors have been deployed in classrooms to support individualised instruction (Koedinger, Anderson, Hadley and Mark 1997).

The new opportunities are, first, to design technology that can support a human teacher to manage and monitor classroom interactions (Alavi, Dillenbourg and Kaplan 2009; Niramitranon, Sharples and Greenhalgh 2010; Nussbaum, Gomez, Mena, Imbarack, Torres, Singer and Mora 2010) and, second, for mobile devices such as smartphones, netbooks, and tablet computers to extend the orchestration of learning outside the classroom, so that the teacher initiates a structured activity and demonstrates it on the mobile devices inside the classroom, then each child continues the investigation in the playground, at home, or in a museum or discovery centre, with the personal mobile technology taking over the function of orchestration, and then shares, discusses and presents results back in class (Vavoula, Sharples, Rudman, Meek and Lonsdale 2009).

Orchestration and the teacher

Although the focus is on taking learning beyond the classroom, it is appropriate to start with the teacher. The Personal Inquiry (PI) project (www.pi-project.ac.uk) has confirmed the essential role of the teacher in explaining the inquiry process, orienting learners to the aims and scope of the inquiry activities, teaching about the inquiry topic, supporting the inquiry activities as they progress, and managing the integration, exploration and presentation of results. The prime requirement, then, is that orchestration should be teacher friendly. It should match the requirements of the curriculum and build upon current teaching practices. When the learning is continued outside the classroom, the teacher needs assistance to integrate each child's investigation back into a shared lesson.

To a teacher, the design and management of effective learning may sound like nothing more than their daily activity of creating lesson plans and running an orderly and productive classroom. A well-constructed lesson plan should set out the objectives of a lesson, the materials required, estimates of time, and an agenda for conducting the teaching, normally including: set-up, instruction, checks or assessments that the students are understanding what is being taught, and a summary or wrap-up of the lesson (Holtrop 2009).

What distinguishes orchestration design from lesson planning is its abstraction away from the specifics of a particular school and teacher, to provide a pedagogic structure that is both universal and relevant. This is a difficult balancing act, since teachers will be reluctant to adopt orchestration designs that are over-general or inappropriate. The approach we have adopted for inquiry science learning is to investigate how the process of inquiry learning has been described and visualised, then to design tools for orchestration that embody and present the essential elements of science inquiry, while allowing the teacher (or, for some activities, the students) to connect the inquiry to a sequence of lessons, to alter or create the teaching materials, and to modify the inquiry framework.

Tools for Orchestration

Since the 1970s there have been academic and commercial efforts to develop computer-based authoring tools for teaching. These enable teachers and educational leaders, with no knowledge of computer programming, to design and deliver a personalised sequence of teaching materials and assessment tasks to students in a classroom or computer lab. Commercial authoring systems have included Hypercard, Authorware and Toolbook. Technology arising from academic research has included REDEEM (Ainsworth, Major, Grimshaw, Hayes, Underwood, Williams and Wood 2003) and CTAT (Aleven, McLaren, Sewall and Koedinger 2009). With all of these, a teacher or instructional designer creates computer-based teaching material and the students learn by interacting with a desktop computer in the classroom or school computer lab. Despite its early promise, this type of adaptive computer-based tutoring has not been widely adopted in schools, due to the intellectual labour of producing effective teaching material and administrative problems of integrating fully-automated tutoring into a conventional school.

More recent work has developed tools to orchestrate teaching in a one-to-one classroom, where all students are equipped with portable devices, such as personal digital assistants (PDA) or netbook computers, to interact with teaching material and manage their learning. These tools enable teachers to combine their own pedagogical expertise in managing a classroom with pre-prepared resources and strategies to manage the flow of a lesson. This differs from development of authoring tools by aiming to support the dynamics of a classroom, with a flow between individual, group and whole class activities. The ManyScripts environment (Dillenbourg and Jermann 2010), for example, was developed to support classroom collaboration. Teachers can choose and edit a teaching script, such as ArgueGraph or ConceptGrid, that guides the flow of a lesson, and then enact it in the classroom, with the system assisting the process of selecting groups, organising the activities, and synthesizing the individual and group responses for classroom discussion. The MCSCL approach from Zurita and Nussbaum (2004) similarly assists a teacher to manage classroom interactions, with students attempting to solve a problem individually, then reach a group consensus, and then present their response to the class.

The SceDer system is an attempt to match the flexibility of authoring systems with the power of learning in a one-to-one classroom (Niramitranon, Sharples and Greenhalgh 2010). A teacher can create or modify a sequence of individual or collaborative learning activities, assigning students to groups and setting tasks that may require the students to view learning materials, answer questions, compare ideas or write responses. This dynamic lesson plan is then stored ready for use in the classroom. During a lesson the teacher can orchestrate the activities, not only by stepping through the sequence of tasks, but also by contributing material, annotating and discussing responses, and monitoring progress of individuals and groups.

All the systems described are founded on knowledge of successful teaching structures, including individual and collaborative inquiry. However, they are restricted to supporting a single lesson, with the students located within conventional classroom. Our aim in the Personal Inquiry project has been to design a toolkit for authoring and conducting inquiry-based learning across lessons, which can include learning activities spanning formal and non-formal settings such as the home or field centre.

Designing orchestration

Dillenbourg and Jermann (2010) provide an authoritative introduction to orchestration of classroom learning, through a set of 14 design principles along with indications of how these have been instantiated as specific scripts to support the dynamics of a technology-enabled classroom (see Chapter 5), so that a teacher can coordinate students and technology to progress towards defined learning outcomes while also allowing scope within the lesson for creativity and improvisation. The design factors they propose are: leadership, flexibility, control, integration, linearity, continuity, drama, relevance, physicality, design for all, curriculum relevance, assessment relevance, minimalism and sustainability.

All these factors are, necessarily, relevant to orchestration of inquiry learning since part of an inquiry activity would normally take place in a classroom (within a school or a field centre) mediated by a teacher. Ones that have equal importance and similar interpretation for inquiry learning as for typical classroom learning are *curriculum relevance* and *assessment relevance*. For the learning activity to be accepted within the school system it has to be relevant to the curriculum and compatible with school assessment. As

Dillenbourg and Jermann note, in practice there may be disjunctions in that the curriculum and assessment were designed to fit within the bounds of the traditional classroom and school timetable, so what is assessed may differ from what is taught, and both may not develop all the skills needed for the workplace or lifelong learning. As with classroom orchestration, it is important for inquiry learning to work with the *physicality*, and physical limitations, of the space and learners' bodies – for example, in moving around a space to study its properties and ecologies, or to investigate personal health, fitness, diet and anatomy. There are opportunities for high *drama* (not all of it positive) as children take ownership of their learning, aided by powerful technology, and explore the world as scientists, performing investigations outdoors or at home (Anastopoulou, Sharples, Ainsworth, Crook, O'Malley and Wright, under review).

Most of the factors need to be interpreted differently for inquiry learning. The principle in Dillenbourg and Jermann of general *relevance*, that the total time needed to teach a method should be proportional to its importance, should be seen not just in relation to the curriculum but in gaining the skills of 'being a scientist' that can enhance learning and attitudes throughout the lifecourse. Good *leadership* is even more important in inquiry learning, since the teachers must not only lead the classroom activities, but also coordinate the learning outside and incorporate the sometimes unpredictable results back into a classroom lesson. Thus, *integration* is an essential element of inquiry learning across contexts. Dillenbourg and Jermann show a notation similar to a musical score to indicate movement over time between interactions of individuals, groups, class, school, community and the world. To continue the analogy, we cannot assume that learners will be 'in harmony' outside the bounds of the classroom. They may collect incorrect data at the wrong locations, or might rush about exploring their environment and collecting material without considering whether this is appropriate to answer the inquiry question, or they may miss opportunities by failing to coordinate and discuss their findings. Such discord can be managed by technology-mediated coordination and sharing of data, so learners can gain awareness of each other's activities and know they need to keep up the pace, or alternatively by setting up meeting times in the classroom or field centres to get the activities back into synchronisation.

The technology can assist with *continuity* of learning, by maintaining a workflow so that the same data, learning objects and activities are being used by all the learners to provide compatibility of results (e.g., the same units of measurement and compatible metadata) to enable rapid integration. The students need to experience continuity across contexts, so that an inquiry activity which starts in the classroom can continue seamlessly into the playground, field centre or home, and then back to the classroom for discussion and presentation. Since the teacher may not be present to guide the activity then there needs to be a handover of control from teacher to student and technology, where the students and technology are mutually supportive in guiding the inquiry process. This means that the software must run in the classroom (on a classroom computer as well as personal devices) to enable the teacher to introduce the computer toolkit and hand off the activity to the combination of students and personal devices. Software such as Adobe® Flash® can run on a variety of desktop and handheld devices, but a more flexible approach is to store the individual and group data on a central server and provide a toolkit that interacts with the server through a web browser (see Chapter 5).

Flexibility for the teacher to improvise around the changing energy and responses of the students is just as important for inquiry learning. A different type of 'contingent flexibility' is also needed for the teacher to interpret data arising from an inquiry activity, uncover and investigate any inconsistencies, and draw implications for teaching from a tangle of results. This may require considerable skill in adapting the lesson to the outcomes of the inquiry so as to interpret specific and possibly contradictory findings as answers to the inquiry questions, guiding the students in how to act as scientists. Although the technology can do little to help a teacher in performing this task of contingent teaching (Wood and Wood 1996), it can ensure the data are stored in a consistent, structured format for comparison and presentation.

With inquiry learning there is a necessary break of *linearity*, as students carry out investigations at different times and locations, sometimes in contrary sequences. *Control* of the learning is not the teacher's sole responsibility, but must be dynamically handed between teacher, student and technology, with mutual understanding of when the teacher should be managing the activity, when individuals or groups of students are controlling their own learning within a clear structure, and when the technology is acting as guide or instructor. This control may cut across contexts – for example, with the teacher handing control to the learners guided by their personal inquiry toolkits during a classroom lesson which they continue outside.

The design principle of *minimalism*, of not providing more facilities or technology than are needed and not replicating existing classroom tools, is extended beyond the classroom. We cannot assume that learners will have (or have easy access to) computers at home, so tools such as word processors and presentation software may need to form part of the personal inquiry toolkit.

Design for all is perhaps the most difficult to achieve, since it requires an understanding of where and how the tools and activities will be enacted, at home, in field centres, or outside. The requirement that the learning should be conducted by most skilled teachers, not just exceptional ones, is essential if the methods are to be widely adopted, but this will require training and guidance for the teachers, not only in how to utilise the technology, but also in understanding the process of inquiry learning and how to orchestrate inquiries that require handover of control, preparation for active learning outside the classroom and integration of results. The *sustainability* of the approach will come from a growing understanding of the importance of personal inquiry as a life skill and how the inquiry process and methods can be applied throughout school and into post-school education.

Two additional factors need to be considered when designing the orchestration of inquiry learning outside the classroom and these are presented in the same style as the original 14.

Contextuality. The learning matches and exploits the physical and social environment (Factor 15).

Context in education can be viewed either as a bounded 'shell' in which the learner is situated, receiving information and accessing resources, or as a dynamic construct that is created and shaped continuously by interactions between people and technology across settings (Sharples, Taylor and Vavoula 2007). Beyond the classroom, learning can exploit the properties of the physical environment so, for example, a field trip to a nature reserve can sensitise children to the variety of wildlife and habitats, and help them to know where to look and how to observe without disrupting the habitats.

Classrooms create an ambience of stability, with a fixed setting, familiar and readily available resources, and a teacher as guide. Outside the classroom this stability is removed, which means the students (and, where appropriate, a teacher or mentor) may have to establish 'micro sites' for inquiry learning (Vavoula and Sharples 2009), where these are ad hoc learning spaces, such as a bedroom at home or patch of grass on a field trip, instrumented with appropriate mobile technologies and resources. This is a significant challenge that has been faced by institutions such as the UK Open University in developing its 'home experiment kits' (Bramer 1980). Although we could hope that the setting where a young person collects data, carries out an interview, or conducts a survey is quiet, physically stable and unchanging, this may not be the case. A child may be doing investigations in a noisy living room, balancing equipment on their lap, with continual distractions from television and interruptions by family members. Technology to orchestrate learning outside the classroom must be suitable for learning in everyday settings: portable, available when needed, easy to switch on and access, operable in bright, wet or noisy environments and either connected to the Internet or (if continual communication is not essential) capable of being synchronized back in the classroom.

Personal meaning. The learning activities make sense to each student and lead to personal understanding and fulfilment (Factor 16).

A tenet of personal inquiry learning is that students should carry out investigations that relate directly to their everyday life and interests. That is not to trivialise the learning; it could require engagement with a deep and complex topic, such as pollution or climate, but in a way that connects from personal understanding and interest to societal concerns or universal principles. The proposal is that children will engage with the scientific process and take a committed stance towards scientific issues by forming questions to which they genuinely want to know the answer, carrying out investigations that relate to their own needs and concerns, and discussing emerging findings with peers and experts (Anastopoulou, Sharples, Ainsworth, Crook, O'Malley and Wright, under review).

Challenges in orchestrating inquiry learning

The central challenge to orchestrating inquiry-based learning is how to manage the flow of control between teacher, students and technology, allowing learners the freedom to explore within a structure that guides their understanding of the inquiry process and supports discussion and sharing of results. Making this structure explicit, as a diagram or table, could provide a common referent for teachers and students that also illustrates the scientific process and matches the curriculum aims. But the more such a structure is specified as a lesson plan or sequence of tasks, the less opportunity there is for spontaneous discovery, to experience the enjoyment of 'doing real science'.

The way to break out of this bind is to see structure and constraint as productive. Constraints allow us to control the multitude of possibilities for action. There are so many ideas that we might have, and so many avenues to explore, that we have to impose constraint to avoid talking gibberish or wandering at random. Constraint is not a barrier to creative exploration, but the framework within which creativity can occur (Boden 1990; Sawyer 2004a). Constraints in science inquiry are both external and internal. External constraints include the scientific process (such as induction or hypothesis testing), the goals, the tools available to probe the world and share understanding, and the surrounding world of human and physical resources. The internal, mental constraints are of two general types: content (personal or consensual knowledge of the world and its properties) and task (how to argue about science, conduct a scientific inquiry and share results). Thus, orchestration of inquiry learning must provide a framework that allows creativity within the constraints of accepted scientific process.

A further challenge arises from integrating learning conducted on portable devices outside the classroom back into a classroom lesson. Say, for example, that a class is engaged in an inquiry that requires collecting personal data at home (such as their habits of watching television and playing computer games). Back at school they work in groups to share, discuss and combine results and then present the findings to the entire class. Issues may include: some children arriving back in class having not performed the task or having been absent when it was set; children failing to collect sufficient or accurate data; dealing with the reluctance of some children to reveal data about their personal habits or their deliberate falsification of data; cross-checking the accuracy of the data before it is merged with the group; and presenting the findings in a way that can lead to productive class discussions about children's habits and about the process of science inquiry. This handover back to the class will require the technology to record and display data in consistent format that can be viewed and merged. The children will need assistance in interpreting their findings in relation those of their peers and the aims of the inquiry. The teacher will need to be helped to correct inaccuracies, bring the results to the attention of the class and conduct a discussion about the findings. This not only requires new skills from the teacher, of managing externally-conducted inquiry and improvising discussion around results that emerge during the lesson, but also for the technology, children and teacher to work in harmony to analyse results and resolve problems. Such improvisational, contingent orchestration is of a different nature to the pre-prepared lesson that initiated the inquiry, or the scripted collaborations of Dillenbourg and Jermann. To support these different types of orchestration there needs to be a framework for orchestration that connects pre-structured learning with improvised inquiry, within and beyond the classroom, controlled by the teacher, or by the learner with the aid of technology.

Personal Inquiry framework and toolkit

The Personal Inquiry (PI) project is described in other chapters of this book, so here we shall examine only those aspects related to the orchestration of inquiry learning. A main objective of PI was that learners and their teachers should be supported throughout an inquiry process, with the teacher managing an investigation within the classroom supported by a computer toolkit running on a mixture of personal devices and fixed classroom computers, then moving control of the inquiry to the students each with a personal toolkit, then viewing, integrating, sharing and presenting results in the classroom. There may be a number of iterations of classroom and outdoor activity either within an inquiry cycle or through a series of investigative cycles.

Thus, the PI software application (named nQuire) was designed to support the cycle of inquiry, with its phases, tools and activities, while overlaying on this a sequence of time-bounded lessons or explorations. It offers templates for generic inquiries that can be adapted to specific lessons, to enable orchestration design, and a simple navigation interface based on the metaphor of a 'dynamic To Do list' (Rogers 1995) that enables dynamic orchestration. The very simplicity of an everyday To Do list (for shopping, etc.) hides its conceptual power. The essential property is that an ordered list structure provides productive constraints on a task, while allowing flexibility in how that task is carried out. List items can be elaborated, annotated and re-ordered, and items can be 'ticked off' to show how the task is progressing and what needs to be done. A dynamic To Do list goes beyond a paper one in

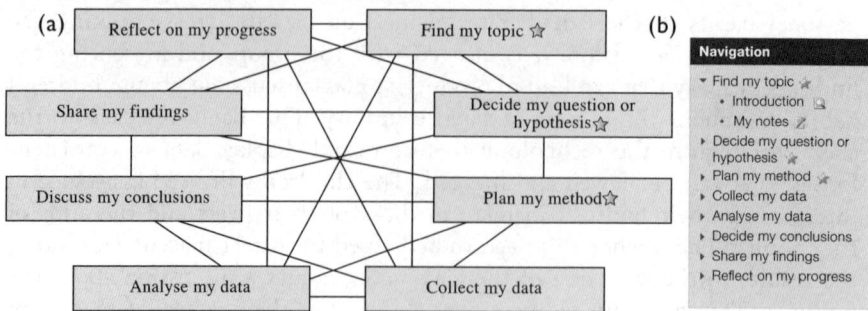

Figure 4.1 The inquiry process of nQuire shown (a) on the initial screen, and (b) for navigation.

allowing computer-based activities to be linked to each item and automatic management of the constraints, so that adding information to one item can alter, add or remove another one.

For science inquiry, the dynamic To Do list acts as an activity guide, to enable exploration and creativity within the constraints of a shared scientific process. The depiction of the scientific process shown in Chapter 1, Figure 1.3 was translated into a visual, clickable guide for nQuire (Figure 4.1a), displayed on its 'home' screen, which is then 'linearised' as a navigation guide on each successive screen (Figure 4.1b). The nQuire authoring system also allows for alternative wordings and visual arrangements for the home screen, to match specific curriculum or teaching needs.

When a user (teacher or student) clicks on an item in the navigation list it expands to show the specific activities and resources needed (such as a software tool to upload a photograph). Thus, a teacher could show it on a classroom

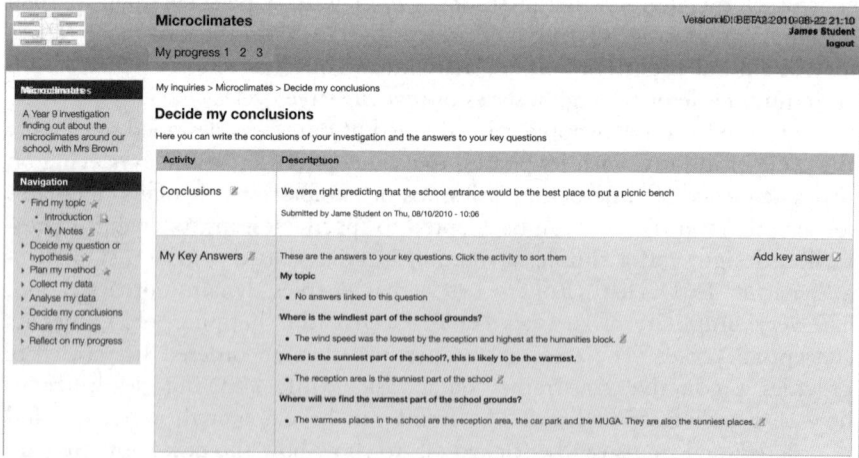

Figure 4.2 The nQuire screen, showing Conclusions and My Key Answers.

display during an orientation lesson as an Advance Organiser (Ausubel 2000) to explain and step through the activities. During an investigation, entering or changing items in one phase of the inquiry process (e.g. 'Decide my question or hypothesis') may then affect another phase (e.g. 'Decide my Conclusions', where the questions are presented again, for the student to add answers based on findings from the inquiry), see Figure 4.2.

The teaching and learning sequence (which might be classroom lessons or more exploratory activities) is shown in 'My Progress' at the top of the screen. This is set in advance as part of the authoring process, so the teacher has control over which phases of the inquiry will be available during a specific lesson (e.g. Figure 4.1a and b shows 'stars' against three phases to indicate they are active for that lesson) or can set specific activities to be undertaken outside the classroom.

Since both teacher and students are working with a shared software application, with an interface based around the phases of inquiry, the handover of control can be eased and supported. A typical sequence might be:

- The teacher introduces the inquiry topic, showing the inquiry cycle on a classroom display and working with the whole class to agree on a wording for 'Find My Topic';
- Students work in groups to propose inquiry questions or hypotheses, which are checked by the teacher;
- In groups, the students plan their methods and set up the investigation;
- Students work individually outside the classroom to collect data. Each student can either see data from other students as it is entered (if there is a network collection) or back in class (if not);
- Groups of students analyse their shared data and reach conclusions, referring back to their initial questions;
- Each group prepares and presents its work for a class discussion.

That is only one of many orchestration designs that nQuire can support. Others include starting from individual or group analysis of pre-prepared data, or reflecting on a previous inquiry as a prelude to designing a new investigation.

Orchestration in practice: 'Healthy Eating' and 'Effect of Noise on Birds'

In this section we analyse how orchestration was enacted in practice during the Personal Inquiry project. The analysis was based on two school trials that were carried out in a Nottingham school in 2008 and 2009, on the topics of Healthy Eating and Effects of Noise Pollution on Birds. The same teacher was responsible for managing both sequences of lessons at Nottingham, with the Healthy Eating trial taking place over nine lessons plus home activities lasting three weeks and the Noise Pollution requiring ten lessons and a field trip over four weeks. The children were equipped with Asus netbook computers running the nQuire toolkit which they kept for the duration of the trial, plus other equipment including a camera for the Healthy Eating trial.

Detailed results of the projects have been presented elsewhere (Anastopoulou, Wright, Sharples, Ainsworth, Crook, Norton and O'Malley 2009; Anastopoulou, Yang, Paxton, Sharples, Crook, Ainsworth and O'Malley 2010; Anastopoulou, Sharples, Ainsworth, Crook, O'Malley and Wright, under review); this section draws implications for orchestration of inquiry learning in practice. Both inquiries were designed around the dual factors of *contextuality* and *personal meaning*, whilst also also account of the other factors in the list of Dillenbourg and Jermann. The Healthy Eating trial connected the classroom as the place for framing and reviewing the work, and the home or other eating locations as sites for collecting data. Noise Pollution also started in the classroom, and then continued in a nature reserve (for observation of bird habitats) and the school grounds (for collecting data on the amount of food eaten by birds from feeders placed in noisy and quiet settings). The personal meaning came from discussions with children about issues that affected their lives and that they wanted to investigate. Healthy Eating was chosen by the teacher as being both relevant to the curriculum and to children's concerns. For Noise Pollution, a discussion amongst the children, researchers and the teacher narrowed it down to the effect of pollution on animals, and further discussion with an expert on animal behaviour resulted in a study that could be investigated through observation, correlation (amount of food eaten by birds from different feeders) and a 'fair test' experiment (setting up two feeders in similar locations in a garden, with a waterproofed radio placed beside one of them, and measuring the food eaten each day).

The experience of the PI project is that the teacher has a central role and one that requires different orchestration skills to conducting a normal lesson. The teacher produced a poster of the inquiry process which provided a visible guide to their activities across the different lessons and locations (Figure 4.3). The teacher referred to the poster during lessons to show where each learning activity was located in the inquiry process. This same workflow was implemented through the nQuire toolkit (Figure 4.2), which also managed the sharing of tasks and data amongst student groups.

Each trial enabled the students to become individually involved in the process of scientific inquiry and understanding of scientific method, which is a part of the UK curriculum but not easy to support within a traditional lesson. This requires investment of time over a series of lessons, so there was a decision to be made as to how much emphasis should be given to preparing and supporting the process of inquiry-based learning at the expense of content-led science teaching. For each trial, the school was willing to commit a sequence of lessons so that the children could gain knowledge of the topic

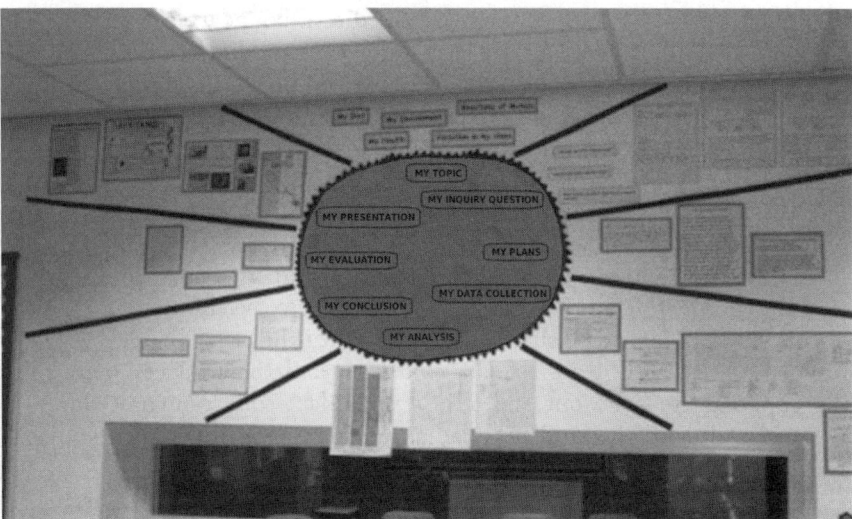

Figure 4.3 A classroom poster showing the inquiry process.

through the inquiry process, with the introduction and synthesis lessons in the classroom having an important function of relating the investigation to established scientific knowledge. For the healthy eating inquiry the children were able to ask questions by email to an expert on nutrition.

When the students first received the netbooks as part of a classroom lesson, the teacher channelled their excitement by giving them time to play with the technology and also by discussing technical problems that they might encounter outside the class. The dynamics of the classroom were immediately altered by the introduction of the netbooks, since each student had an individual machine with a screen that the teacher could not see from the front of class, so she was unable to tell what they were looking at and found it difficult to get their attention. As with many interaction or orchestration issues in technology-mediated learning, there might be a longer term technical solution (designing a means of wirelessly locking or synchronising the screens) or a more immediate social one (telling the students to close the lids and pay attention). Thus, orchestration involves consideration of trade-offs, in this case of designing and managing another layer of technology against disrupting the flow of the lesson by shutting and restarting the netbooks.

The learning designs for each trial were complex, requiring a coordinated sequence of activities over multiple lessons with synchronization of results back in the classroom, leaving little opportunity for creativity or improvisation by the teacher. In one lesson, the teacher had a few minutes left before the end, so decided to spend time on discussing technical problems that the students had encountered at home. In this, as in other lessons, the combination of inquiry cycle and computer toolkit acted as a boundary object (Star and Griesemer 1989), connecting the learning within and outside the classroom, through discussions about the technology use and mediating discussion about results collected at home or in the school grounds (Anastopoulou, Yang, Paxton, Sharples, Crook, Ainsworth and O'Malley 2010).

Integration of inquiry activities conducted outside the classroom back into the lesson was a central issue of the project. In both trials, the children collected data outside using the nQuire toolkit. These then needed to be shared, analysed and extracts presented on the classroom display for the whole class to see. The teacher played a key role to prepare the children for the need to collect valid data to be shared with the rest of the class. She devoted class time to discuss difficulties in data collection and the students were given the opportunity to go out and adjust their data collection procedures. It was made clear to the students that unreliable or invalid results would be questioned.

Furthermore, decisions needed to be made, by the students or teacher, as to which data were to be presented and in what format. The challenge is how to manage this integration for data that are not known in advance, and that might be messy and inconsistent. Again, this might be managed by technical or social means. Social management requires artful improvisation by a teacher within a lesson, to interpret the data and decide which to display to achieve the aims to the lesson without distorting the scientific findings. The data entry forms in nQuire ensured that the data were compatible and capable of being shared, but left selection and presentation of results to negotiation between the teacher and students.

Both trials were successful in that the children completed the task and there is evidence that children learned about the science topics as well as practising and understanding the process of science inquiry (Anastopoulou, Sharples, Ainsworth, Crook, O'Malley and Wright, under review). With regard to orchestration, the main issue was the burden that technology-mediated inquiry placed on the teacher, in managing a class of children engaging with netbooks, and in preparing the children for activities outside the class, then interpreting results they bring back to reach a satisfactory closure. Managing the expectations of children who expect a neat resolution where one may not be possible, yet demonstrating how the scientific method contributes to understanding the natural world is the fundamental challenge of orchestrating inquiry learning.

Conclusions

There are many similarities between orchestration for inquiry learning and orchestration in the classroom, especially when inquiries start and end as classroom lessons. This means that current practices of classroom management, as well as new research into the orchestration of learning, are

relevant to technology-mediated inquiry. There are, however, two fundamental differences.

First, the teacher must balance the need to teach the fundamentals of
science topic in a well structured way against the value of open-ended inquiry
where students conduct open-ended investigations that might produce an
unexpected result or no conclusive result at all. For the Noise Pollution investigation, the results went counter to expectations in that more bird food was
eaten in a noisy area of the school grounds. The teacher helped the children to
examine the evidence from their observations that a large pigeon, seemingly
unaffected by noise, was eating most of the food. The separate 'fair test'
experiment in the controlled setting of a garden did indeed show less food
being eaten in the noisy condition. It requires different skills from a teacher
to design and manage such inquiries, with their unforeseen results and the
need to interpret findings from multiple groups and settings, compared to
conducting a typical curriculum-led lesson.

Second, the teacher must be able to initiate and guide activities taking
place beyond the classroom. On some occasions, such as a field trip or museum
visit, the teacher may be present to check that the activities are going to plan.
External visits already form part of the standard school curriculum so teachers
should generally be well equipped to deal with contingencies. But organising
inquiry learning for the home or places where the teacher is not present is
a different proposition. This is not the same as traditional homework, since
the conduct of the investigation is as important as its outcome. Each child
should take responsibility for carrying out personally meaningful activities,
so that not only can the results be integrated and shared, but they can
individually and jointly reflect on the process of doing science. Our aim with
the Personal Inquiry project has been to design a mobile toolkit to support
this process of orchestrating learning activities across formal and non-formal
settings, providing a seamless handover from teacher orchestration supported
by the technology to technology-guided personal inquiry. The initial results
are encouraging and the next, substantial, step is to explore the value of
extending both the technology and the personal inquiry approach across
science education.

References

Ainsworth, S., Major, N., Grimshaw, S., Hayes, M., Underwood, J., Williams, B. and Wood,
D. (2003) 'REDEEM: Simple intelligent tutoring systems from usable tools', in T. Murray,
S. Blessing and S. Ainsworth (eds) *Authoring Tools for Advanced Learning Environments*,
Dordrecht, the Netherlands: Kluwer Academic Publishers.

Alavi, H. S., Dillenbourg, P. and Kaplan, F. (2009) 'Distributed awareness for class orchestration', in U. Cress, V. Dimitrova and M. Specht (eds) *Learning in the Synergy of Multiple
Disciplines, Proceedings of the 4th European Conference on Technology Enhanced Learning, EC-TEL
2009*, Heidelberg: Springer-Verlag.

Aleven, V., McLaren, B. M., Sewall, J. and Koedinger, K. R. (2009) 'A New Paradigm for

Intelligent Tutoring Systems: Example-Tracing Tutors', *International Journal of Artificial Intelligence in Education*, 19 (2): 105–154.

Anastopoulou, S., Wright, M., Sharples, M., Ainsworth, S., Crook, C., Norton, B. and O'Malley, C. (2009) 'Personal Inquiry: Lessons Learned', in *Proceedings of the mLearn Conference, 2009*. Florida: University of Central Florida.

Anastopoulou, S., Yang Yang, Y., Paxton, M., Sharples, M., Crook, C., Ainsworth S. and O'Malley, C. (2010) 'Maintaining continuity of inquiry learning experiences across contexts; teacher's management strategies and the role of technology' in M. Wolpers, P. A. Kirschner, M.Scheffel, S.Lindstaedt and V.Dimitrova (eds) 'Sustaining TEL', from *Innovation to Learning and Practice*, Lecture Notes in Computer Science, 2010, Volume 6383/2010: 17–29.

Anastopoulou, S., Sharples, M., Ainsworth, S., Crook, C., O'Malley, C. and Wright, M. (under review) 'Creating personal meaning through technology-supported science learning across formal and informal settings', *International Journal of Science Education*, (under review).

Ausubel, D. P. (2000) *The Acquisition and Retention of Knowledge: a cognitive view*, Dordrect: Kluwer.

Boden, M. (1990) *The Creative Mind: myths and mechanisms*, London and New York: Routledge.

Bramer, M. (1980) 'Using computers in distance education: The first ten years of the British Open University', *Computers and Education*, 4 (4): 293–301.

Dillenbourg, P. and Jermann, P. (2010) 'Technology for classroom orchestration', in M. S. Khine and I. M. Saleh (eds) *New Science of Learning: Cognition, Computers and Collaboration in Education*, New York: Springer.

Dillenbourg, P. and Jermann, P. (2007) 'Designing interactive scripts', in F. Fischer, I. Kollar, H. Mandl and J. Haake (eds) *Scripting Computer-Supported Collaborative Learning: cognitive, computational and educational perspectives*, New York: Springer.

Dillenbourg, P., Jarvela, S. and Fischer, F. (2009) 'The evolution of research in computer-supported collaborative learning: from design to orchestration', in N. Balachef, S. Ludvigsen, T. de Jong, A. Lazonder and S. Barnes (eds) *Technology-Enhanced Learning*, New York: Springer.

Dodd, B., Sime, M. and Kay, H. (1968) *Teaching Machines and Programmed Instruction*, London: Penguin Books.

Forman E. A. and Ansell E. (2002) 'Orchestrating the multiple voices and inscriptions of a mathematics classroom', *Journal of the Learning Sciences*, 11 (2/3): 251–274.

Goodyear, P. and Retalis, S. (eds) (2010) *Technology Enhanced Learning: Design Patterns and Pattern Languages*, Rotterdam: Sense Publishers.

Holtrop, S. D. (2009) *Writing Lesson Plans: An Introductory Page*. Huntington, Indiana: Huntington College. Available at: http://www.huntington.edu/education/lessonplanning/Plans.html (accessed August 2010).

Koedinger, K. R., Anderson, J. R., Hadley, W. H. and Mark, M. A. (1997) 'Intelligent tutoring goes to school in the big city', *International Journal of Artificial Intelligence in Education*, 8 :30–43.

Mitrovic, A. and Koedinger, K. (2009) 'Authoring intelligent tutoring systems', *International Journal of Artificial Intelligence in Education*, 19 (2): 103–104.

Niramitranon, J., Sharples, M. and Greenhalgh, C. (2010) 'Orchestrating learning in a one-to-one technology classroom', in M. S. Khine and I. M. Saleh (eds) *New Science of Learning: Cognition, Computers and Collaboration in Education*, New York: Springer.

Nussbaum, M., Gomez, F., Mena, J., Imbarack, P., Torres, A., Singer, M. and Mora, M. E. (2010) 'Technology-supported face-to-face small group collaborative formative assessment and its integration in the classroom', in D. D. Preiss and R. J. Sternberg (eds) *Innovation in*

Educational Psychology: Perspectives on Learning, Teaching and Human Development, New York: Springer.

Rogers, I. (1995) 'The use of an automatic "To Do" list to guide structured interaction', in I. Katz, R. Mack and L. Marks, (eds) CHI '95 *Conference Companion on Human Factors in Computing Systems*, New York: ACM.

Sawyer, K. R. (2004) 'Improvised lessons: Collaborative discussion in the constructivist classroom', *Teaching Education,* 15 (2): 189–201.

Sawyer, K. R. (2004a). 'Creative Teaching: Collaborative discussion as disciplined improvisation', *Educational Researcher,* 33 (2):12–20.

Sharples, M., Taylor, J. and Vavoula, G. (2007) 'A theory of learning for the mobile age', in R. Andrews and C. Haythornthwaite (eds) *The Sage Handbook of E-learning Research*, London: Sage.

Star, S. L. and Griesemer, J. R. (1989) 'Institutional ecology, "translations" and boundary objects; Amateurs and professionals in Berkeley's Museum of Vertebrate Zoology, 1907–39', *Social Studies of Science*, 19: 387–420.

Vavoula, G. and Sharples, M. (2009) 'Meeting the challenges in evaluating mobile learning: a 3–level evaluation framework', *International Journal of Mobile and Blended Learning*, 1 (2): 54–75.

Vavoula, G., Sharples, M., Rudman, P., Meek, J. and Lonsdale, P. (2009) 'Myartspace: Design and evaluation of support for learning with multimedia phones between classrooms and museums', *Computers and Education*, 53 (2): 286–299.

Wood, D. and Wood, H. (1996) 'Contingency in teaching and learning', *Learning and Instruction*, 6 (4): 391–397.

Zurita, G. and Nussbaum, M. (2004) 'MCSCL: Mobile computer supported collaborative learning', *Computers and Education*, 42 (3): 289–314.

Chapter 5

Scripting personal inquiry

Trevor Collins, Paul Mulholland and Mark Gaved

Introduction

Personal inquiry learning involves students in undertaking personally relevant investigations that can span home, school and field trip contexts. Over the past few years we have been developing and testing nQuire, a web-based application to guide secondary school students in designing, conducting and evaluating their inquiries (Mulholland et al. 2010). nQuire guides the learner according to a script that specifies the structure and process of the inquiry.

The ways in which the scripts are authored and customised has to be accessible to teachers and students as the inquiries should be personally relevant. A teacher needs to be able to specify the structure of the inquiry and options available to the learner. Choices made by the student need to be reflected in the script and guidance that will be provided. Given the difficulties students have with inquiry learning, the script needs to explicitly represent and support not only the step-by-step learning flow through the inquiry, but also the flow of data. For example, as well as leading the student through data collection then on to data analysis, the script should also pass the collected data in a form appropriate for analysis.

In this chapter we explain how scripting can be applied to support personal inquiry learning. Through the chapter we identify five aspects of personal inquiry learning that scripting can address, namely: personal choice, collaboration, regulatory process support, transformative process support and orchestration. The following section briefly introduces personal inquiry learning, the role of technology to support inquiry projects, and the role of scripting to support personal inquiry. We then summarise some of the challenges students face with inquiry learning, and present an overview of some of the key approaches to scripting that we have used. Our application of scripting to support personal inquiry is then explained through a set of four scripting constructs along with the rationale for using them. The penultimate section presents a set of examples illustrating how these constructs can be used in a scripting environment to help address the identified challenges of inquiry. The chapter closes with a summary of how this approach to scripting personal inquiry addresses the five aspects of personal choice, collaboration, regulatory process support, transformative process support and orchestration.

Inquiry learning

Inquiry learning seeks to engage students in a question-driven, open-ended process of investigation where they can extend their knowledge of a subject and further practise their scientific skills (Edelson et al. 1999). Inquiry learning is intended to help motivate students by arousing their curiosity and building on their existing interests, knowledge and skills. With regard to project-based learning, Blumenfeld and her colleagues (1991) make the case that students are more likely to be motivated to engage in projects that they perceive to be interesting and valuable, that they feel able to complete, and where the teacher's focus is on guiding the students' learning rather than their assessment performance. Therefore, personal inquiry learning focuses on supporting students so that they can take an active role in driving the inquiry process.

Considering the role that technology can play to enhance student and teacher motivation, Blumenfeld and her colleagues also identify six potential contributions – namely, to enhance interest; facilitate access to information; support the creation and manipulation of graphs or other representations; structure and guide the process; diagnose or correct errors; and help manage complexity and aid the production of reports or other artefacts. Within the broader scope of computer-supported collaborative learning (CSCL), computers have been likened to a 'Trojan horse', in that when used effectively they affect everything else in the classroom (Salomon 1992, p. 63). Orchestrating such a classroom requires the coordination of the students' activities, their learning processes and the technological support (Dillenbourg and Jermann 2007).

Based on a theatrical metaphor, scripts are used as a means for describing a set of activities that engineer and exploit differences between students' opinions or knowledge in order to encourage interactions, such as discussion, explanation and consensus. Scripts offer a means for specifying and adapting a set of activities, at a level of abstraction that can be reused in different learning contexts. Personal inquiry is not just about personally meaningful questions and motivational contexts, the students' actions and decisions also need to be reified through the tools they use to support their inquiry. Applying scripting techniques to represent the inquiry process offers a level of abstraction that can be used in a software application to enable teachers and students to specify inquiries. Furthermore, during enactment, the script can help manage the inquiry process and reflect the decisions students make in the guidance and support it provides.

The challenges of inquiry learning

In categorising problems that students encounter in inquiry, de Jong and van Joolingen (1998) distinguish between transformative and regulatory processes. Transformative processes are defined as those that yield knowledge during the inquiry, such as generating a hypothesis or designing an experiment. Regulatory processes are those needed to manage the inquiry. These two categories relate directly to the two goals of inquiry learning introduced above – that is, to extend students' subject knowledge and develop their scientific skills. Approaches to alleviate the problems associated with transformative processes include providing direct access to domain knowledge, structured templates for constructing hypotheses and support for making predictions. For regulative processes, examples of support include help with planning, monitoring and structuring the inquiry process.

A comparable set of challenges, motivated by the development of a series of technology-supported inquiry-based learning tools, are presented by Edelson et al. (1999). These highlight the importance of a motivational context, the accessibility of investigation techniques, access to background knowledge, the management of extended activities and the practical constraints of the learning context. In response to these challenges, they propose a design framework based on four interdependent components: the motivational context, the selection and sequencing of activities, the design of investigation tools and the creation of process supports.

Strategies for selecting a motivational context for learners relate to identifying meaningful, controversial and open issues (Blumenfeld et al. 1991; Dillenbourg and Schneider 1995; Barron et al. 1998; Linn et al. 2003). The selection and sequencing of activities are intended to structure the students' learning process to ensure their knowledge builds through the course of the inquiry process. The design of investigation tools is targeted at supporting specific tasks within the inquiry, such as access to background information, support for creating graphs or other representations, and the production of reports. The process supports relate to the tasks students need to undertake to manage the inquiry process, such as planning and monitoring their progress. In developing environments that support the scripting of inquiries by both teachers and students, we need to be mindful of the challenges of inquiry learning and, where possible, incorporate the strategies and techniques that have been used successfully to help address them.

Scripting: An overview of key approaches

Dillenbourg and Hong (2008), stress that the effectiveness of collaborative learning depends on the richness of the interactions during collaboration. Collaborative learning scripts are 'activity models that aim at enhancing the probability that knowledge generative interactions, such as conflict, resolution, explanation or mutual regulation occur during the collaboration process' (Tchounikine 2008, p. 193).

The granularity used to specify a script ranges from coarse-grained 'macro' scripts, where the sequence of tasks is described as a pedagogical model, to fine-grained 'micro' scripts, where the activities are described moment-to-moment as a dialogue model (Dillenbourg and Hong 2008). Macro-scripts typically exploit differences in students' opinions or knowledge to create situations that require the students to interact (e.g. to argue their case or explain and discuss the issues) in order to find a resolution. When played out, a fine-grained micro-level version of a script will include the means of interaction, for example a model of argumentation, which through use the students are intended to learn. The role of scripts to support collaborative learning relates directly to inquiry learning: at the macro-level, the inquiry process can be described as a set of phases that reflect a model of scientific inquiry which, through enactment (at the micro-level), the students are intended to both further their understanding of the subject domain and develop their scientific abilities.

ArgueGraph is summarised here to illustrate how scripts can be used to structure collaboration (Jermann et al. 1999; Dillenbourg and Hong 2008). The ArgueGraph script is an example of a macro-script that uses differences in students' opinions to motivate discussion. ArgueGraph has five stages, in the first of which students are asked individually to complete a multiple-choice questionnaire that elicits their opinions on open-ended topics. For each answer, the students are asked to write a few lines justifying their choice. The students' opinions expressed through their responses to the questionnaire are then presented as a scatter plot and discussed with the class, and pairs are formed that match students with widely differing opinions. In the third stage, each pair of students discusses their answers and justifications from the first stage; together they select a single answer, and add a justification for their choice. In the fourth stage, the teacher debriefs the students on the topics discussed, and synthesizes and clarifies the class's arguments. In the final stage, each student selects one of the questions and writes a summary of the arguments.

One of the dangers of applying scripts is to over-constrain the collaboration in such a way that inhibits naturally occurring collaboration (Dillenbourg and Tchounikine 2007). Scripts that have too many constraints about what can be done may stifle opportunities for collaboration. Dillenbourg and Tchounikine (2007) categorize the constraints affecting the flexibility of scripting as either intrinsic or extrinsic constraints. The core elements that define a macro-script can be viewed as a set of 'intrinsic constraints', which cannot be altered without changing the pedagogical intention of the script. In the case of personal inquiry learning, the intrinsic constraints relate to the model of scientific inquiry being applied and the students' active role in running their inquiry. Any other constraints (e.g. regarding the technology, learning context or group characteristics) that do not directly impact upon the intended pedagogy can be referred to as 'extrinsic constraints'. These can potentially be altered by the teacher or students in order to take advantage of unanticipated collaboration opportunities.

As noted previously, the purpose of collaboration scripts is to engineer conflicts (or splits) between students in order to necessitate interactions that are more likely to improve the students' understanding (Dillenbourg and Hong 2008). As well as using scripts to trigger interactions through differences of opinion or knowledge between students, scripting the inquiry process also seeks to highlight differences caused by false assumptions, misconceptions, and unrealised predictions. Intentionally structuring activities that help externalize assumptions, challenge misconceptions, validate data and justify interpretation are some of the scaffolding strategies used to support scientific inquiry (Quintana et al. 2004).

Within the context of developing support for inquiry learning, our interest in scripts is motivated by their suitability for specifying and guiding inquiries. As in a theatrical production, the full elaboration of a learning script will only be complete when the script is enacted. Although the inquiry cycle provides a model of scientific inquiry that describes and regulates the macro-level activities to be undertaken, inquiry is an open-ended process of investigation. For example, the question being investigated will help determine the nature of evidence required, and the means of data collection and analysis. Particularly in the case of personal inquiry, these decisions are made during the process rather than at the beginning. Scripting can be used to identify the structure of the inquiry and the options available for the students, but it does not require the elaboration of every possible outcome. Therefore, an inquiry script should support the students' decision making during the inquiry process and reflect those decisions in the support provided, without over-constraining the students' scientific inquiry method or collaboration opportunities.

Consolidating the previous work on CSCL scripts, Kobbe and his colleagues (2007) proposed a generic framework for specifying scripts, which considers the structural components and implementation mechanisms of the script. The components include descriptions of the type of participants involved, the activities they undertake, the roles adopted, the resources used to support the script, and the groupings used to structure the interaction between participants. The mechanisms used to implement the script consist of the task distribution (in terms of how activities, roles and resources are distributed across participants), the process of allocating participants to groups, and the temporal sequencing of groups and components (i.e. the order of events and activities).

In applying scripts as a means for teachers and students to specify and undertake inquiries, we are interested in how scripts can be effectively represented. Macro-scripts can be described in scenarios (as in the above

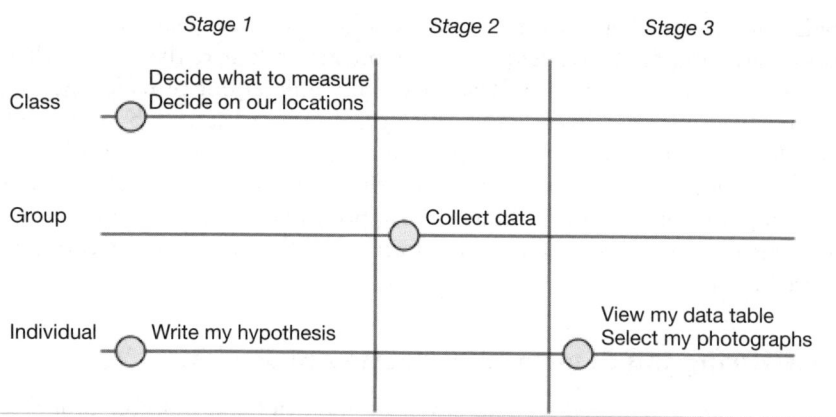

Figure 5.1 The nQuire open data model used to support the flow of information within an inquiry.

ArgueGraph example), but a more structured representation describes a script in terms of a 'workflow, i.e. a time-based sequence of operators that transform data structures, the social structure (student, groups, classes, roles) and object structures (resources and products)' (Dillenbourg and Hong 2008, p. 16). To specify a script, the social and object structures can be listed in tables to illustrate how the structures change at each stage of the script.

Within most school and university contexts the social structure active at each stage of a script can be described as that of the individual, small groups or the whole class. Dillenbourg and Jermann (2010) relate these to Vygotsky's three planes of psychological development: the intra-psychological plane (individual), inter-psychological plane (small groups) and the social plane (culture and society). At each stage of the inquiry, the level of social interaction can then be illustrated as a musical score notation showing the movements between the individual, group and social plane (see Figure 5.1).

In summary, scripts provide a flexible means for describing a set of activities. Collaborative learning scripts engineer and exploit differences between students' opinions and knowledge in order to motivate learning through discussion. Scripting techniques could also be applied to inquiry learning to encourage discussion between students, and to motivate students' engagement with the intermediate products of their inquiry, such as alternative hypotheses, conflicting data or differing interpretations.

Applying scripting to personal inquiry learning

To support personal inquiry the nQuire application has been developed to help guide students to design, conduct and evaluate their inquiries. Using the application the teacher can specify the overall structure of the inquiry and the options available to the students. As the students undertake the inquiry their choices are reflected in the application and the guidance it provides. nQuire provides web-based support for scripting inquiries that can be authored, extended and reused by both teachers and students. Here, we describe the key set of design constructs that enable the scripting of personal inquiries in the nQuire application. Although the application was implemented using the Drupal content management platform, the design constructs could be realised in other platforms.

Structuring inquiries and reflecting progress

Three constructs are used to help structure inquiries and monitor progress: stages, activities and phases. As with other scripts, our inquiries are structured into temporal 'stages', which can be managed by the teacher (or the student) as a means to progress the inquiry. The 'activities' to be undertaken are functionally grouped into 'phases'. Using this structure, the author of a script can identify a set of focal activities and phases in each temporal stage. These can then be highlighted as the inquiry progresses to guide the students' attention to their current tasks.

The status of each activity is shown as one of four states that reflect the currently available action for that activity, namely: 'unavailable', 'start', 'edit' and 'view'. These status values are altered by a set of operators when the user undertakes an activity or by changing the stage. For example, within an experiment, the activity to select a set of available measures, referred to as 'Decide what to measure', only becomes available once the hypothesis generation stage has been completed. The status of the 'Decide what to measure' activity will then be changed from 'unavailable' to 'start', and changed again from 'start' to 'edit' once a selection has been made.

Authoring a script can be done by either entering a new inquiry or cloning an existing one. This involves identifying the temporal stages, activities and phases, and setting the initial status and set of operators for each activity. A compact view of the script structure can be shown as a table containing the phases and activities as rows, the temporal stages as columns, with the initial status and change of status within each cell (see Figure 5.2). These constructs also support the monitoring of progress by both students and teachers. As noted above, the student's view of the inquiry can highlight the important activities and phases for the current stage, and the student's progress through them will be reflected by the status of each activity. Similarly, for any activity the teacher can see an overview of the class's progress by viewing the activity's status for each student or student group.

Figure 5.2 An extract from a script structure table showing how each activity's status changes during an inquiry.

Phase	*Activity*	*Stage 1*		*Stage 2*		*Stage 3*	
Decide my hypothesis	Write my hypothesis	start	edit	edit	edit	edit	edit
Plan my methods	Decide what to measure	start	edit	view	view	view	view
	Decide on our locations	start	edit	view	view	view	view
Collect my data	{Locations}		unavailable	start	edit	edit	edit
Present my data	View my data table	unavailable	unavailable	unavailable	unavailable	start	edit
	Select my photographs	unavailable	unavailable	unavailable	unavailable	start	edit

Icon descriptions: unavailable, start, edit, and view

An open data model for inquiry (data flow)

Within an inquiry, the result of each activity will typically create intermediate products, such as a hypothesis, predictions, an experimental design and data. How this information flows through the inquiry is referred to as 'data flow'. One of the key challenges of supporting open-inquiry is to identify a data model that is flexible enough to support a range of scientific methods, but also includes sufficient dependencies to ensure that the relevant information is available to support each activity. For example, the questions to be asked in a questionnaire need to be associated with their responses, and should be available during analysis.

Therefore, the data model needs to include dependencies between the products created in related activities. We modelled these dependencies explicitly for a generalised set of activities which are instantiated when the script is enacted. The activities undertaken during an inquiry that create intermediate inquiry products, such as a research question or hypothesis, can be mapped to this general data model. The key dependencies in our

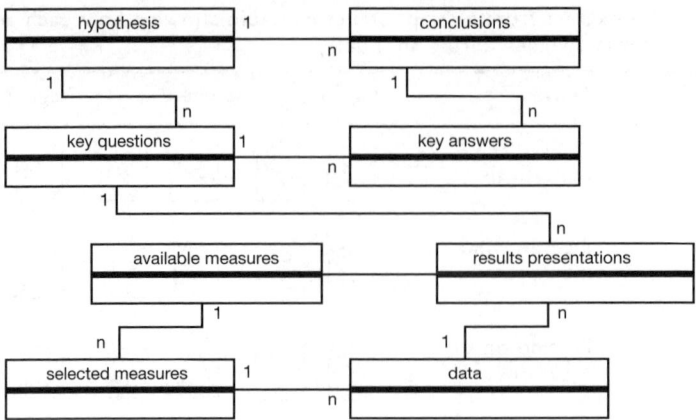

Figure 5.3 An example screen image from a Microclimate inquiry showing a student's 'Add data' activity.

model link the conclusions and hypothesis, the available and selected set of measures, and the data and presentation of results (see Figure 5.3). In order to help support experimental design, we also introduced an optional activity to break a hypothesis into one or more key questions that can be used to guide the choice of measures, the presentation of results and conclusion activities.

Activity actors, content and audiences (control flow)

As well as linking the intermediate products that are created as a result of the teacher and student activities, a scripting application also needs to allocate ownership to those products. The 'musical score' notation typically used to describe activities (see Figure 5.1) refers to whether the activity is being undertaken at the individual, group or class level. Scenarios describing the use of a script often implicitly refer to how the intermediate products are later used, but within the script this needs to be made explicit in order for an application to support the flow of control through the inquiry. Therefore, as well as specifying who can undertake an activity, we also identify who is intended to use the products that get created as a result. Following the theatrical script metaphor, we refer to these, respectively, as the activity 'actor' and 'audience'. The actor is identified directly when the activity is created, either individually by (user) name or as a group (such as class-10c or group-g). In contrast, the audience refers to a social level relative to the actor (i.e. individual, group or class). The audience is then used to identify a specific person, group or class during the script's enactment.

An example may help to illustrate this point. During the data collection stage of an inquiry, the students could be collecting data individually that they then share within their group. In this case, the actor for the 'Add data' activity could be the specific class (e.g. class-10c), but the audience would be set at the 'group' level, which would then be instantiated to a specific group (such as group-g) when a student in that group added data. A status of 'start' would be used throughout the data collection stage for the 'Add data' activity, and each of the data points would be created with an initial status of 'edit' so that anyone within the student's group could (if needed) correct the data.

Groups in use (groups and groupings)

This set of constructs is used to help support changes in groups during the enactment of a script. This collaboration technique is referred to as the JIGSAW technique (Aronson and Patnoe 1997). As explained in the previous subsection, defining the audience for an activity is attributed relative to the actor undertaking that activity. In scripts applying the JIGSAW technique, if the group is directly associated with the activity then changes to a group's membership would affect who could access that activity. Therefore, we introduced the concept of groupings that can be used to identify which set of groups are in play at any given point in an inquiry (i.e. for a given stage, phase and/or activity).

An example of how grouping works in practice would be an inquiry in which groups are formed to study a set of political viewpoints on a given issue, one group of students per viewpoint. After the first stage, the class is reorganised into another set of groups so that each group contains one member with knowledge of each viewpoint. In the second stage, the new groups then debate the issue from the perspective of each viewpoint. This JIGSAW technique would be supported by two groupings, where one grouping would identify the set of groups (and their members) in the first stage, and the second would identify the groups in use during the second stage. An important point to make here is that, in the second stage of the inquiry, each of the students could still access the activities (and intermediate inquiry products) from the first stage. Each student is a member of two groups, but the grouping in use changes from the first to second stage in order to handle the change in the social structure.

Addressing the challenges of personal inquiry learning through scripting

The constructs introduced in the previous section enable collaborative scripts to be authored and enacted in a web-based content management platform to support personal inquiry learning. In this section we give a set of examples from two versions of the nQuire application to illustrate how these features enable us to address some of the challenges associated with the regulatory and transformative processes involved in inquiry learning and group work. The examples shown are from two secondary school geography inquiry projects – one on Microclimates, and another on Urban Heat Islands.

Regulatory processes

Structuring the inquiry according to the activities to be undertaken at each (temporal) stage of the inquiry (either by individuals, groups or a complete class) provides a set of constructs that enable the inquiry process to be specified, monitored and (if needed) modified. These constructs can be used by a scripting application to help guide students through the inquiry process. For example, Figure 5.4 shows an 'Add data' activity for a Microclimates inquiry. The current inquiry stage is indicated in the top bar of each page, directly below the title of the inquiry (i.e. '**My progress:** $1 \rightarrow 2 \rightarrow 3$'). The set of activities in the current stage requiring the student's attention are highlighted in the navigation panel on the left of the screen (highlighted with a star i.e. the 'Collect our data' phase).

The structure of the inquiry is reflected in a 'breadcrumb trail'. The actor and audience for each activity can be used to reinforce the student's confidence and sense of control over their inquiry by indicating who can do the current activity (i.e. the actor) and who will see what is produced as a result (i.e. the audience). For example, Figure 5.4 shows that the 'Add data' activity can be carried out by any student in the group and the data point created will be seen by the same group members.

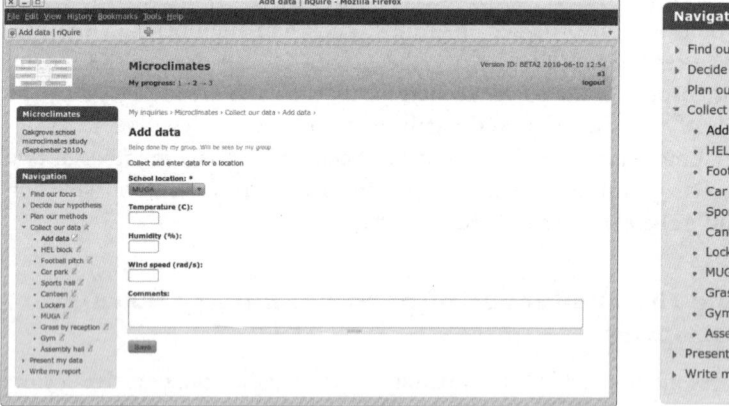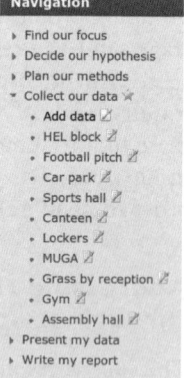

Figure 5.4 An example screen image from an Urban Heat Islands inquiry showing the introductory resources for the inquiry.

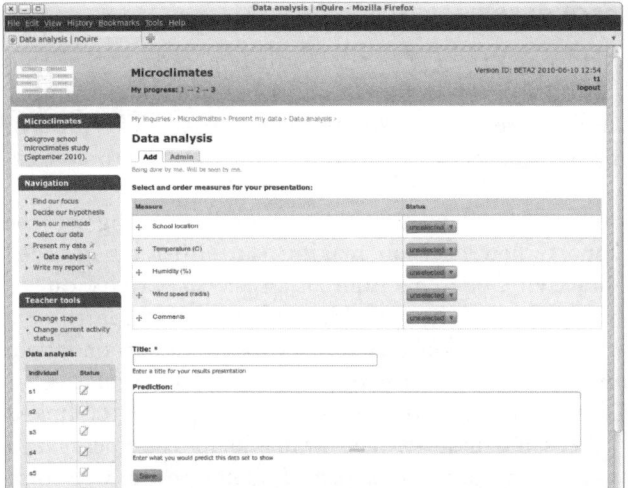
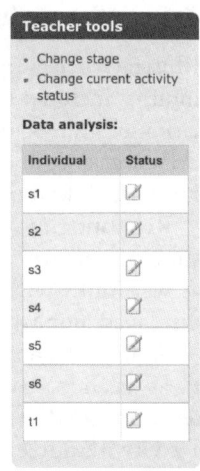

Figure 5.5 A microclimate inquiry screen image showing a teacher's view of the 'Data analysis' activity. An expanded view of the teacher's tools area is shown to the right to illustrate the activity status view (i.e. no one has yet created an analysis table).

The same structural elements can also be summarised to support the monitoring of a class's progress. For example, when a teacher accesses an activity, the current status of that activity for each actor could be displayed. Figure 5.5 shows the teacher's screen for the 'Data analysis' activity in our Microclimates inquiry. In this case, none of the six students (anonymised as s1 to s6) have yet created a data analysis presentation. Using authoring interfaces based on the script structure table illustrated in Figure 5.1, a teacher (anonymised as t1) can also add additional resources or edit activities, in order to address emerging misconceptions during an inquiry. Similarly, activities can be revised if the class is taking longer than expected to complete them.

Regulating the available activities according to the inquiry stage is a commonly used scripting mechanism, but some flexibility is required to handle cases of absent students or individual students that take longer to complete their activities. Stage changes are usually carried out by the teacher selecting the next stage in the proposed sequence. However, to handle exceptions to the intended sequencing of activities, an option in the 'Change stage' activity can be used to keep open activities from more than one stage. Another option is to progress the stage in the usual fashion and then access individual activities to change the activity's status (see the example 'Teacher tools' panel in Figure 5.5).

Transformative processes

Illustrative examples of support for the transformative processes within inquiry include: facilitating access to information; the creation and manipulation of graphs, or other representations; aiding the production of reports or presentations; and supporting experimental design and data interpretation. Here we describe examples of each in turn.

Relevant information to supplement students' understanding of the subject domain or support their decision making can either be included as web links within an activity, or items from an associated activity can be displayed alongside the current activity (providing contextual support).

Figure 5.6 shows an example introductory activity for an inquiry on Urban Heat Islands that provides students with direct links to a set of teacher recommended resources. Figure 5.8 (top) shows an example set of linked activity resources for the same inquiry. The available measurements and potential locations for collecting data are displayed alongside the web form students use to enter and edit their hypothesis.

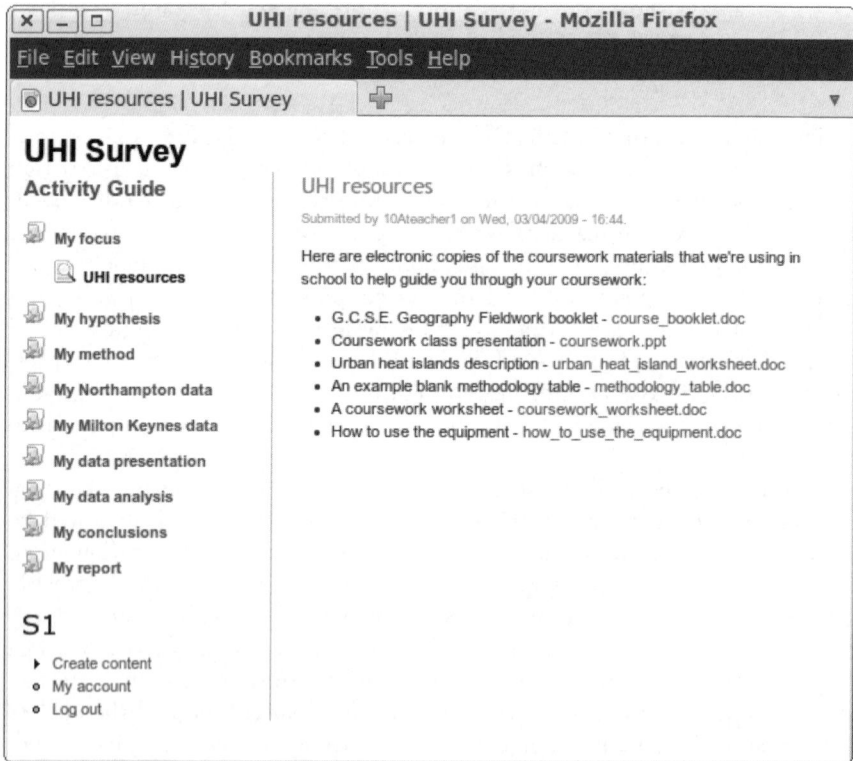

Figure 5.6 An example screen image from an Urban Heat Islands inquiry showing the introductory resources for the inquiry.

Facilitating the creation and manipulation of graphs (or other representations) can be automated according to the types of measures created in the open
data model for inquiry. For example, in the Microclimates inquiry where data
is collected at a number of distinct locations, the numerical data collected
can be presented as one or more bar charts with the locations marked on the
horizontal axis (see Figure 5.7). However, the students may want to create
their own representations using spreadsheets or other software. In which case,
displaying data tables that can be copied into other applications, or providing
links to data files in commonly used formats, facilitates the use of additional
software applications for producing reports or other presentations.

Figure 5.7 shows an example data presentation activity that includes a
bar chart, data table and links to data files. According to the selected set of
measures in the 'Data analysis' activity (see Figure 5.8 bottom), the bar chart
displayed in the resulting data presentation can be saved as an image file or
copied into another application. Similarly, the data table (or selections from
it) can be selected and copied into other applications. Clicking on either of the
data file links, the student can either open the file in an associated application

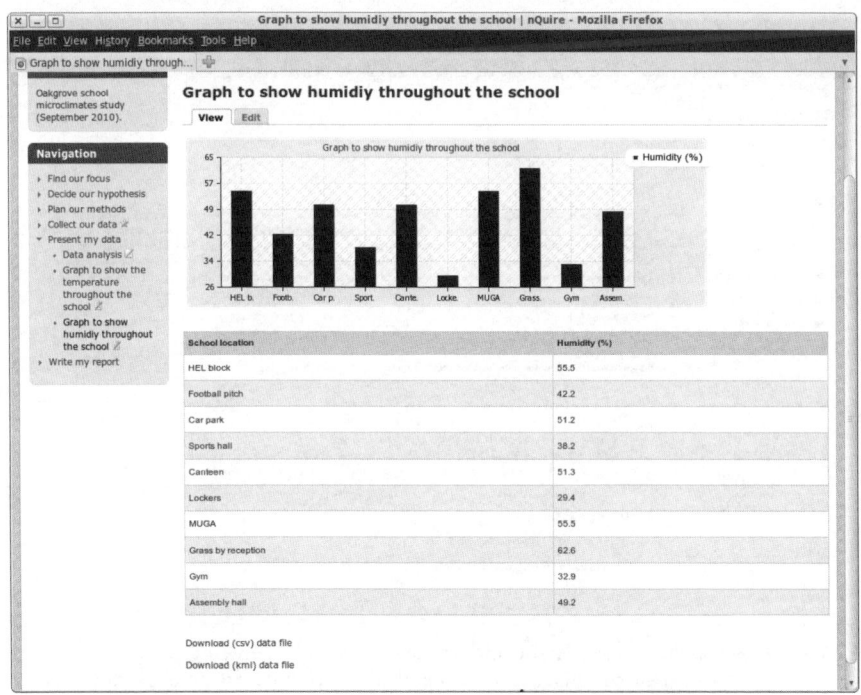

Figure 5.7 A Microclimates inquiry screen image showing the graph, data table
and data export links for a results presentation activity. The csv
and kml data formats enable the data to be easily transferred to
spreadsheet and map visualization applications (such as Microsoft
Excel and Google Earth).

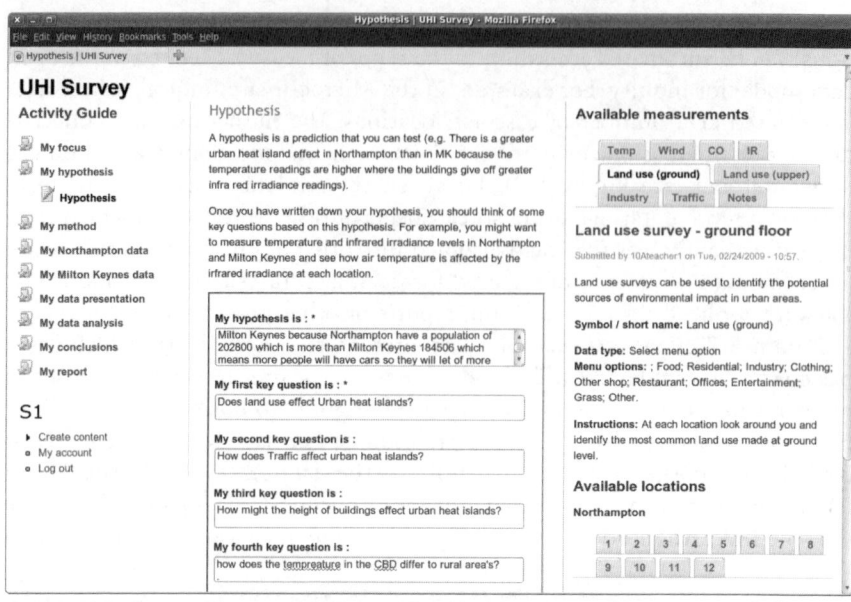

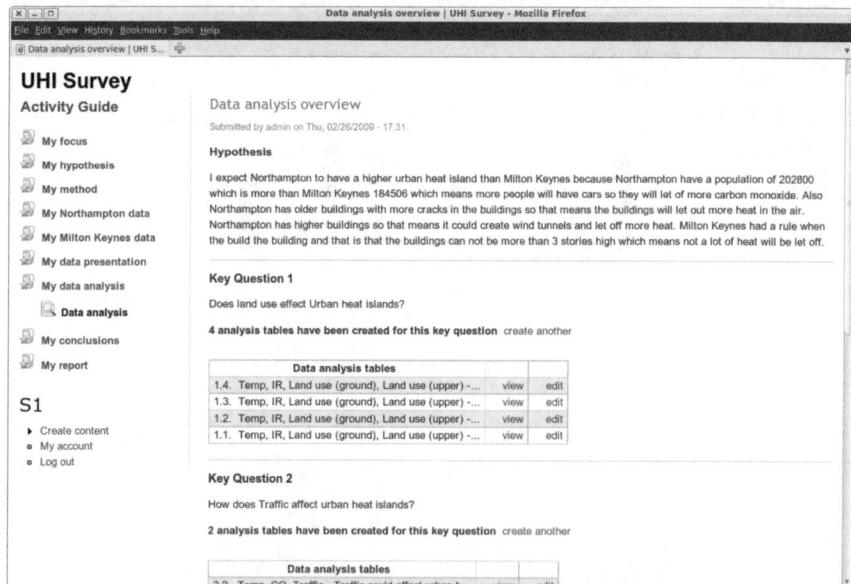

Figure 5.8 An Urban Heat Island inquiry screen image showing how a structured template can be used in an activity to help break a hypothesis into a set key questions (top), which can in turn be used to help guide the student's data analysis (bottom).

or download it. The 'csv' (comma-separated-value) data file format is used in spreadsheet applications, and the 'kml' (keyhole mark-up language) scheme is used in mapping applications, such as Google Earth. In this example, the latitude and longitude data associated with each location is used, along with the collected data, to generate a set of pins on a map that display the data associated with each location.

Designing an experiment and interpreting data are two other areas that some students can benefit from support. Figure 5.8 shows two screen images from an Urban Heat Islands inquiry, one for a student editing their hypothesis (top) and a second for the same student analysing their data (bottom). In this inquiry, the hypothesis activity made use of a structured template to encourage students to break their hypothesis into key questions. These questions were then used in an associated data analysis activity to help guide the student to select relevant data to answer each question.

Summary

These examples of regulatory and transformative process supports illustrate how the scripting constructs, introduced in the previous section, can be applied within an inquiry scripting environment. The temporal stage and functional phase structuring of activities enables the distribution of tasks that can be used to reflect the stages of an inquiry process. The open data model provides a means for sharing information between activities and can be used to either inform other activities, such as providing access to relevant information, or explicitly structure other activities, such as generating a data entry form based on a selected set of measures. The actors and audience associated with each activity, and the operators that set an activity's status, help to manage the completion of the activities throughout the inquiry. Finally, the application of groupings to identify the 'groups in use' at an appropriate level of granularity (i.e. the inquiry, each stage, specific phases or individual activities), enable flexible support for complex collaboration groupings, as in scripts applying the JIGSAW technique.

Conclusions

Scripting support for personal inquiry requires an open approach that enables teachers and students to author or customise inquiries on personally relevant topics. The five aspects of personal inquiry learning that can be addressed through scripting support are: personal choice, collaboration, regulatory process support, transformative process support and orchestration. Scripting supports personal choice by enabling the specification of activities that include interdependencies between individuals and their actions. These are crucial elements in both collaboration and inquiry. Genuine interdependencies between students necessitate the types of interactions that facilitate learning (Salomon 1992). Interdependencies between the student's actions, their consequent options, and guidance within an inquiry are equally important to ensure the inquiry reifies their personal choices.

Scripting support to help manage collaboration enables the allocation of activities to individuals and groups, and the handling of the resources required for and produced by their collaboration activities. Associating an actor and an initial status with each activity identifies who can do each task. The actor for any additional activities that are created when an activity is carried out is computed according to that activity's audience (specified as the individual, group or class level relative to the actor). Using a relative social level to describe the audience for an activity is necessary in order to support the flexible allocation of tasks involving individuals, groups and whole classes. Support for changes to groupings within an inquiry (as in the JIGSAW technique) need to be handled through a flexible distribution structure. The proposed 'groups in use' structure ensures that each student can continue to work with their resources and activities across every stage of the inquiry.

The regulatory processes of planning, managing and monitoring the inquiry can be supported through scripting by the structural model of temporal stages, phases and activities; the identification of focal phases and activities in each stage; and the initial status and status operators associated with each activity. The musical notation and script structure table illustrated in Figure 5.1 and Figure 5.2, respectively, show how the structural model can be used to plan an inquiry as a macro-level script. Managing the inquiry process for each student is then supported through the status of each activity and the highlighting of focal activities and phases at each stage of the inquiry. Monitoring progress through the temporal stages and activities can be reflected in an application (such as nQuire). The user's current activities and available actions will depend on the groups and classes of which that user is a member.

Transformative processes within an inquiry are supported through the tools used to complete each activity. The tools need to reflect the dependencies between the activities and therefore some form of generalised data model is required. In the case of web-based systems, distinct content types provide a means for structuring content items which can be associated with activities. Based on a generalised open data model for inquiry, the content types used in our activities enable the sharing of information within an inquiry between hypotheses and key questions; key questions, data collection and analysis; and data analysis, key answers and conclusions.

Scripting provides a set of representations that are used for orchestration. Orchestration, either to specify an inquiry or facilitate the running of it, involves the identification and coordination of the students' activities, their learning processes and the technological support used. Scripting enables teachers to specify the overall structure of an inquiry and the options available to the students. The activities to be undertaken and the students' progress through them can be shown in a scripting application. Furthermore, changes to the script can be made at any time by the teacher in response to the students' progress: to add or remove activities, to provide additional information, or to change an activity's status so a previously absent student can complete it.

Acknowledgments

The examples presented in this chapter are taken from some of the inquiries carried out with the teachers and students at Oakgrove School, Milton Keynes. The authors would like to thank them for their collaboration. We would also like to thank David Crellin and Ewan Bingham at ScienceScope for their advice and support throughout the project.

References

Aronson, E. and Patnoe, S. (1997) *The Jigsaw Classroom: building cooperation in the classroom,* 2nd edn, Longman.

Barron, B. et al. (1998) 'Doing with Understanding: lessons from research on problem- and project-based learning', *The Journal of the Learning Sciences,* 7 (3/4): 271–311.

Blumenfeld, P.C. et al. (1991) 'Motivating Project-Based Learning: sustaining the doing, supporting the learning', *Educational Psychologist,* 26 (3): 369.

De Jong, T. and Van Joolingen, W.R. (1998) 'Scientific Discovery Learning with Computer Simulations of Conceptual Domains', *Review of Educational Research,* 68 (2).

Dillenbourg, P. and Hong, F. (2008) 'The mechanics of CSCL macro scripts', *International Journal of Computer-Supported Collaborative Learning,* 3 (1): 5–23.

Dillenbourg, P. and Jermann, P. (2007) 'Designing Integrative Scripts', in P. Dillenbourg et al. (eds) *Scripting Computer-Supported Collaborative Learning: computer-supported collaborative learning,* New York: Springer, Available at: http://dx.doi.org/10.1007/978–0–387–36949–5_16.

Dillenbourg, P. and Jermann, P. (2010) 'Technology for Classroom Orchestration', in M. Khine and I. Saleh, (eds). *New Science of Learning: cognition, computers and collaboration in education.* New York: Springer.

Dillenbourg, P. and Schneider, D. (1995) 'Mediating the Mechanisms Which Make Collaborative Learning Sometimes Effective', *International Journal of Educational Telecommunications,* 1 (2): 131–146.

Dillenbourg, P. and Tchounikine, P. (2007) 'Flexibility in macro-scripts for computer-supported collaborative learning', *Journal of Computer Assisted Learning,* 23 (1): 1–13.

Edelson, D., Gordin, D. and Pea, R. (1999) 'Addressing the Challenges of Inquiry-Based Learning through Technology and Curriculum Design', *Journal of the Learning Sciences,* 8 (3and4): 391–450.

Jermann, P., Dillenbourg, P. and Brouze, J. (1999) 'Dialectics for collective activities: an approach to virtual campus design', in *International Conference on Artificial Intelligence in Education.* Le Mans, France. Available at: http://hal.archives-ouvertes.fr/hal-00197379/en/ (accessed November 2010).

Kobbe, L. et al. (2007) 'Specifying computer-supported collaboration scripts', *International Journal of Computer-Supported Collaborative Learning*, (2): 211–224.

Linn, M. C. Clark, D. and Slotta. J. D. (2003) 'WISE design for knowledge integration', *Science Education*, 87 (4): 517–538.

Mulholland, P. Collins, T. and Gaved, M. (2010) 'nQuire: a customizable toolkit for inquiry learning across school, home and field trip locations', in *The Proceedings of the Ninth World Conference on Mobile and Contextual Learning (mlearn 2010)*, Valletta, Malta. Available at: http://oro.open.ac.uk/25765/ (accessed February 2011).

Quintana, C. et al. (2004) 'A Scaffolding Design Framework for Software to Support Science Inquiry', *Journal of the Learning Sciences*, 13 (3): 337.

Salomon, G. (1992) 'What does the design of effective CSCL require and how do we study its effects?' *ACM SIGCUE Outlook*, 21: 62–68.

Shimoda, T. (2006). 'The Web of Inquiry: Technology for learning inquiry and reflective assessment'. In *The Proceedings of the Annual Conference of the American Educational Research Association*, San Francisco, CA. April 2006.

Tchounikine, P. (2008) 'Operationalizing macro-scripts in CSCL technological settings', *International Journal of Computer-Supported Collaborative Learning*, 3: 193–233.

Chapter 6

Learning and technological designs for mobile science inquiry collaboratories

Roy Pea, Marcelo Milrad, Heidy Maldonado, Bahtijar Vogel, Arianit Kurti and Daniel Spikol

Introduction

Learning the content and inquiry strategies involved in the sciences is one of the core concerns of education (Kali and Linn 2008). The National Science Foundation (2000) provides one of many meritorious definitions of inquiry learning: "an approach to learning that involves a process of exploring the natural or material world, and that leads to asking questions, making discoveries, and rigorously testing those discoveries in the search for new understanding." The 1996 National Science Education Standards (NSES) notes that: "Inquiry is central to science learning. When engaging in inquiry, students describe objects and events, ask questions, construct explanations, test those explanations against current scientific knowledge, and communicate their ideas to others. They identify their assumptions, use critical and logical thinking, and consider alternative explanations. In this way, students actively develop their understanding of science by combining scientific knowledge with reasoning and thinking skills."

The pedagogical strategies developed for engaging learners in inquiry science have been extensively researched over the past decade (Edelson 2001; Kali and Linn 2008; Kali, Linn and Roseman 2008; Krajcik, Czerniak and Berger 2003; Minstrell and Van Zee 1998; Quintana et al. 2004). Given the multi-faceted nature of inquiry competencies, the challenges for educators are substantial, and new requirements for teacher professional development to support inquiry science have been the focus of significant programs of research (Fishman, Marx, Best and Tal 2003; Fogleman, Fishman and Krajcik 2006).

What are the challenges for educators in supporting inquiry science? And how can these pedagogical problems be addressed in part with technology-enhanced design strategies? Unlike traditional science education that devotes itself to frontal instruction, demonstrations, having students solve textbook problems and work through cookbook lab experiments, inquiry science pedagogy seeks to engage learners' interests with authentic inquiry problems in their lives beyond schools and to guide their asking of researchable questions; to foster the norms, uses of language and argumentation activities that relate evidence to knowledge claims as a part of the science community of practice; and to prepare students to employ the cognitive, social and technological practices that, when pursued, hold promise to advance scientific understanding of the focus of inquiry.

Inquiry science pedagogy increasingly recognises that a key vehicle for implementing these desirable changes in the focus of science education is to leverage new computing and communication tools for learners' pursuits of science inquiries. The reasons why include a greater authenticity and relevancy to the inquiry activities, as the actual conduct of science by adults is also increasingly incorporating new technologies, such as sensors for real-time data capture and display (e.g., http://research.cens.ucla.edu/research/), information visualization techniques for data analysis and sense-making (Card 2009), and low-cost mobile computers and smartphones for field-based science to exploit the communication and computing infrastructure with its open internet and web standards (Silva et al. 2009; Vogel, Kurti, Spikol and Milrad 2010).

Science education with an inquiry pedagogy becomes more of a breathing, living, socio–technical process in the world and not simply about learning novel vocabulary and solving equations. Incorporating contemporary technologies in inquiry science pedagogy also has the additional advantage of foregrounding the social nature of inquiry, including team-based collaborations, assignments of inquiry roles to reflect the distributed nature of expertise in science teams, interactive data visualization environments for analysing data from research inquiries and creating scientific graphics to function in the processes of defensible scientific argumentation from evidence, and communication tools for research report writing. Each of these features of an integration of current and emerging technologies into inquiry pedagogy has the further benefits of fostering learner engagement and the social construction of identity for participants as inquiring learners in science (Barton 2003; Bell et al. 2009).

The design opportunity for technology-enhanced inquiry science pedagogy is that K-12 learners can now learn science by participating in science inquiry in the field as well as in classrooms, and by incorporating the distinctive affordances for science inquiry of desktop/laptop computers and mobile smartphones/tablets for their fieldwork. Environmental sciences education is one of the more important and exciting fields for advancing the required new activities, pedagogical models and technological supports. In our view, learning the inquiry strategies and content associated with ecological science should increasingly use these newly accessible science tools. They include sensors for data capture, information visualization technologies for data-analysis, low-cost mobile computers and mobiles for field-based science, and geo-tagged digital photos and videos for documenting field settings for research. Why? Because they provide persistent conversational resources for science learning discussions back in the classroom.

Inspired by the distributed collaboratories increasingly used in the scientific community (Bos et al. 2007), we envision the growth of inquiry-oriented agency of learners and educators when using mobile science collaboratories for inquiry learning. NSF program officer William Wulf first defined a 'collaboratory' as a "center without walls, in which the nation's researchers can perform their research without regard to physical location, interacting with colleagues, accessing instrumentation, sharing data and computational resources, [and] accessing information in digital libraries" (Wulf 1989; see also Wulf 1993). The pedagogical needs of a mobile science inquiry collaboratory are to support the workflow of inquiry science. We define a *mobile* science collaboratory as the technologies and services that enable distributed collaborative science inquiry: a set of mobile, laptop and other devices for network access and computing, sensors as instrumentation for capturing data, and open software tools that enable interactive analyses of data, and which provide support for online participation frameworks to engage learner collaborations and inquiries.

Our chapter describes a collaborative international project in which we are developing, implementing, studying and scaling with our partners (Intel, National Geographic Society, Pasco Scientific) novel ways for fostering secondary school student learning in teams for ecological and environmental sciences. To these ends, we are working to integrate geopositional data sensing, multimedia communication, data visualization and Web 2.0 tools in specific ecology learning scenarios to create mobile science inquiry collaboratories, using co-design methods (Penuel et al. 2007; Spikol et al. 2009) with teachers, learners, developers, and learning and domain scientists on topics such as water quality, soil quality, ecosystems and biodiversity.

The major objective of our project is to provide educational activities and tools for students to participate in collaborative scientific inquiry as they formulate questions and hypotheses, and collect, analyse, discuss and compare data while studying problem topics in environmental and ecological sciences.

In workshops with teachers from participating school sites, learning scientists, technology developers and domain experts, we have been co-designing hands-on learning activities. Our central purposes for co-design are to tackle the problems of inquiry pedagogy that teachers experienced in their practices while seeding design discussions with prospective applications of new tools for supporting different facets of inquiry pedagogy. These co-designed activities should offer students a learning environment with enhanced opportunities for scientific inquiries, systems thinking and conceptual change mediated by the iterative cycles of scientific inquiry, in and out of the classroom. We came to see how handheld-based data-collection sensors could augment inquiry-driven investigations with real-time data and visualizations that have the promise of increasing students' engagement, enabling concentration on science rather than logistics. Students would use sensors to collect and analyse data in real time in their groups, and compare it in near-real time with data from other locations. New opportunities for learning occur (Novak and Gleason 2002, contributions to this volume) when students are encouraged and supported by teachers, domain experts and peers, as they ask their own questions while collecting scientific data. Our technology-augmented environment provides an experimental arena for student learning on complex science topics by exploring a particular natural phenomenon in its natural setting – using sensors for systematic data collection and software tools for collaborative data investigations.

In this chapter we describe our project rationale, and review an emerging framework for an open learning platform using mobile and web technologies to support science inquiry learning using different portable sensing devices. We describe several illustrative curriculum activity structures and scenarios that exploit these tools, and report pilot research on the kinds of experiences learners have when supported by these mobile science collaboratory environments.

Inquiry learning engaging new technologies

Inquiry learning in science education is often embodied in project-enhanced science learning (PESL), as students engage in authentic and motivating tasks mediated by various tools and expertise extending over days. These tasks require collaboration and communication within – and sometimes beyond – the classroom, taking advantage of online data resources (Blumenthal et al. 1991; Pea 1993; Quintana et al. 2004; Scanlon et al. 2005; Tinker and Kracjik 2002). These conditions aim to support the social "cognitive apprenticeship" model of teaching and learning (Collins, Brown and Newman 1989), where problem definition and problem-solving processes are guided by mentors, with learners gradually taking on increasingly complex tasks and autonomy as support fades.

This inquiry model is congruent with recommendations from influential science learning standards projects (e.g., NRC 1996, NRC 2010, Project 2061: AAAS 1993). Our project continues a line of work in technology-enhanced inquiry science learning from the microcomputer era (e.g. Hawkins and Pea 1987; Linn, Layman and Nachmias 1986) and with an earlier generation of mobile personal digital assistants (PDAs) (Soloway et al. 1999; Tinker and Krajcik 2002) before today's smart phones and inexpensive sensors. Earlier projects using desktop computing for PESL include the pioneering student–scientist partnership studies on water quality developed by TERC (Technical education Research Center, in Cambridge Massachusetts), such as National Geographic Society-KidsNet and the environmental science Global Lab Project (TERC, 1996), the Learning through Collaborative Visualization (or CoVis) Project (Gordin and Pea 1995; Pea 1993; Pea et al. 1997; Pea 2002), and recent Concord Consortium curriculum projects employing probeware

(Zucker et al. 2007) and advances in web-based inquiry environments (Kali and Linn 2008).

For example, the GLOBE Project (globe.gov) attracted educators and students from over 100 countries to collect and upload to the web environmental data according to scientific protocols (e.g., atmosphere, hydrology, land cover, phenology, soil), providing aggregate environmental data visualization for classrooms, but very little in way of interactive data visualization for learner inquiries. Student teams collected data locally and used computer and telecommunications tools for pooling and interpreting results (Penuel and Means 2004). These works pre-dated ubiquitous mobile phones, low-cost consumer-ready GPS, and open standards and APIs (Application Programming Interfaces) for web browser data visualization.

More recently, rapid developments in mobile, wireless, and sensor technologies have opened up new possibilities for learning activities, which can be orchestrated over different educational contexts – schools, nature and science centers/museums (Rogers and Price 2006; Roschelle and Pea 2002; Scanlon, Jones and Waycott 2005; Sharples, Taylor and Vavoula 2007). Such technology-enhanced learning activities can be spatially distributed and incorporate different physical and environmental sensory data (Wu et al. 2008). Sensor-based technologies generate new perspectives on how learning activities can be embedded in different settings and across contexts (Chang, Wang and Lin 2009).

Building on this work, we have been creating new learning opportunities enhanced by technologies: to plan for, capture, upload, and interactively analyse new datasets to address science inquiry questions and projects. The tools that enable these new opportunities are new mobile multimedia technologies, sensors, digital maps and interactive data visualization tools (Giemza, Bollen and Hoppe 2010; Vogel, Spikol, Kurti and Milrad 2010). Despite such technology advances, it is important to emphasise many challenges remain in the integration of diverse technological resources and the pedagogical orchestration for their use in educational inquiries. Our ongoing research asks: *How to best support mobile science inquiry in activity structures and software 'scaffolding'?*

The activities and tools we have been designing explicitly support inquiry, integrating sensor data collection from sites near to the school with a collaborative learning system using locally networked mobile devices. One of the expected outcomes of this project is to provide a flexible architecture that supports the easy integration of different technological resources in order to facilitate the deployment of inquiry-based learning activities. In the following sections, we provide an overview of our current efforts.

Related work on technological supports for mobile inquiry and sensing

Context sensing (Salber et al. 1999) has become an important line of exploration in the ubiquitous computing field, with research projects developing context-aware applications for technology-enhanced learning, exploring their potentials by combining sensor information with context awareness (Collins et al. 2008; Hansen and Bouvin 2009; Hwang et al. 2009; Silva et al. 2009: Yeh et al. 2006). For example, Hansen and Bouvin's HyCon framework developed a learning platform employing diverse mobile technologies and software applications, experimenting with hypermedia mechanisms in mobile, context aware environments. HyCon offers a four-layered framework: storage, server, terminal, and sensors. Apps employing the HyCon framework supported mobile learning activities such as field trips and problem-based education, using different sensors to collect context information used to link, annotate, and tag different learning resources.

Related approaches tackling context awareness in inquiry-based learning activities coming from the Stanford Human-Computer Interaction Group are *ButterflyNet* for field biology, and the *iDeas* project for design education (Maldonado et al. 2006; Yeh et al. 2006), each built upon a software architecture encompassing systems for data capture, structure, access, and transformation. These systems provide the capacity of visualising and synchronizing photographic and sketched images and notes captured during inquiries with a camera and digital pen. Visual codes, digital pens, cameras, GPS devices, and audio and video recorders were all resources incorporated into this architecture, responding to the needs of field biologists and Human Computer Interaction designers.

Hwang et al. (2009) advocate using context awareness systems for supporting learning during complex scientific experiments with the aide of a distributed expert system. The adaptive features of such a system, they suggest, provide benefits to learners while experimenting in complex scientific domains, even recognising the difficulties of authoring learning materials with such systems. Silva et al. (2009) reports the use of sensory information with mobile devices to support learning activities, providing a long list of research projects that exploit spatial and sensory dimensions of their environment for educational benefits. They argue for an emphasis on space and sensing to achieve an engaging learning environment with mobile learning. And in the Personal Inquiry project, Collins and colleagues (2008 and this volume) have developed and studied uses of a system that scaffolds location-based inquiry learning across school, field and home contexts using mobile, sensor and web technologies. These researchers have been particularly concerned to design tools for technology-supported inquiry activities that scaffold and bridge sequences of learning activities, and highlight the use of digital maps and sensor data visualization for establishing bridging representations across field and classroom activities – a focus of our own work, too.

We see several areas for further research in relation to these prior works, which do not fully utilise sensory data in supporting inquiry processes, and have not fully developed tools for visualising sensory data as an anchoring medium for supporting learners' reflections about their inquiry processes. Why are sensed data important in inquiry? First, they represent the results of the agency of learners capturing data from their local environments. Secondly, they become an authentic, locally relevant and persistent resource for discussing both the processes and results of inquiries back in the classroom.

We also consider the *extensibility* of such systems vital when it comes to different open systems and available Application Programming Interfaces (APIs) in the Web. In comparing our research efforts with the above-mentioned projects and the identified issues, our approach will utilise and visualise sensory data to support different learning processes in the cycle of inquiry science (Edelson et al. 1999). We have designed and implemented a software system to enable wireless and sensor technologies to connect with mobile and other computational devices to provide complementary ways to support science inquiry learning. We now present our efforts related to the co-design activities that originated the learning and technical requirements for our system architecture.

LET'S GO! learning activity co-design

Our approach to designing the mobile science inquiry collaboratory as an educational innovation has been guided by the use of co-design method-ologies (Penuel, Roschelle and Schechtman 2007), in which the entire process from design of learning activities to defining functional requirements learns from co-design workshops teaming different stakeholders – teachers, experts, science educators, learning researchers, software developers, and learners. Educational innovations resulting from co-design processes have been successful in science education, generating a wide range of innovative curriculum materials for productive implementation (Edelson et al. 1999; Edelson 2002; Reiser et al. 2000; Roschelle et al. 1999; Shrader et al. 2001).

Co-design workshops were launched first in Sweden and then in northern California with local teams, in one-day or two-half day sessions (Maldonado and Pea 2010; Spikol et al. 2009). We came to the co-design process with pedagogical design and technical requirement considerations. For design, we wanted to explore inquiry pedagogy issues for how to support students in the process of data collection, reflection, and analysis of scientific data in the lab and the field. Design resources for consideration included uses of mobile sensors, geo-tagged learning content, data visualization, and collaborative inquiry tools. For technical requirements, we needed to achieve acceptable levels of classroom usability, to support different applications, to utilise open standards, and to keep costs down. During the first half of the workshops the team discussed the pedagogical roots and goals of science inquiry learning, and engaged in a showcase of different technologies for seeding design. Team members, including teachers, science educators, learning science researchers, and software developers walked from station to station, completing hands-on demonstrations of the technologies considered. The technology-enhanced activities demonstrated include geo-tagging phone-uploaded photos, journaling with interactive digital pens (paper-based computing), exploring different commercially available science education sensors, and others. During the second half of the workshop, participants created interdisciplinary teams for a brainstorming activity to define learning scenarios using mobile science inquiry collaboratories for students enrolled in middle- and high-school (15 to 18 years of age). We adopted a systematic approach where each team member quickly came up with at least three ideas, and presented them to the full group on sticky notes, placed on a wall, and categorized by the team. Ideas included an interactive field notebook, climate change studies (past, present and future changes), natural habitat restorations, international science data sharing between students, and water and soil quality testing, among others.

The ideas were then refined by teams as they described more concretely in scenarios what a trajectory of learning activities in the classroom and in the field would look like where these ideas would be developed. Template categories for design included: defining activity locations, prior conceptual and technological knowledge for students, prior technology set-up and measurements to be made, learning goals (e.g., whether whole group, small group, or individual), grouping rationale, activity type, technology resources needed, desired outcomes, success goals, and deliverables at the activity's conclusion. As a co-design discussion anchor, these template categories proved valuable in helping different kinds of experts co-design a feasible activity. It required integration of the different competencies of team members for jointly understanding the limits of the technology, constraints of lesson plans in limited class time, lesson flow, curriculum standards, and so on. From these initial scenarios a simple functional list was created to guide the design of the system architecture for the implementation of mobile science collaboratories (Spikol et al. 2009)

From the three top activities chosen in each country, one was then picked for piloting. The Swedish teachers and researchers opted in the first year to develop a Soil Quality unit (Vogel, Spikol, Kurti and Milrad 2010), the US team members focused on the complementary Water Quality unit (Maldonado and Pea 2010). Trial sites were reversed in the second year to incorporate feedback from these cross cultural trials into adapted materials for greater utility across contexts and student populations.

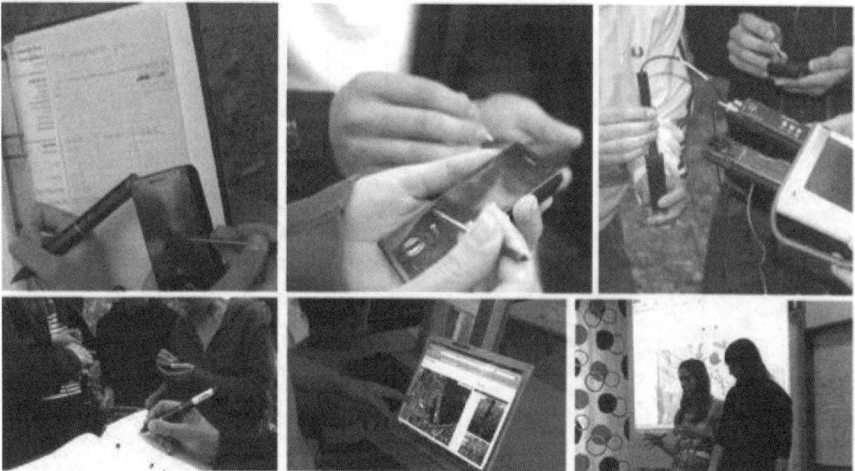

Figure 6.1 The different technologies in use by students.

Proposed architecture for mobile science collaboratories for inquiry learning

As part of the co-design process, our interdisciplinary team of teachers, science educators, learning science researchers, and software developers settled on four devices they considered both useful to the students' outdoor inquiry activities, and feasible to incorporate easily into their science class schedule. These are shown in Figure 6.1 and are:

(1) A *smartphone* with built-in sensors (camera, GPS), and a mobile client (application) developed by the Linnaeus University team for students' data collection and related observations, and using 3G networking for communication purposes.

(2) *Pasco's SPARK Science Device* (specially designed for inquiry science learning) with built-in sensor interface, additional sensors, and connection options such as Bluetooth and USB. This science appliance is used for data plotting and collection through different sensor probes such as pH, temperature, humidity, dissolved oxygen, among three hundred others.

(3) *Livescribe's* Pulse digital pen digitises the users' notes, and records audio in sync with the pen strokes. Student groups use this digital pen for data collection and recording of discussions during field investigations, which are replayed by student teams when they reflect on their inquiry processes and compose their reports.

(4) A *portable computer* to visualise geolocated data by the groups, as well as to compose and project aggregate visualizations in the classroom, to the group at large for comparison and discussion.

Our system architecture (Figure 6.2) is comprised of five different blocks, matched to the students' inquiry activities in the field and class, a design

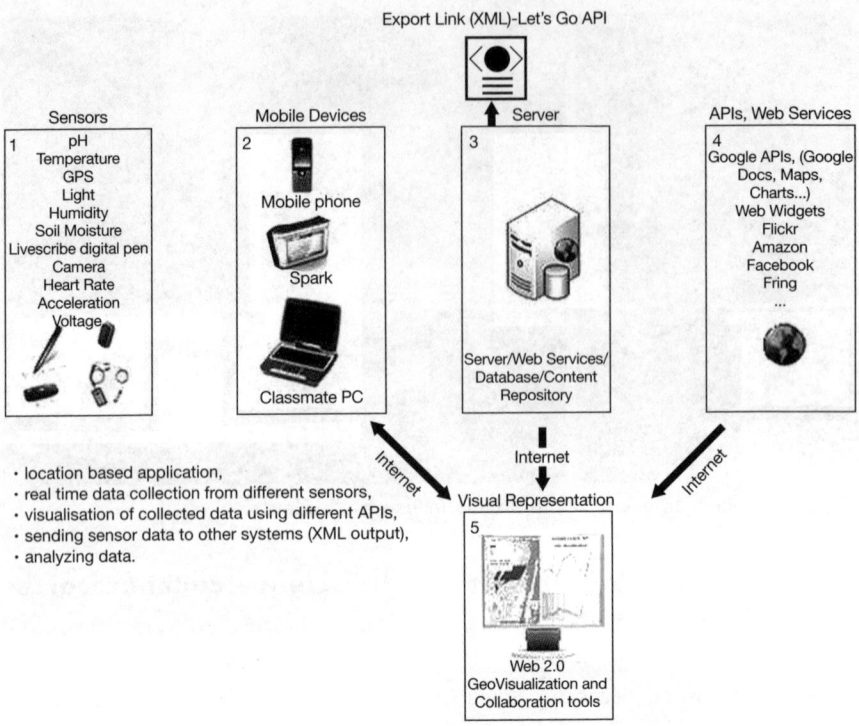

Figure 6.2 Proposed system architecture.

emerging from the functional requirements during the project's co-design phase (Spikol et al. 2009), and from earlier work noted above. The architectural blocks differentiate logical divisions of system resources: sensors, mobile devices (and transmission of sensor data), repositories, external APIs, and visualization. The diagram depicts the complete lifecycle for data capture, storage, export, sharing, and visualization. Our aim is to develop a flexible architecture useful for supporting different aspects of inquiry science learning. This architecture also provides expandable mechanisms to enable various reconfigurations that can be implemented by other research groups.

We now describe the Water Quality Inquiry and Soil Quality Inquiry activities, focusing on findings from Spring 2009 school trials that tested the validity of our system architecture and the functionality of its blocks in supporting the students' inquiry-based learning activities in ecological sciences.

Technical infrastructure including mobile client and visualization tools

We needed a mobile application for supporting learning activities that incorporated geo-gridded data gathering in the field. For our trial developments,

Figure 6.3 Collecting water quality samples at the creek and pond locations using Pasco's SPARK, then visualising data in Google Maps.

we used mobile devices running Windows Mobile 6.0[1]. The mobile app enabled students to collect sensor data and images during their inquiry activities, to automatically geo-tag images and sensor data with a built-in GPS sensor, and to annotate the data captured and content created in their current learning activity with metadata (Figure 6.4). The mobile application is connected via 3G networks to the SQL database server, and student data collection populates a mobile application form comprised of predefined fields for different types of data (coordinates, annotations, sensor values, which can be customised for specific inquiries by the teachers). The database contents created from geo-tagged sensor data or content entries are stored as unique objects in the content repository, and become very useful during the data visualization discussions following fieldwork.

1 The development of the mobile application employed C# using Compact Framework 3.5.

Figure 6.4 Mobile client screenshots.

As we note, visualization of sensor data aggregated by the mobile app was important for creating a reflection and collaboration space for use in activities following fieldwork, so we developed a web-based geo-visualization tool enabling different media content and sensor data to be visualised at the location where the learners collected them. The metadata annotations done with the mobile application, digital pen, and Spark devices are treated with the same significance as other sensor data sources (Figure 6.5, caption a).

We designed our visualization tool to present three different views of the collected data, to facilitate data comparison, analysis, and discussion: *General* view; *Instant* view (positions at any selected date and time) and *Dynamic* view (interactive). Students can now interactively explore the gathered sensory data with two information visualization techniques (see Figure 6.5, caption b): timelines and time plots.

A timeline is the most frequently used technique for interacting with time-linear visual information and allows learners to explore relationships among historical data. Students can select date and time intervals for a particular activity, and the timeline can be moved back and forth to dynamically visualise the collected data. The time plot technique is used to visualise time series data, and in our implementation, it is connected to the timeline. This technique visualises the sensor data while allowing reading of the value of each data point, and gives students the capability to further analyse the data collected. These two techniques were integrated with Google Maps APIs dynamically. Using these techniques and approaches, the data collected through the different mobile sensors (pH, relative and absolute humidity, and temperature altogether with GPS), annotations and pictures are integrated and visualised utilising these visualization tools. The tool allows students to

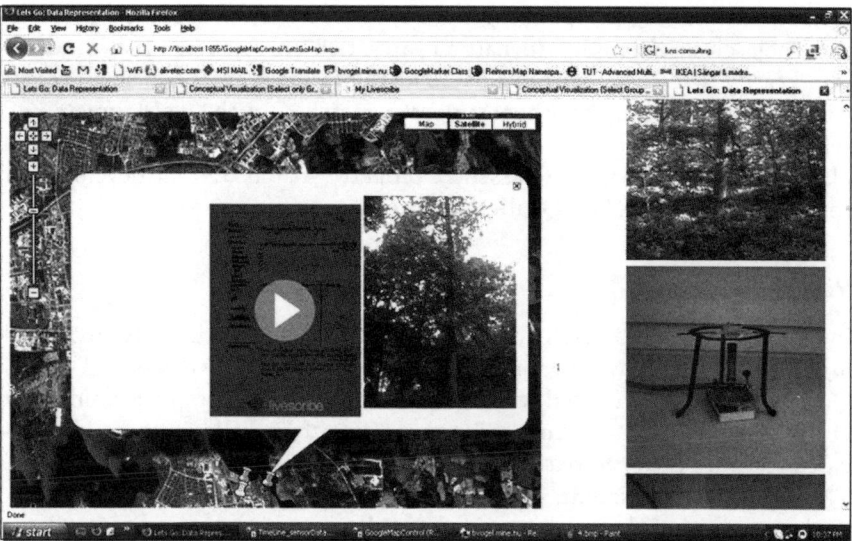

(a) Geo-visualization of the collected data.

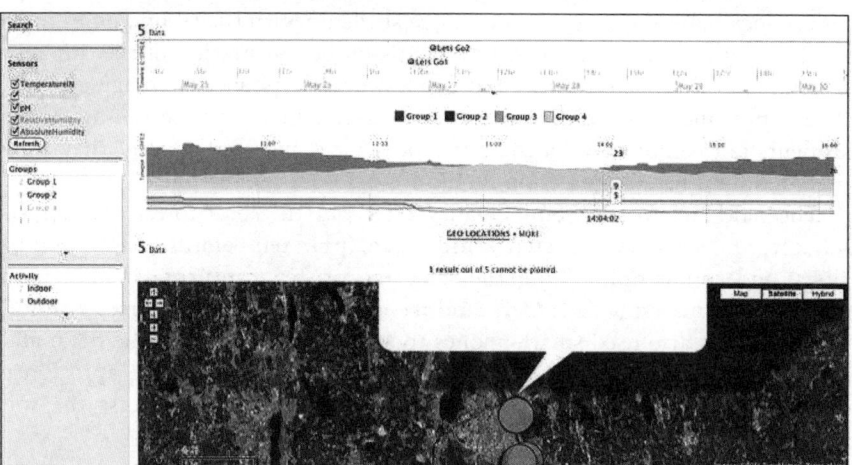

(b) Spatial-temporal visualization.

Figure 6.5 Visualization tool.

select geographical information in a simple way by retrieving location-based sensor data together with pictures and annotations as one unique object.

LET'S GO! field trials across sites

Target groups for field trials were 15–18 year-old students from four schools, two in northern California (USA) and two in southern Sweden, chosen due to their interest in incorporating inquiry in everyday pedagogical practice, and their close proximity to natural sites rich in resources that students could easily investigate within a day. The California schools had small creeks within or adjacent to the school property, matched to the development and evaluation of the Water Quality activity, while Swedish schools had woodland glades within or adjacent to the school property, matched to the development and evaluation of the Soil Quality activity.

Växjö, Sweden

In our (spring) 2009 trials in Växjö, Sweden, eight students from a local high school participated in three two-hour sessions over two weeks. The Soil Quality activity was framed within the woodland ecology topic forming part of the students´ environmental science elective class. Following the inquiry-based learning cycle, activities were divided into three sessions that included learning in the classroom, outdoors, and in the lab. In the initial session, students explored current issues of woodland ecology. Activity students formulated questions about the local forest's health, and generated hypotheses about the impact of pH, soil temperature, light, soil moisture, and soil type on the local environment. To familiarise students with the technologies to be used, the students participated in a hands-on demonstration of the different instruments: scientific sensors and probes; mobile phone for image capture, data input and field work control; and digital pen for note taking. Once students felt confident with the different devices and applications, they were prepared for a hands-on session including field data collection.

The field-site for this Soil Quality trial was the local forest behind the schoolyard. Students collected sensor data (pH, temperature, light condi-tions) and soil samples using the scientific probes, capturing images with the built-in smart-phone camera, and recording observations with the digital pen. Students also used smart-phones to send data collected in the field, and upload it to the LET'S GO! server using a customised mobile app. Once fieldwork was completed, students returned to the lab to process the soil samples, analyse and compare the collected data.

In the second session, the students analysed their soil samples, reflecting on the data collected and their field notes. The analysis was followed by a discussion session, where students used the LET'S GO! web visualization tool. These discussions paved the way for the third session, where the students discussed in depth their hypotheses, explorations, observations, and analysis. During a third session, students interactively visualised data from soil analyses, comparing and discussing the relationship between the health of trees across the sampled locations in relation to their soil quality. The session concluded with students generating new questions for further inquiries about the woodlands ecosystem.

Figure 6.1 illustrates the different phases of the learning activities and the technology used in each stage. The students all reported that they enjoyed the collaborative work and the different roles they were assigned, like the sensor operator, digital note taking, and smart phone operator. The visualization tools provided a new window for the students to use to reflect, discuss, and share different opinions in the group and overall.

Bay Area, California, USA

In California, 20 students (eleven male, nine female) agreed to participate in this 90–min Water Quality activity designed and led by the LET'S GO! team as part of an established Environmental Leadership Academy on the school campus. The creek and student-built pond on the school property are defining characteristics of this school, with the latter providing a natural contrast to the creek's riparian habitat. The students in this continuation high school come primarily from underserved populations, and attend school to complete credits needed for graduation.

In this Water Quality trial, the teacher introduced the learning activities and scientific concepts (such as pH, total dissolved salts, temperature, dissolved oxygen, etc.) and the essential questions for weekly units. Groups of four students answered questions about their current understanding of concepts involved in the activity, and then developed hypotheses investigating the qualities of water in the pond as compared to the adjoining creek. After recording their predictions and reasoning, the groups changed to waterproof boots and moved to a randomly selected GPS coordinate location in the creek. In designing the activities, we followed Lotan's (2003) conception of group-worthy activities, as follows: Lotan argues that the strength of group work in classroom is best realised when the activity is designed to embody the following five features: (1) the task to complete is open-ended and requires complex problem solving; (2) the activity allows students to make significant contributions to the group effort by using their various talents and multiple intellectual competencies; (3) the activity answers a discipline-based, relevant, intellectually important question; (4) the activity requires positive interdependence (for example, when students have to reach a consensus regarding the next step to follow), as well as individual accountability; and (5) the activity must include specific evaluation criteria as to what makes a successful group product.

One way we applied this notion of 'group-worthy' activities was in creating clear roles in the data collection process for every student: one was responsible for acquiring the water samples; another used the SPARK to take measurements of the creek. The other two students recorded the activity and results, one using the LiveScribe pen and notebook, another using the camera. These roles were assigned by consensus – teammates had to agree on who would complete each role.

As depicted in Figure 6.3, once back on dry land, the students analysed their samples after they have measured and recorded the physical appearance of the creek water (clarity, dissolved solids, etc), pH, temperature, dissolved oxygen, and conductivity. They repeated the sample collection and analysis procedure for the pond location, also recording general observations of both environments (including ambient temperature). In their groups, the students then discussed possible reasons for any differences observed, making explicit references to the proximity of the creek to a nearby industrial compound.

The students then returned to their classroom, wrote up their conclusions, and reported their theories and reflections about possible explanations for differences between samples. The data collected by all class groups, at different locations throughout the creek, was visualised on Google Maps or similar systems for class-wide discussion (Figure 6.3). Students completed an individual questionnaire on their understanding of the subject, perception of their learning, and reflections on the learning activity.

Results from the field trials

In terms of technology and pedagogical design, the outcomes of our trials generally validated our proposed system architecture and inquiry learning activities, as they were easily used and well received by participating students. Students individually completed a pre- and post-experience questionnaire with fill-in long-answer questions designed to probe their understanding of the scientific concepts and phenomena, and their opinions on the experience. Content questions in the pre-experience questionnaire included: "What do you think the pH of the creek will be? Why?" and "I predict the CO_2 of the pond will be _____ because." In the post-experience questionnaire students were asked to reflect on their predictions with questions such as: "Why do you think the creek and the pond had different O_2 values?" and "If you had to do it again, what would you do differently?" Attitudinal questions included: "What did you think of the experience as a whole today?" and "What did you think of the technology we used today: the digital pen, the sensors, the video camera?" Students' responses on the questionnaires and during interviews were overwhelmingly positive towards the learning activity and the technologies: "a great way to collect data, made it more exciting and much easier," wrote one student in California. "It is very interesting to get data, I enjoyed doing it and learned a lot," wrote another.

During interviews, the students and one of the teachers in Sweden thought that using the smartphone in the field and lab expedited their work by reducing paper recording needs, when compared to other similar experiments conducted by their class in the field of environmental sciences. A student in a Swedish group reported: "The tools made the experiment go faster and it was fun to use them in the field. I think we saved a lot of time by feeding the data directly into the phone instead of via paper, like we did before." Through the worksheets a Swedish student reported that the scientific sensor kit was "easy to use, a better way, and more precise in measurements, along with getting your results right in the forest." One possible reason for these claims may be the fact that the sensor data collected in the field using mobile devices (including geo-tagged information) was uploaded to our servers directly from mobiles and integrated in the aforementioned system. Once in class, the data sets were visualised in Google maps.

In Sweden and the US, the digital pens were of great interest to students, especially the audio playback feature, as they could listen back in the classroom to the conversations they had in the field while conducting the experiment and solving a number of problems associated with their task. Students in both countries expressed significant interest in additional visits to repeat measurements for different seasons and conditions, as well as to study other variables and sites (soil, water, oceans). Such positive responses are encouraging, and bode well for fostering the students' interest in the subject matter.

In terms of learning from the experience, the students' post-questionnaire responses seem to indicate that the students increased their understanding of the topic – "the creek moves so more oxygen goes into the creek and the pond just stays in place" wrote a student explaining the difference in O_2 measurements between the creek and the pond. Reflecting on the difference between the total dissolved salts (TDS) measurements, one student stated: "The creek moves, so it collects more erosion." Another stated: "TDS in the pond is lower because it is rain water, there is nothing flowing into it like the creek ... the creek is collecting more things as it flows." One student group not initially predicting any differences in temperature between the creek and the pond wrote in their worksheet that: "The pond is warmer than the creek because the water stays in the same place and the sun hits [sic] it a lot."

One of the most striking changes in preconceptions came from a student in California whose predictions for the difference between the two locations (over four questions in the pre-test) were that: "The creek is much clearer than the pond because the creek flows and the pond not." Linking water flow and turbidity was a very common misconception the students faced early on. This student's explanation after the activity reflected an increased understanding of the factors to consider when analysing water quality: "I think there's a difference because the pond was filled with drain water and the creek is always flowing. The pond is always in the sun and has no cover or shade. The pond water is still and the creek water comes from miles away, from the mountains."

Beyond survey responses, the digital pens used by all teams recorded students' discussions during inquiry activities, as well as their written notes when the pen tip was pressed down. Through these digital traces, we can hear how the students incorporate their classroom knowledge into inquiry processes. For instance, common sense-making conversations on methodology – including how many measurements are needed to comply with the scientific method, or why the values displayed by the probes change rapidly when jostled – would not be captured by the written responses. We are currently developing a coding scheme to interpret these data across contexts in order to derive new insights of what happened in the field.

These trials were the proving ground for our architecture and inquiry activity designs – and we've continued to iterate the design of both in synergy. From March 2009 to June 2010 more than 150 students from three schools in Sweden and two schools in US have participated in the different trials, although the results presented in this chapter describe only the activities that were carried out until June 2009.

Discussion and Implications

Our chapter provides an account of how we moved from visions of mobile science inquiry, to co-design activities with educators, to system architecture design and technical developments enabling LET'S GO! trials of our first iterations of mobile inquiry science collaboratories. We are developing an innovative environment to engage learners in exploring and experimenting with multiple representations of causal interactions and functional relationships typical in science, to promote inquiry methods and deeper domain understanding. With sensors, data visualization, GPS and Web 2.0 tools, the components for realising our vision are available, but they need to be integrated into a scalable system with solid pedagogical foundations and data-driven mechanisms for continuous improvement.

One critical issue we share with many projects is the lack of open standards in education technology tools. Each device is largely a closed system approach restricting development of customised and integrated approaches advocated by our requirements. The scientific sensor system, the digital pen, and to some extent the smart-phone, required manual synchronization of data before we could provide the visualization tools. In addition, the data visualization tools had some trouble rendering the data in older versions of web browsers prevalent in school IT systems. One fundamental technical challenge for LET'S GO! and projects with scalability aspirations is to explore how to create software and hardware solutions for educational uses for easy integration into schools, making the potential of Science 2.0 (Dede and Barab 2009) accessible to students.

Our system architecture enables off-the-shelf technologies to be used with the newly developed infrastructure by allowing multiple streams of data to be aggregated and analysed for use in science learning activities. The system architecture and technical overview provide a future roadmap for development with context sensing and awareness integrated with smart-phones, sensor-based technologies, and digital pens. One of the salient features of our software system is centered on the visualization of collected sensor data, and the guided discussions these visualizations allow, within and across groups of students. We continue to iterate our design, implementing and testing in field trials ever-improving tools to further support learning activities through collaborative interactions with collected data.

Our work ahead involves expanding our approach to the mobile application, database design, and visualization tool by adding more automatic functionalities; we are especially interested in supporting practices of co-located and distributed collaboration during the activity. Given that our system architecture is still in the initial phase, we still need to develop applications (interfaces) for some of the building blocks of our architecture.

The development and implementation of the technological solutions and learning activities presented in this chapter indicates the growing potential towards the usage of mobile, sensor, and web technologies to support data collection, data interoperability, analysis, and visualization in the context of inquiry-based science learning. In the activities we have described, data interoperability simplifies the integration of data generated by various technological resources and applications. This approach enables a relatively rapid development and reuse of technological resources for supporting different aspects of the learning activities, resulting in the seamless integration of data coming from multiple devices – with important implications for improving the orchestration of inquiry-based learning activities taking place in and out of classrooms. From a practical perspective, the added value for the classroom is the seamless integration of different sensor data combined with devices that enable powerful visualizations to support students´ work with regard to the analysis and reflection upon their collected data. One issue we aim to deepen in our future work is the full utilization of the visualization component of inquiry, by incorporating different techniques that provide interactive spaces for discussion, sharing, and collaboration around data-focused sense-making.

Acknowledgements

The LET'S GO! project is principally funded by the Knut and Alice Wallenberg Foundation of Sweden, as part of the Wallenberg Global Learning Network. We also thank Pasco Scientific, Intel Research, and the National Geographic Society for their contributions and partnership in the project. Special thanks to Chen Kee Tan, Hans Willstedt, and colleagues from the LET'S GO! teams at Stanford University (Rodolfo Dirzo, Cindy Wilber, Amy Wong, and Janelle Austin) and at Linnaeus University (Katrin Lindwall, Sadaf Salavati, and David Johansson). We are very grateful to participating teachers, students, and administrators from the California and Swedish schools for their creative engagement in these studies.

References

American Association for the Advancement of Science (1993) *Benchmarks for Science Literacy*, New York: Oxford University Press.

Barron, B., Walter, S. E., Martin, C. K. and Schatz, C. (2010) 'Predictors of creative computing participation and profiles of experience in two Silicon Valley middle schools', *Computers and Education*, 54: 178–189.

Bell, P., Lewenstein, B., Shouse, A. and Feder, M. (eds) (2009) *Learning Science in Informal Environments: people, places and pursuits,* Washington, D.C.: National Academies Press.

Blumenfeld, P., Soloway, E., Marx, R., Krajcik, J., Guzdial, M. and Palincsar, A. (1991) 'Motivating project-based learning: Sustaining the doing, supporting the learning', *Educational Psychologist,* 26: 369–398.

Bos, N., Zimmerman, A., Olson, J., Yew, J., Yerkle, J., Dahl, E. and Olson, G. (2007) 'From shared databases to communities of practice: a taxonomy of collaboratories', *Journal of Computer-Mediated Communications,* 12: 652–672.

Calabrese Barton, A. (2003) *Teaching Science for Social Justice,* New York: Teachers College Press.

Card, S. (2009). 'Information visualization', in A. Sears and J. A. Jackos (eds) *Human-Computer Interaction: design issues, solutions, and applications,* Boca Raton, FL: CRC Press/Taylor and Francis Group.

Chang, B., Wang, H. Y. and Lin, Y. Sh. (2009) 'Enhancement of Mobile Learning Using Wireless Sensor Networks', *IEEE Computer Society's Technical Committee on Learning Technology (TCLT),* 11: 22–26.

Collins, A., Brown, J. S. and Newman, S. E. (1989) 'Cognitive apprenticeship: teaching the crafts of reading, writing, and mathematics', in L. B. Resnick (ed) *Knowing, Learning, and Instruction: essays in honor of Robert Glaser,* Hillsdale, NJ: Lawrence Erlbaum Associates.

Collins, T., Gaved, M., Mulholland, P., Kerawalla, C., Twiner, A., Scanlon, E., Jones, A., Littleton, K., Conole, G. and Tosunoglu, C. (2008) 'Supporting location-based inquiry learning across school, field and home contexts', in *Proceedings of the MLearn 2008 Conference,* October 7–10, Ironbridge Gorge, Shropshire, UK.

Chan, T. W., Pea, R., Milrad, M. et al. (2006) 'One-to-one technology-enhanced learning: an opportunity for global research collaboration', *Research and Practice in Technology Enhanced Learning Journal* (RPTEL), 1: 3–29.

Dede, C. and Barab, S. (2009) 'Emerging technologies for learning science: a time of rapid advances', *Journal of Science Education and Technology,* 18: 301–304.

Edelson, D. C. (2002) 'Design research: What we learn when we engage in design', *The Journal of the Learning Sciences,* 11: 105–121.

Edelson, D. C. (2001) 'Learning-for-Use: A framework for the design of technology-supported inquiry activities.' *Journal of Research in Science Teaching,* 38 (3): 355–385.

Edelson, D. C., Gordin, D. N. and Pea, R. D. (1999) 'Addressing the challenges of inquiry-based learning through technology and curriculum design', *The Journal of the Learning Sciences,* 8: 391–450.

Eissele, M., Weiskopf, D. and Ertl, T. (2009) 'Interactive Context-Aware Visualization for Mobile Devices', in A. Butz, B. Fisher, M. Christie, A. Krüger, P. Olivier and Therón, R. (eds) *Lecture Notes In Computer Science: proceedings of the 10th international symposium on smart graphics,* Berlin: Springer-Verlag, 5531: 167–178.

Elsafty, A., Aly, G. S. and Sameh, A. (2008) 'The context oriented architecture: an augmentation of context awareness and reactivity into web services', in M. Wallace, M. Angelides and P. Mylonas (eds) *Advances in Semantic Media Adaptation and Personalisation,* Berlin: Springer.

Fishman, B., Marx, R., Best, S. and Tal, R. (2003) 'Linking teacher and student learning to improve professional development in systemic reform', *Teaching and Teacher Education,* 19 (6): 643–658.

Fogleman, J., Fishman, B. and Krajcik, J. S. (2006) 'Sustaining innovations through lead teacher learning: a learning sciences perspective on supporting professional development'. *Teaching Education,* 17 (2): 181–194.

Frohberg, D., Gšth, C. and Schwabe, G. (2009) 'Mobile Learning projects – a critical analysis of the state of the art', *Journal of Computer Assisted Learning*, 25: 307–331.

Giemza, A., Bollen, L. and Hoppe, U. (2010) 'LEMONADE: a flexible authoring tool for integrated mobile learning scenarios', in *Proceedings of Wireless Mobile Ubiquitous Technologies in Education 2010*, Kaohsiung, Taiwan.

Gordin, D. and Pea, R. D. (1995) 'Prospects for scientific visualization as an educational technology', *Journal of the Learning Sciences*, 4: 249–279.

Hansen, A. F. and Bouvin, N. O. (2009) 'Mobile Learning in Context – Context-aware Hypermedia in the Wild', *International Journal of Interactive Mobile Technologies*, 3: 6–21.

Hawkins, J., and Pea, R. D. (1987) 'Tools for bridging everyday and scientific thinking', *Journal of Research in Science Teaching*, 24(4): 291–307.

Hwang, G. J., Yang, C. T., Tsai, C.C. and Yang, S. J. H. (2009) 'A context-aware ubiquitous learning environment for conducting complex science experiments', *Computers and Education*, 53: 402–413.

Kali, Y. and Linn, M. C. (2008) 'Technology-Enhanced Support Strategies for Inquiry Learning.' in J. M. Spector, M. D. Merrill, J. J. G. Van Merriënbocr and M. P. Driscoll (eds), *Handbook of Research on Educational Communications and Technology* (3rd edn), Mahwah, N. J: Lawrence Erlbaum Associates.

Kali, Y., Linn, M. C. and Roseman, J. E. (eds). (2008) *Designing Coherent Science Education*, New York: Teachers College Press.

Krajcik, J., Czerniak, C. and Berger, C. (2003) *Teaching Children Science in Elementary and Middle School Classrooms: a project-based approach (2nd edn)*, Boston: McGraw-Hill.

Kurti, A., Spikol, D. and M. Milrad, (2008) 'Bridging outdoors and indoors educational activities in schools with the support of mobile and positioning technologies', *International Journal of Mobile Learning and Organization*, 2: 166–186.

Linn, M. C., Layman, J. W. and Nachmias, R. (1986) 'Cognitive consequences of micro-computers: graphing skills development', *Contemporary Educational Psychology, 12*(3): 244–253.

Lotan, R. (2003, March) 'Group-worthy tasks', *Educational Leadership*, 60: 72–75.

Maldonado, H. and Pea, R. D. (2010) 'LET'S GO! To the Creek: Co-design of Water Quality Inquiry using Mobile Science Collaboratories', *Proceedings of the 6th International IEEE Conference on Wireless, Mobile, and Ubiquitous Technologies in Education (WMUTE)* pp. 81–87, Kaohsiung, Taiwan.

Maldonado, H., Lee, B. and Klemmer, S. (2006) 'Technology for Design education: a case study. Work in Progress', in *Extended Abstracts of the 2006 Association for Computing Machinery's Conference on Human Computer Interaction (CHI 2006)*, pp. 1067–1072. New York, NY: ACM Press.

Minstrell, J. and Van Zee, E. (eds) (1998) *Inquiring into Inquiry Learning and Teaching in Science*, Washington, D.C: American Association for the Advancement of Science.

National Research Council (1996) *National Science Education Standards*, Washington, D.C: National Academy Press.

National Research Council. (2010) *Conceptual Framework for New Science Education Standards*, Washington, D.C: National Academy Press.

Novak, A. M. and Gleason, C. I. (2002) 'Incorporating Portable Technology to Enhance an Inquiry, Project-Based Middle School Science Classroom', in R. F. Tinker and J. S. Krajcik (eds) *Portable Technologies: science learning in context*, New York: Kluwer.

Pea, R. D. (1993) 'The Collaborative Visualization Project', *Communications of the ACM, 36*: 60–63.

Pea, R. D. (2002) 'Learning science through collaborative visualization over the Internet', in N. Ringertz (ed), *Nobel Symposium: Virtual museums and public understanding of science and culture*, Stockholm, Sweden: Nobel Academy Press.

Pea, R. D., Gomez, L. M., Edelson, D. C., Fishman, B. J., Gordin, D. N. and O'Neill, D. K. (1997) 'Science education as a driver of cyberspace technology development', in K. C. Cohen (ed), *Internet links for science education*, pp. 189–220. New York, NY: Plenum.

Pea, R. and Maldonado, H. (2006) 'WILD for learning: interacting through new computing devices anytime, anywhere', in K. Sawyer (ed) *Cambridge Handbook of the Learning Sciences*, pp. 427–442. New York: Cambridge University Press.

Penuel, W. and Means, B. (2004) 'Implementation variation and fidelity in an Inquiry Science Program; Analysis of GLOBE data reporting patterns', *Journal of Research in Science Teaching*, 41: 294–315.

Penuel, W. R., Roschelle, J. and Shechtman, N. (2007) 'Designing formative assessment software with teachers: an analysis of the co-design process', *Research and Practice in Technology Enhanced Learning*, 2: 51–74.

Quintana, C., Reiser, B. J., Davis, E. A., Krajcik, J., Fretz, E., Duncan, R. G., Kyza, E., Edelson, D. and Soloway, E. (2004) 'A scaffolding design framework for software to support science inquiry', *The Journal of the Learning Sciences*, 13: 337–386.

Reiser, B. J., Spillane, J. P., Steinmuler, F., Sorsa, D., Carney, K. and Kyza, E. (2000) 'Investigating the mutual adaptation process in teachers' design of technology-infused curricula', in B. Fishman and S. O'Connor-Divelbiss (eds), *Fourth International Conference of the Learning Sciences (ICLS)*, pp. 342–349. Mahwah, N. J. Erlbaum.

Rogers, Y. and Price, S. (2006) 'Using ubiquitous computing to extend and enhance learning experiences', in M. van´t Hooft and K. Swan (eds) *Ubiquitous Computing in Education: invisible technology, visible impact*, Mahwah, N. J. Erlbaum.

Roschelle, J., DiGiano, C., Koutlis, M., Repenning, A., Phillips, J., Jackiw, N. et al. (1999) 'Developing educational software components', *IEEE Computer*, 32: 50–58.

Roschelle, J. and Pea, R. D. (2002) 'A walk on the WILD side: How wireless handhelds may change computer-supported collaborative learning (CSCL)'. *The International Journal of Cognition and Technology*, 1: 145–168.

Salber, D., Dey, A. K., Orr, R. J. and Abowd, G. D. (1999) 'Designing For Ubiquitous Computing: A Case Study in Context Sensing', *GVU Technical Report*, GIT-GVU Online. Available at ftp://ftp.cc.gatech.edu/pub/gvu/tr/1999/99–29.pdf (accessed April 2010).

Scanlon, E., Jones, A. and Waycott, J. (2005) 'Mobile technologies: prospects for their use in learning in informal science settings', *Journal of Interactive Media in Education* 2005(25). Online. Available at http://jime.open.ac.uk/2005/25 (accessed April 2010).

Sharples, M., Taylor, J. and Vavoula, G. (2007) 'A theory of learning for the mobile age', in R. Andrews and C. Haythornthwaite (eds), *The Sage Handbook of e-learning Research*, pp. 221–247. London: Sage.

Shrader, G., Williams, K., Lachance-Whitcomb, J., Finn, L.-E. and Gomez, L. (2001) 'Participatory design of science curricula: The case for research for practice'. Presented at the Annual Meeting of the American educational Research Association, Seattle, WA.

Silva, M. J., Gomes, C. A., Pestana, B., Lopes, J. C., Marcelino, M. J., Gouveia, C. and Fonseca, A. (2009) 'Adding space and senses to mobile world exploration', in A. Druin (ed) *Mobile Technologies for Children*, pp. 147–169. Boston: Morgan Kaufmann.

Soloway, E., Grant, W., Tinker, R., Roschelle, J., Resnick, M., Berg, R. and Eisenberg, M. (1999) 'Science in the palms of their hands', *Communications of the ACM*, 42: 21–26.

Spikol, D., Milrad, M, Maldonado, H. and Pea, R. (2009) 'Integrating co-design practices into the development of mobile science collaboratories', *Proceedings of the 9th IEEE International Conference on Advanced Learning Technologies* (ICALT 2009), July 2009, Riga, Latvia, IEEE Press.

TERC (1996) *Student and scientist partnerships.* Online. Available at: http://ssp.terc.edu/ssp.html (accessed June 2010)

Tinker, R. F. and Krajcik, J. S. (2002) (eds) *Portable Technologies: science learning in context,* New York: Kluwer Academic/Plenum Press.

Vogel, B., Spikol, D. Kurti, A. and Milrad, M. (2010) 'Integrating mobile, web and sensory technologies to support inquiry-based science learning', in *Proceedings of Wireless Mobile Ubiquitous Technologies in Education 2010*, pp. 65–72. Kaohsiung, Taiwan.

Vogel, B., Kurti, A., Spikol, D. and Milrad, M. (2010) 'Exploring the benefits of open standard initiatives for supporting inquiry-based science learning', *Proceedings of the Fifth European Conference on Technology Enhanced Learning*, EC-TEL 2010, *Lecture Notes in Computer Science,* pp. 596–601. Springer-Verlag, Berlin/Heidelberg.

Wichmann, A., Gottdenker, J., Jonassen, D. and M. Milrad (2003) 'Scientific inquiry learning using computer supported experimentation, *Proceedings of The International Conference on Computers in Education*, pp. 1247–1251. Hong Kong.

Wu, T. T., Yang, T. C., Hwang, G. J. and Chu, H. C. (2008) 'Conducting Situated Learning in a Context-Aware Ubiquitous Learning Environment', *Fifth IEEE International Conference on Wireless, Mobile, and Ubiquitous Technology in Education*, pp. 82–86. Hong Kong.

Wulf, W. (1989) 'The National Collaboratory', in J. Lederberg and K. Uncapher (eds) (1989). *Towards a National Collaborator; Report of an invitational workshop at the Rockefeller University, 1989,* Washington D.C: National Science Foundation Directorate for Computer and Information Science.

Wulf, W. (1993) 'The Collaboratory Opportunity', *Science,* 261: 854–855.

Yeh, R. B., Liao, C., Klemmer, S. R., Guimbretiere, F., Lee, B., Kakaradov, B., Stamberger, J. and Paepcke, A. (2006) 'ButterflyNet: 'A mobile capture and access system for field biology research', *CHI: ACM Conference on Human Factors in Computing Systems*, Montreal, Quebec, Canada, pp. 571–558.

Zucker, A., Tinker, R., Staudt, C., Mansfield, A. and Metcalf, S. (2007) 'Increasing science learning in Grades 3–8 using computers and probes'; Findings from the *TEEMS II Project'*, *Proceedings of the NARST Annual Meeting*, New Orleans, LA, United States.

Chapter 7

Infrastructures for technology-supported collective inquiry learning in science

Marjut Viilo, Pirita Seitamaa-Hakkarainen and Kai Hakkarainen

Introduction

The purpose of this chapter is to examine an elementary-school teacher's practices of supporting collaborative inquiry. In many present-day classrooms, teachers are trying to create a collaborative student-centred learning culture with students who are used to following teacher-centred schooling activities. Therefore, instead of portraying the classroom teacher either as a transmitter of knowledge or a facilitator of learning, it is essential to understand in detail the diversity of roles that a teacher may enact and consider appropriate within the diversity of day-to-day classroom-based activities. We argue that whilst the teacher has a crucial role to play in inducting students into collaborative inquiry learning practices, the significance of teacher guidance has often remained unexplained (Hakkarainen 2009). Even when the pedagogical setting is organised towards collaboration and student-driven inquiry, it does not mean that students will, as a matter of course, collaborate and take collective responsibility for their own learning. Deliberate guiding efforts, on the part of the teacher, oriented toward establishing, cultivating, and sustaining corresponding classroom practices, are needed. Thus, getting teachers more effectively involved in designing their own inquiry-oriented curriculum would better capitalise on their creative potential, as well as facilitate deeper engagement in developing their own teaching and pedagogy (Sawyer 2004).

In this chapter, we will examine how one classroom teacher organised and promoted computer-supported collaborative inquiry in her classroom. We firstly describe the salient pedagogical infrastructure framework (Lakkala et al. 2008) and the pedagogical model of progressive inquiry that informed her work, and continue by addressing the role of teacher guidance in a collaborative inquiry project. Using the teacher's reflective project diaries, we will describe how she organised and supported the collective work by aligning community effort and collaborative tools in the pursuit of shared objects of inquiry. We also describe how the teacher, in her diaries, first considered and reflected on what was going on in the classroom, and then used these reflections to re-design and re-organise the subsequent activities. The teacher's efforts of orchestrating the subsequent inquiry process will be illustrated by presenting excerpts of a videotaped 'heated moment' and associated teacher–students interaction regarding one particular collective classroom situation. Finally, implications for teacher guidance and cultivation of inquiry practices are discussed.

Towards collaborative inquiry learning

Studies of successful knowledge-building classrooms have been reporting promising results regarding engaging students in collaborative inquiry learning (Hmelo-Silver, Duncan, and Chinn 2007; Hakkarainen 2004; Scardamalia and Bereiter 2006). Such classrooms are oriented toward putting the students' own questions and ideas at the heart of their working practices, treating ideas and knowledge generated as continually improvable objects of collaborative inquiry efforts (Scardamalia 2002). The aim is that students would set their own learning goals and assume collective cognitive responsibility for the advancement of collective inquiry under teacher guidance. A teacher is a part of an inquiry community, learning and building knowledge together with students; simultaneously, he or she has a crucial strategic guiding role without which students' inquiry would not be successful (Hakkarainen 2009).

In the settings where the process and the object of inquiry are designed in collaboration with students, the outcomes of the inquiry cannot be fully known in advance – neither the phases of the process, nor the content to be studied. In order to prevent novice performers' frustration, the students should be provided with sufficient support (Hmelo-Silver et al. 2007). That said, there are also serious concerns that too rigid a structure undermines higher-level inquiry learning objectives, because it makes the pursuit of advancing students' own ideas peripheral (Scardamalia and Bereiter 2006; Lakkala et al. 2008). However, many knowledge-building studies have focused particularly on students' accomplishments and overlooked the teacher's guiding role or the value of particular classroom practices (Hakkarainen 2009). When novice teachers try to implement knowledge-building culture in their classrooms, they may become discouraged when students initially fail to pose meaningful questions, generate relevant intuitive theories or engage in productive discourse interaction. The advancement of knowledge-building communities can be attributed to the ways in which the teachers have iteratively developed methods of socializing students into the evolving inquiry culture (Hakkarainen 2004; 2009). In order to expand advanced inquiry practices, the teacher's invisible work in guiding classroom practices has to be rendered visible and analysed in detail. Consequently, there are clear needs for research focusing on productive pedagogical practices in collaborative inquiry settings.

Supporting technology-enhanced collaborative progressive inquiry

Lakkala and her colleagues (2008) proposed that the fostering of technology-enhanced collaborative learning depends upon interrelated *technical, social, epistemic* and *cognitive* support structures. The development of the infrastructure framework is inspired by Bielaczyc (2006), who notes that when implementing computer-supported collaborative learning, the central challenge lies in building the appropriate social infrastructure around the technical one (Bielaczyc 2006). A proper technological infrastructure for students requires that they be provided with suitable technological learning tools for supporting inquiry (*technological infrastructure*). Technical arrangements include both the affordances of the tools that promote inquiry activity, and the arrangements for providing students with guidance for using the technology. A *social infrastructure* involves social arrangements (i.e. explicit rules, agreements and organisational structures) that entice the participants to collaborate and create a common ground. For a proper *epistemological infrastructure,* educators also need to encourage learners to treat knowledge as something that can be shared and jointly developed (Bereiter 2002). Lastly, a productive *cognitive infrastructure* depends upon educators' efforts to facilitate the participants' understanding and reflection on practices and processes by providing concrete conceptual tools, such as guidelines, models or templates, for supporting self-regulative competencies and meta-skills for planning,

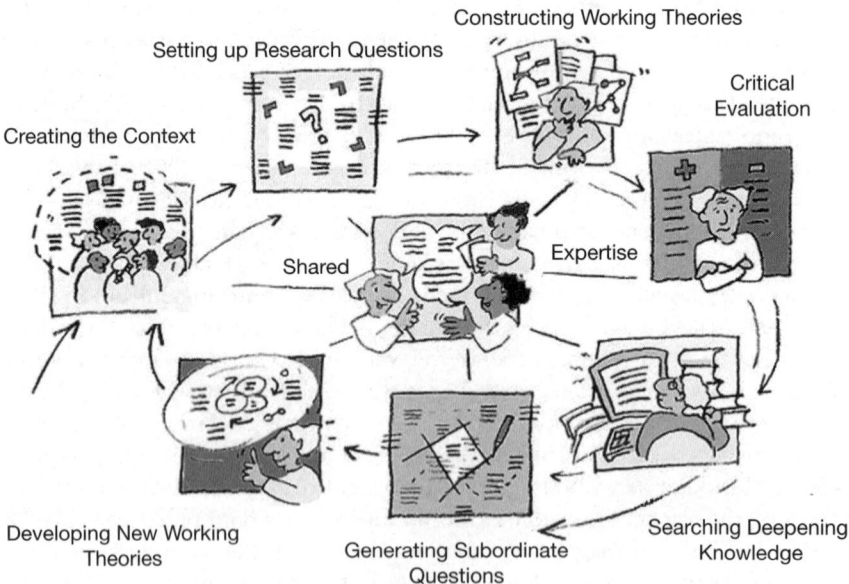

Figure 7.1 The progressive inquiry model.

monitoring, and reflecting. The aim of the *pedagogical infrastructure* is to highlight, for educators, the fundamental factors that need to be designed and addressed, which we have outlined.

Hakkarainen and colleagues have developed a pedagogical model of progressive-inquiry learning called the 'Progressive Inquiry' model as detailed in Hakkarainen, (2004) and inspired by Scardamalia and Bereiter's knowledge-building framework (see Scardamalia and Bereiter 2006 for an account of this framework). The progressive inquiry model is a tool that assists teachers in engaging their students in expert-like creative knowledge practices (see Figure 7.1).

The basic presumption of such inquiry is that the teachers should guide students to assume responsibility for all aspects of inquiry, such as goal-setting, questioning, explaining and evaluating; and crucially, they must guide students' process of inquiry through their own examples. The model consists of several elements of the inquiry that constitute essential aspects of a cyclic process of building local, collective knowledge. Shared expertise means that the participants of knowledge-creating inquiry function as a community that pursues joint investigation by sharing all elements of inquiry. The starting point for the process of inquiry is the creating of a context for the project; engaging participants in pursuing a challenging project that supports the development of their understanding of complex real-world problems and deep principles of knowledge. The participants are encouraged to set up their own research problems and questions oriented toward explaining the objects being investigated. The construction of working theories guides the participants to stretch their understanding for creating shared epistemic artefacts for supporting subsequent inquiry efforts. By critically evaluating their advancement, individuals, teams, and the whole inquiry community are able to focus their subsequent inquiry efforts in promising directions. The question-driven process of inquiry provides heuristic guidance in the search for deepening knowledge for directions and sources not determined by the teachers or initially anticipated by the participants. The process of inquiry starts with very general, unspecified and 'fuzzy' questions and tentative working theories; advancement of inquiry entails that the participants focus on improving their ideas by generating subordinate questions and searching for new information for directing further investigations (Hakkarainen and Sintonen 2002).

The desired classroom culture that sustains collaborative learning practices would not appear without the intensive practical work of the teacher or whole learning community (Hakkarainen 2009; Roth 1998). The teacher's active role is highlighted in the ways in which she or he guides the students' activities of questioning, explaining and giving feedback to each other. In an inquiry classroom with two or three dozen students and a single teacher, the teacher has to base their guidance, not only on what any individual or team requires at the moment, but also what they believe the advancement of collective inquiry project requires to be successful in attaining its higher-level objectives (Puntambekar and Kolodner 2005; Mercer and Littleton 2007). Hence, orchestration of serious technology-mediated inquiry learning is not only focused on real-time improvisational efforts of supporting productive participation in discourse interaction, but also sustained and long-standing efforts stretched across many sessions to create conditions for advancement of the inquiry (guiding participants to documenting advancement of inquiry, organizing and structuring evolving epistemic resources, and planning and envisioning further pursuit of inquiry). Such an expanded approach to orchestration creates opportunities for collaboration and sustains progressive classroom discourse focused on attaining the higher-level objectives.

Sawyer (2004) emphasised that classroom collaboration requires the teacher to manage the participatory aspects of social interaction – for example, turn taking, the timing and sequencing of turns, participants' taking on roles and relationships and asserting rights to speak. The teacher does well to observe, reflect and comment on students' reciprocal interlinkages, as well as their relations to the materials and objects of inquiry. The most effective classroom interaction balances structure with flexibility and improvisation. Sawyer (2004) particularly emphasises the value of 'improvisational' teaching, where learning is shared social activity in which all participants are participating and managing the collective process, not only the teacher. In this kind of instruction, the teacher seeks to give students the freedom to construct their own knowledge, while providing the elements of structure that effectively scaffold the co-constructive process. Improvisation can work only if all participants have internalised many joint conventions and appropriated shared practices.

Context for collaborative learning settings

In the section that follows, the role of teacher guidance in orchestrating inquiry learning will be examined by presenting a case study: 'The Artefact Project: 'Past, Present and Future' was designed together with the class teacher and took place in her classroom in Laajasalo Elementary School, Helsinki, Finland (see Seitamaa-Hakkarainen, Viilo, and Hakkarainen (2010) for detailed descriptions of the project). The Artefact Project started with 32 participating 10- to 11-year-old elementary students at the beginning of their second term of fourth grade and continued across 13 months until the end of their fifth grade. The technical infrastructure of the projects was provided by Knowledge Forum (KF) (Scardamalia and Bereiter 2006), which allows visual organization in creating an interlinked series of views (background pictures with interlinked computer notes). The project was based on the following commitments: 1) intensive collaboration between the teacher and researchers; 2) integration of many school subjects for solving real-world problems; 3) engagement in extended technology-mediated inquiry across a long period of time; 4) breach of the boundaries of traditional schoolwork by engaging a

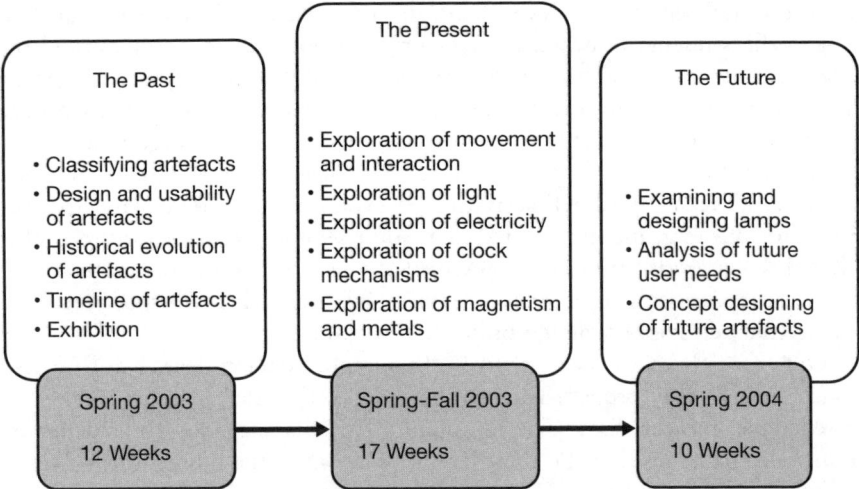

Figure 7.2 Phases of the Artefact Project.

professional designer to support students' inquiry, which involved designing artefacts.

The aim of the Artefact Project was to support students' understanding of the diversity and development of artefacts in their cultural context. In the first phase – The Past – the historical investigation of artefacts and their functionalities were carried out. Each student team chose the history of one type of handheld artefact – i.e. ball, clock, jewellery, lamp, lock and key, money, spoon – for investigation, and the students' ideas drove the historical investigation. In the second phase – The Present – the students investigated physical phenomena of artefacts, such as the functioning of a lamp, its light and the characteristics of the metals used in its construction. They were guided to ask questions and carry out their own scientific experiments as well as those based on pre-given science tool-kits. The third phase of the project – The Future – took ten weeks. Under the leadership of a professional designer and a teacher, the participants designed future artefacts in teams.

In total, the Artefact Project took 139 lessons (each lesson takes 45 minutes) over three terms. The teams were the main actors in about half of the overall project time. About half of the time, the participants worked with KF (Seitamaa-Hakkarainen et. al. 2010). In the first phase of the project, the students worked in heterogeneous 'home teams' (about 4 students per group, consisting of boys and girls, as well as less and more advanced students) which investigated the chosen artefacts and produced knowledge (made postings) representing their own team-based views in KF (i.e. views created and organised by each team). During the second phase of the project, all students worked with topics shared by the whole classroom and created collective KF views (i.e. views shared by the whole classroom). In the last phase, the students returned to their original home teams, and worked on the collective views of the whole class community. In the last phase, notes were mainly written in teams rather than individually; i.e. all team members participated in creating the content of their notes. The classroom activities were organised during the project so that there were a) joint classroom sessions, b) team-based KF activities, c) experiments, and d) participation in excursions (e.g. museum visits). The joint session took place in front of a shared screen (video projector showing KF views or notes); sometimes these were short meetings in order to organise activities, whereas other occasions involved extensive knowledge-building discussions.

Our research relies on extensive ethnographic data collected during the longitudinal study project. During the process, the teacher wrote weekly in a reflective, project diary. The template of the diary guided the teacher to reflect on the issues that she considered important at the moment of writing: 1) how were practices organised; 2) what themes and contents were addressed and how was the inquiry developing; 3) how did the community function; and 4) what was the role of supporting technology in the process. The teacher filled in one project diary template several times during the weeks that involved participation in shared project activities. This method of repeatedly collecting teachers' contextual reflections regarding the inquiry corresponds to the method of event sampling (Bolger, Davis, and Rafaeli 2003). The diaries were analysed with qualitative content analysis using Atlas.Ti software (Viilo, Seitamaa-Hakkarainen and Hakkarainen 2011). The video recordings captured the overall classroom setting and activities. The aim was to ensure that the teacher's role in the process was included. The diary-based method provided access to the teacher's orchestration in the background of the project in conjunction with the observational work of video data. For this study, we concentrated on the collaborative whole-class sessions. In what follows, we give an overview of the teacher's reflections on the classroom process, drawing on the contents of her reflective project diaries. In addition, we illustrate the nature of the teacher's presence in the classroom by selecting one represent-ative example of her practice and of the guidance pattern in the longitudinal project.

Teacher's reflections in the diary

The reflective diary entries underscored the teacher's active role in organizing and guiding the students' inquiry practices. She appeared to be committed to teaching, and contributed a great deal of her own time and effort. Her activ-ities relied on the continuous assessment of the students' ongoing inquiry processes. She emphasised that the learning community should decide collec-tively, in joint knowledge-building sessions, how to pursue further inquiries. After the community had planned how to advance, she proceeded to herself consider how to implement the practical support required for attaining the project objectives. In her diary, the teacher described her real-time support and concerns during the unfolding practice. As the students' work unfolded, she needed to rely on her own guiding principles based on the higher-level objectives (i.e. facilitation of progressive inquiry) of the project, the pedagogical infrastructure created, as well as her subject domain knowledge and skills.

The reflections indicated how the teacher instructed, reminded and continuously gave supportive feedback in order to guide students to participate in inquiry activities. When necessary, she also structured activities and tasks from the background so as to assist students in performing the inquiry activities needed for advancement of the project; such orchestrating activity taking place in the background appeared to be complemented with real-time guidance. Simultaneously, she sought to support students' own thought and their assumption of responsibility for the development of the project. The diaries revealed that her main concerns regarding student guidance related to progressive questioning, eliciting searches for deepening information, producing written notes for knowledge advancement, and organizing KF views for mediating inquiry efforts.

The higher-level objective of the project was to investigate cultural artefacts; the exact nature of the activities to be conducted were not determined beforehand beyond the main stages of the project, but emerged collaboratively across the project (i.e. studying light or designing lamps). The teacher emphasised that the students should create their own questions or problems within the overall frames of the project. Simultaneously, she was, however, concerned that the participants' initial personal theories and questions frequently tended to be superficial rather than explanation-seeking in nature. Her solution was to reiterate the initial questioning stage, and encourage students to provide deeper-level explanations. Sometimes she provided supporting questions herself in order to foster the investigative orientation of the students. Continually, she faced the contradiction that too much guiding could lead to predominantly teacher-centred activities, and too little guiding could leave the students directionless.

> They needed to be urged to wonder and make more in-depth how- and why-questions.
>
> PR:339–341

Evaluating the process: Should I have given the questions literally? It could have made the pupils' focus clearer. On the other hand in this phase it is good to see where the students are spontaneously focusing their attention. The students themselves are creating questions which are better than the advising questions. We are again facing the situation where we are forced to evaluate what is too much guidance and how much guidance is needed.

F:195–202.

The teacher paid considerable attention to guiding students to search for further information in order to deepen their partial explanations, and prompt a further consideration of their inquiry topics. The teacher often guided students to use information sources which she herself found useful so as to prevent students from getting lost whilst using the Internet. In addition, she sought to ensure that the student teams were aware of each other's information sources and their achievements, and focused the students' attention on the significance of collaborative efforts so that the products of team-based activity would be shared by the whole community.

According to the reflective diary, the teacher encouraged the students in making notes and expressing ideas in their own words so as to make their own thinking processes visible and the subject of collective evaluation. The note making was supported with mind maps or sometimes with a structured form, which guided students to write down specific aspects of the phenomena under investigation. The reflections also indicated that the teacher emphasised the use of subject domain tools (e.g. cables and light bulbs, or prisms and glass sticks, when doing experiments), or just their earlier notes and summaries, to facilitate inquiry processes and the mutual sharing of methods.

> When students were doing their experiments, I said again and again, to write down as much as possible, write down how you are doing the experiment, and what is happening, and what you observed. I spent my time shepherding the children in different rooms. I had to make sure that everyone had a good place to work.
>
> PR:269–276.

While monitoring the students' inquiry, the teacher followed their development in sharing responsibilities and work, and made remarks concerning the emergence of the student community. These reflections addressed group structures, division of work, and commitment to collaborative work. She had organised the group to be as heterogeneous as possible. The students' own interests or research questions and, in some cases, their relations with others – especially friends – affected the composition of teams. The teacher remarked in her diary how the organization of team processes or the division of labour were managed, and sometimes she mentioned that her own presence was needed so as to get everyone involved. She felt that, through the course of pursuing a successful project and accumulating experiences, the commitment to inquiry increased. She was also pleased when the students assumed responsibility for the whole community, i.e. taking care of their team members by guiding them and offering help.

The students are working a lot in teams or in pairs. They are pleased to advise each other and other teams as well in using new tools. They are eager in writing notes and raising questions about artefacts.

P:929–932.

Underpinning the enacted classroom situations were teacher-made plans and the arrangements needed for building a supportive basis for the students' working, even though the teacher could not predict how events would develop within the learning community. Her organizational processes concentrated on managing the timetable and the process of inquiry, eliciting searches for background information, and fostering the continuous documentation of knowledge-building processes. The teacher gave much thought to what the students had achieved and how the deepening of inquiry could be facilitated. By following the students' process, she was able to prefigure the forthcoming discussions, assist students in the completion of tasks and prepare them for emerging inquiry challenges. The teacher linked the activities with their past achievements and grounded forthcoming events in the current tasks. She took care that the various activities were completed, and considered, when it was time to discuss and make decisions collaboratively, how and when to support individual teams in these processes. In addition, student teams were guided to pursue parallel lines of activities and encouraged to interlink diverging lines of inquiry. However, she continuously needed to consider how to avoid being too directive whilst still providing the required assistance.

I let the teams choose their topics by themselves, which was a little risky in my opinion, because I was a bit bothered about whether or not the students would choose the kind of questions that would help them to learn the essential aspects from physics. I don't really know, what I would have done, if the students' decisions had been completely 'off'.

PR:246–252.

The teacher estimated that the KF database integrated various aspects and levels of the inquiry process; it mediated the teacher's general efforts in her organisational processes, with her real-time hands-on guidance activity. Moreover, it structured the social responsibilities in respect of the activities and assisted in interlinking personal efforts toward collaborative aims. The KF database was both the tool which organised inquiry and the object of the participants' knowledge-building activity. It stored all the inquiry efforts and represented gradually accumulating bodies of information as well as associated Internet links. The notes constructed during the process constituted a rich collective memory of the community. One crucial element in the teachers' background orchestration was the preparation of support for the externalization of the process. She organised the database, created new views to work with, and saved the information sources, notes and results of the collaborative discussions in the database. She stated that the process should be documented continuously. She herself often prepared the following collaborative whole-class discussions by collecting the students' writings – for example, from their own theories, wonderings and questions on the new KF view:

> In the next collaborative session I will try to get the students to make observations from everybody's achievements. But for that, I have to put everybody's work into the same view, where the notes can be compared, opened and handled easily.
>
> P:490–494.

The various computer views from Knowledge Forum and the Internet were typically reflected on the shared screen for collective examination. When the class was collaboratively talking and generating ideas, the teacher collated the emerging ideas and process-organizing plans using the computer, and displayed these on the wall using the data projector. The collaborative results were then saved to the KF environment. Instead of having the whole responsibility for the development of the collaborative session herself, it was shared with the classroom community.

The teacher's practice in the collective classroom situation – in the heat of the moment

The following project session shows the continuity of the teacher's reflections. The excerpts that follow each other also exemplify the teacher's typical practices. The students had earlier constructed their initial working theories and questions regarding the main question, 'What the light is and how does the lamp produces the light?' that the teacher and researchers had jointly agreed. Relying on her evaluation of knowledge produced by students, the teacher guided the participants, in this session, to participate in 'strategic planning' regarding how to make Light View more comprehensive and how to continue their collaborative inquiry. The teacher wrote in her diary:

> I decided to do a new view named 'lamp and related phenomena' for the purpose [i.e., make specific theories and questions for answering the main question "What the light is and how does the lamp produce the light?"].
>
> Theories were written. I don't remember the date. I read the theories. I was thinking that they should somehow be organised, because the view seemed to be rather chaotic. The theories were still quite superficial.
>
> PR: 110–119.

In the classroom, her direction was needed for the students to be able participate using their own initiative. The community was collectively discussing how to proceed. The plan was created by developing their collective objective at the same time. When they had together created an understanding as to how to proceed, they continued in smaller groups while the others were reading further information about electricity. The teacher could not know beforehand how this would be done.

Excerpt 1. Episode 1: 'Discussing about previous task'

Teacher: ... Well, I put our main page on display and we'll look at what you've done during last week. I think that, we really need to think about how we're going to proceed from this, but you might have some previous experience of dealing with situations like this, and I think that now we should think together as a group, how to go forward from here as you have put up your theories on the view from the lamp and the phenomena related to it. This is the kind of work we have ahead of us. What does this look like? What does it look like? When there is so many of them, they are coming forth little by little. What kind of first impressions does this give you? Michael?
Michael: It's quite confusing.
Teacher: So it appears to be.
Tom: There is now a big pile of work

First the teacher tried to orientate the students towards strategic activity and planning what to do next. She started by reminding them of their previous phase. The students were highlighting the same chaos that the teacher referred to in her diary. Whilst discussing of the previous task, the class followed the current situation from the shared screen.

Excerpt 2. Episode 2: 'Discussion about strategy and deepening inquiry, Connection to past events, Collecting rising ideas'

Teacher: Previously we have had these kinds of big projects, if you remember anything about the Pohjola (Nordic) project, or from the early phases of the Artefact project where we had this kind of large amount of information in front of us. What did we do then? And what can we do now? With this kind of pile of data? Suggest something.
I'm going to put up some ideas that come to mind. Ethan?
Ethan: To sort them.
Teacher: Ah. Sorting is a good start. Other ideas? Theo?
Theo: Sorting them in rows.
Teacher: Sorting them in rows. Anything else? Anna?
Anna: Mind map.

Teacher: You were thinking of some kind of mind map of this. How did you expect to organise it on a mind map? We have used mind maps to organise our previous work.

The students remained quite passive in the first episode, so the teacher opened the discussion about inquiry in the second episode. The content of the episode had changed from the previous task to strategic. First, the teacher helped the students to connect the situation to their past activity by reminding them of the previous phases. Then, the teacher collected and wrote up ideas emerging in discussion. Such orchestrating epistemic activity, intended to assist the community in advancement of inquiry, often took place in the background.

Excerpt 3. Episode 2: 'Discussion about strategy and deepening inquiry'

Teacher: Well, organization is our goal, surely. And sorting them in rows. Actually, there were two parts to this question, what were the two parts when I asked the question? Tom?

Tom: How to get the lamp to light and I don't remember the other one.

Teacher: Let's look at the topic, someone else. Lara?

Lara: What the light is.

Teacher: Yes, that's where we'll find both of these answers. We could start from just one, right? Well then? If we look at one or the other first. Yeah, what should we do with the notes where there is already a subject in the info screen because you've already made – Mike, has already made it a light, so we can just pick up from there. What should we do to it? Nina?

Nina: Put them together?

Teacher: Yeah. But, in order to know what to put into one group. Tom?

Tom: If we make two mind maps, where one would have what light is and the other how to get a lamp to be alight.

Teacher: Yeah, we have to probably group it like that. But I don't know if we'll be able to get it into a mind map right away. Ethan?

Ethan: Well, that we could put, put some subtitles from the essence of light.

The students were still slightly passive, and the mutual collaboration has not been started – the teacher needed to urge and help them once more. First, she connected the situation to the previous task, their subject of wonder, very mechanically using the 'initiation-response-evaluation' pattern (Mehan 1979). It encouraged students to start discussing the inquiry strategy in a more equal manner. At the end of exchange, Ethan suggested 'subtitles from the essence of light'. The situation continued with a short discussion regarding what Ethan meant by 'essence', and it became evident that Ethan meant to search for qualities or core characteristics. To continue, the teacher also asked them to remember what kind of phenomena they had been considering in the earlier, historical phase of the Artefact Project that could be useful in the present organizational effort. The students rasiesd ideas about 'utility' and 'purpose'. The teacher concluded: 'Will we be fine with these ideas? Well let's look as we open these, what else will come out and we need to get it up there to the title so they'd differ.'

Excerpt 4. Episode 2: 'Discussing about strategy and deepening inquiry'

Lara: I was just thinking that, we could probably get it organised easier if we hold the shift key and press activate everything in the other area and move them somewhere lower.

Teacher: Ah, yeah.

Lara: Then it would be easier to organise.

(Skipped: searching volunteer (Lara) for mechanic organizing. Students are pointing and telling to Lara where the right notes are).

Teacher: Thank you, Lara. Great! And what about next? Well, there is nothing for it but to open them and look what we find.

Tom: Let's start with the upper one.

Teacher: Okay, good; let's start with the upper one.

The discussion about inquiry continued and students started to participate, suggesting what to do. One student organised some notes about light in the classroom computer with the help of others. The teacher had urged and engaged students to participate in creating plans as to how to proceed together. The teacher concluded by suggesting that they now needed to open the notes. The following, last excerpt (Excerpt 5) is from a longer episode in which they discuss the content of the inquiry. In this episode, they are opening the notes and examining them.

Excerpt 5. Episode 3: 'Discussing about content'

Teacher: In the dark you can't see anything. What about in the light. That's the meaning. We can't see without light. We need light to see. Well this is all well said, light lights the darkness. You can move it from place to place ... Well, that is those lamps' businesses. But light can be ... what does it depend on or does what determines if a light is bright or dim? What causes it? What causes it children? Michael, what do you think?

Michael: (unclear) Fire requires oxygen which it then burns and then requires more energy. The less it's in use the dimmer it is.

Teacher: Yeah but what question does that answer? Now it's so that, we need to think up new questions. Who hasn't said anything yet? Everybody with raised hands has already said something. Tom?

Tom: Well, it answers the question that what a lamp needs to be.

Teacher: Well, now we need to do so that, I'm going to put a new subject there, so what kind of light there is. Good. There. Was it John also? Yeah it was that, let's put that there too. This is pretty slow work, but let's look at a few more if we can get this kind, where does this belong, does it belong to either group?

Excerpt 5 shows how the notes were opened one at the time, putting the students' own thoughts at the centre of the discussion, analysing them further, and categorizing the notes under self-made subtitles. The students were able to participate in the creation of the organizing procedure; even though the teacher directed and mediated the discussion. After they had modelled the organizing procedure together, the students were able to continue it within their individual teams. The teacher wrote in her diary afterwards, addressing a number of questions generated by students and emerging through inter-action with the teacher.

> 30.9. We were examining what kind of notes had been done. We were organizing notes under the headings that we had created together. At the same time, we were considering what kinds of questions the notes were answering: Where does the light come from? What is producing the light? The source of light. What is light? How can the light be used? What is light like? Burning.
>
> PR:221–229

Later on, she also reflected on the advancement of collective inquiry in her diary. These reflections indicate that she still was not satisfied with the progress of the project thus far. She wanted the students to continue and reiterate the question–explanation process in teams:

> 2.10. I urged them to wonder and make more in-depth why-questions. I remember explaining that the theories were not yet detailed and deeper-level enough.
>
> More wonderings, questions and deepening questions were collected and commented in teams.
>
> Now we were getting deeper into things. The questions started to become more detailed and focus on some specific phenomena related to light. In fact we discovered many-sided things about light, and the groups chose themselves a topic that they wanted to start to study.
>
> PR: 231–244.

After the re-iteration of the question-explanation process, she was satisfied and let the students choose their own research topics. While the present investigative project involved the pursuit of genuine inquiry with emergent problems and directions, it was not open-ended in respect to allowing spontaneous and free production of ideas as there were higher-level objectives of learning that guided the teacher's efforts of orchestrating collective inquiry activities.

Concluding remarks

This study depicts and analyses an elementary-school teacher's practices, and her efforts to promote pupils' cognitive responsibility for advancing their own collaborative object-oriented inquiry process. The teacher assumed the role of organiser for collaborative progressive inquiry and designing activities. This role involved the continuous monitoring of the pupils' current state within the inquiry process. We have reported this example of the implementation of the pedagogical infrastructure framework to highlight, for educators, the fundamental factors of inquiry learning that need to be designed and addressed. The teacher's diary revealed how she promoted the *epistemic infrastructure* of the class – for example, when she showed concern for guiding and supporting students' deepening inquiry, and when she encouraged them to propose 'why' questions without guiding them too much. With regard to fostering the *social infrastructure*, she considered the students' team activities and their interaction, although the decision in respect of grouping had been made at the beginning of the project. During the project, she reflected on individual student's roles, highlighted their special area of expertise, and supported the creation of a collaborative culture with its rules for behaviour and interaction. Further, she constructed a *technological infrastructure* of inquiry use, developing of ways of using Knowledge Forum, creating and sharing 'views', and making collective discussion notes during the process. Knowledge Forum structured the process and mediated activities, and rendered their objects visible and accessible to the whole learning collective. The video excerpt highlights our interpretation of the *cognitive infrastructure*; it shows how the teacher sought to encourage students to take responsibility for the organisation of the inquiry process. The teacher's efforts were focused between real-time guidance in the emerging classroom situations and background organizing that aimed to support the community to pursue inquiry across long periods of time. In the enacted classroom situations, the teacher's aim was to support students' own ideas and responsibility for the process, whereas in the background she evaluated the current directions of inquiry, and created aims and plans to guide and scaffold the students' process. These efforts involved creative and situationally-varying combinations of improvising and structure which were all based on the present enacted inquiry process.

While discourse interaction between the teacher and the students reported by the present investigation may appear as teacher-centred for Anglo-American readers, it is, however, typical for a Finnish school, where students are not oriented toward sharing their spontaneously generated ideas in the social space of the classroom in the same way (Hakkarainen et al. 1998). On the other hand, the nature of discourse interaction may reflect the very nature of the inquiry project in question: It was not oriented toward free and spontaneous production of ideas, as promoted in student-centred pedagogy, but was driven by disciplined pursuit of shared higher-level objectives of the inquiry project. The present account of our investigation reports on a collective inquiry project carried out at elementary-level focused on investigating cultural artefacts over a period 18 months. The present teacher has perfected a practice of pursuing such challenging projects in which she is learning together with the students. Her efforts at orchestrating inquiry learning were oriented to strategically guiding the classroom learning community in pursuing higher-level objectives at multiple levels by a) providing real-time guidance in classroom discussions (micro-level); b) doing background work between sessions in order to create conditions for the advancement of the project (meso-level); and c) using lessons learned in an earlier inquiry project for finding fresh perspectives for advancement of the project in hand (macro-level). Such an approach suggests that serious inquiry is object-oriented rather than totally open-ended in nature, and this state of affairs also affects the nature of teacher guidance.

Acknowledgements

Contributions were made by all authors. The present project is funded by the Academy of Finland (project 217068), MEd Viilo studies in the Doctoral Programme for Multidisciplinary Research on Learning Environments (Finland).

References

Bereiter, C. (2002) *Education and Mind in the Knowledge Age*, Hillsdale, NJ: Erlbaum.

Bielaczyc, K. (2006) 'Designing social infrastructure: Critical issues in creating learning environments with technology', *Journal of the Learning Sciences*, 15: 301–329.

Bolger, N., Davis, A. and Rafaeli, E. (2003) 'Diary methods: Capturing life as it is lived', *Annual Review of Psychology*, 54: 579–616.

Hakkarainen, K. (2004) 'Pursuit of explanation within a computer-supported classroom', *International Journal of Science Education*, 24: 979–996.

Hakkarainen, K. (2009) 'A knowledge-practice perspective on technology-mediated learning', *International Journal of Computer Supported Collaborative Learning*, 4: 213–231.

Hakkarainen, K., Järvelä, S., Lipponen, L. and Lehtinen, E. (1998) 'Culture of collaboration in computer-supported learning: Finnish perspectives', *Journal of Interactive Learning Research*, 9: 271–288.

Hakkarainen, K. and Sintonen, M. (2002) 'Interrogative model of inquiry and computer-supported collaborative learning', *Science and Education*, 11: 25–43.

Hmelo-Silver, C., Duncan, R. and Chinn, C. (2007) 'Scaffolding and Achievement in Problem-Based and Inquiry Learning: A Response to Kirschner, Sweller, and Clark (2006)', *Educational Psychologist*, 42: 99–107.

Lakkala, M., Muukkonen, H., Paavola, S. and Hakkarainen, K. (2008) 'Designing pedagogical infrastructures in university courses for technology-enhanced collaborative inquiry', *Research and Practice in Technology Enhanced Learning*, 3: 33–64.

Mehan, H. (1979) *Learning Lessons: social organization in the classroom,* Cambridge, MA: Harvard University Press.

Mercer, N. and Littleton, K. (2007) *Dialogue and the Development of Children's Thinking: a socio-cultural approach*, Abingdon: Routledge.

Puntambekar, S. and Kolodner, J. (2005) 'Toward implementing distributed scaffolding: Helping students learn science from design', *Journal of Research in Science Teaching*, 42: 185–217.

Roth, W. M. (1998) *Designing Communities*, Boston: Kluwer.

Sawyer, K. (2004) 'Creative teaching: Collaborative discussion as disciplined improvisation', *Educational Researcher*, 33: 12–20.

Scardamalia, M. (2002) 'Collective cognitive responsibility for the advancement of knowledge', in B. Smith (ed) *Liberal Education in a Knowledge Society*, Chicago: Open Court.

Scardamalia, M. and Bereiter, C. (2006) 'Knowledge building: Theory, pedagogy, and technology' in K. Sawyer (ed) *The Cambridge Handbook of the Learning Sciences*, New York: Cambridge University Press.

Seitamaa-Hakkarainen, P., Viilo, M. and Hakkarainen, K. (2010) 'Learning by collaborative designing: technology-enhanced knowledge practices', *International Journal of Technology and Design Education,* 20: 109–136.

Viilo, M., Seitamaa-Hakkarainen, P. and Hakkarainen, K. (2011) 'Supporting the technology-enhanced collaborative inquiry and design project – A teacher's reflections on practices', *Teachers and teaching theory and practice*, 17 (1): 51–72.

Chapter 8

Participatory learning assessment for organising inquiry in educational videogames and beyond

Daniel T. Hickey and Michael Filsecker

Introduction

Science educators and theorists have long argued that more specific concepts and skills of scientific domains should not be divorced from the process of scientific inquiry (Barrow 2006). As elaborated in the other chapters in this volume, proponents of inquiry-oriented instruction argue that students should engage in the same "authentic" thinking processes as practicing scientists, and that they should discover scientific knowledge through scientific investigation. For many, the debate is not whether science should be taught via inquiry, but rather how to do so. For example, some argue that inquiry learning should be organised around social problems that emerge from modern society (e.g. Sadler 2004) rather than laboratory contexts. Within particular inquiry contexts, some argue for more open-ended student-directed activities (e.g. Tamir 1983), while others have emphasised the need for guided inquiry that leads to currently accepted scientific laws and principles (Magnusson and Palinscar 1995). These debates in turn lead to more specific issues such as teacher question-answering practices (e.g. Furtak 2006) and the appropriate roles for technology (e.g. Edelson, Gordon and Pea 1999; Linn, Clark and Slotta 2003).

Nonetheless, science instruction has continued to focus on relatively direct exposition of scientific facts, skills, and concepts (Olson and Loucks-Horsley 2000). This chapter briefly considers some of the challenges facing inquiry-oriented instruction. It then illustrates how newer theories of cognition can be used to transform two key challenges – classroom assessment and external testing – in order to directly support the design of and participation in inquiry-oriented instruction. This illustration takes the form of assessment design principles that emerged over four annual cycles of design-based refinements of an inquiry-oriented science curriculum in one immersive educational videogaming platform.

Challenges for inquiry-oriented instruction

Of course, many teachers give students opportunities to collect data, draw conclusions, and contribute to the questions that direct their inquiry. This is particularly the case for teachers who have had more coursework in the particular scientific discipline, and who have had access to sustained professional development concerning inquiry-oriented instruction (Smith, Desimone, Zeidner, Dunn, Bhatt and Rumyantseva 2007). Yet careful analyses reveal that even for expert teachers, school-based activities and investigations tend not to contextualize the inquiry more generally, and they often have little, if any, connection to science as it is practiced professionally, or to the lived experiences of the students themselves (e.g. Roth 1996).

Like many enduring debates in education, much of the disconnection between science education rhetoric and science education practice can be traced back to competing assumptions about human cognition and learning (Greeno, Collins and Resnick 1996). Generally speaking, inquiry-oriented approaches reflect modern cognitive-rationalist views of knowledge as higher-order conceptual schema and representations (e.g. Piaget and Brown 1985). These assumptions support more constructivist approaches to science education that help learners build and refine these schemas by making sense of new information and solving problems in the world around them. These assumptions are also consistent with the use of performance and portfolio assessment methods. In contrast to multiple-choice tests, such open-ended formats allow extended problem solving. By capturing solutions to extended problems and asking students to explain their reasoning, open-ended formats are presumed to provide evidence of conceptual understanding and higher-order schema.

Much of the resistance to inquiry-oriented instruction reflects associationist views of cognition that characterise knowledge in terms of organised structures of more specific elements (e.g. Skinner 1953; Anderson 1996). These assumptions support much more direct teaching of specific science facts and concepts, and efficient testing of those elements (e.g. Kirshner, Sweller and Clark 2006). Some of the resistance to inquiry-oriented instruction is tacit, as teachers retreat from the challenges of school-based inquiry (e.g. Tobin, Tippin and Gallard 1994) to the relative comfort of direct instruction and testing. More explicit support for "expository" approaches comes from experimental comparisons (e.g. Klahr and Nigam 2004) and from large scale studies of learning outcomes (e.g. Ruiz-Primo, Shavelson Hamilton and Klein 2002) that generally show greater impact on science achievement. In recent years, and particularly in the US, this tendency has been exacerbated by accountability-oriented educational reforms which rely on externally developed multiple-choice achievement tests and the corresponding demise of large scale performance assessment.

Debates over inquiry-oriented instruction have certainly been a factor in the establishment and refinement of science content standards (see Olson and Loucks-Horsley 2000). Much of the initial support of organised standards in science education reflected a desire to ensure that scientific inquiry was not overlooked amidst exhaustive lists of science content. From our perspective, the coupling of science education standards with test-driven accountability has actually made it harder to include scientific inquiry. The development of standards requires broad consensus, a process that is likely to de-emphasise current-but-controversial topics that students are likely to find personally meaningful, motivating, and ideal for engaging in inquiry (see Orpwood 2001). Consider, for example, the single most relevant content standard for fifth-grade students in the US state where the present study was conducted:

> **5.1.6:** Explain how the solution to one problem, such as the use of pesticides in agriculture or the use of dumps for waste disposal, may create other problems.

While this standard certainly *could* serve as the basis for meaningful scientific inquiry experiences, it could also be readily addressed without engaging or even raising the underlying social issues. Indeed, simply helping students link this point – that solutions to some problems can cause other problems – with basic understanding of environmental issues should suffice.

Such standards lose additional meaning when translated into inexpensive, externally-developed achievement tests. In the case of the present study, a search of the relevant state's released fifth-grade test items and published classroom practice assessments failed to uncover a single item even indirectly addressing Standard 5.1.6. A search of released items from other states eventually turned up an item with a drawing of a town downstream from a river with two potential industrial sources of pollution. The question asked students what the pollution agency should do *first* when the residents complained about pollution. The correct answer was (a) testing water quality upstream and downstream from the industry sites, while the foil answers were (b) close one of the industries, (c) close the other industry, or (d) stop drinking the water. Most elementary science curricula in the US include river ecology and directly instruct students about both testing for point source pollution and the need to test hypotheses before acting. Given such standards, as represented to teachers and curriculum designers by test items like these, teachers have few incentives to engage students in messy and potentially controversial inquiry practices that the standard-setting committee might have had in mind when Standard 5.1.6 was adopted. When coupled with the lack of curricular activities that go beyond the shallow representations in the textbooks, even teachers whose personal orientation and professional development is supportive of more inquiry-oriented approaches end up not implementing them in their classrooms (see Sadler, Amirshokoohi, Kazempour and Allspaw 2006).

A comprehensive alternative for supporting inquiry-oriented instruction

The enduring debate between proponents of constructivist instruction and direct instruction is quite relevant to this chapter. But this chapter does not aim to enter into this debate (see Tobias and Duffy, 2009 for a recent comprehensive consideration). Rather, this chapter summarises a comprehensive approach to instruction and assessment that essentially sidesteps these tensions. It does so by using situative theories of cognition (e.g. Greeno 1998; Gee 2004) participatory views of learning (e.g. Barab and Roth 2006; Wenger 1999), and design-based methods (e.g. Cobb, Confrey, diSessa, Lehrer and Schauble 2003). This approach uses these perspectives and methods to transform classroom assessment and educational testing, two educational practices that have long fueled this debate. In practice, this approach pragmatically adopts a much broader view of assessment and testing than has previously been the case. This view is used to align learning within embedded assessments of communal discourse to classroom assessments of individual understanding. This alignment is done in a way that protects the communal discourse in the enactment of inquiry-oriented activities from the distortion that occurs when inquiry-oriented practices are formally represented on individual classroom assessments. This activity is then aligned to external tests of aggregated achievement, but in ways that protects classroom discourse and assessment from the corrosively simplistic representations of that knowledge in typical achievement tests. By optimizing the value of the very different forms of feedback provided at each level, this approach enhances student participation in the practices of inquiry, while directly ensuring that each student takes away valued understandings of science and scientific inquiry, and indirectly ensuring that overall science achievement is improved.

Research context and methods

Quest Atlantis and the Taiga Ecological Sciences Curriculum

Quest Atlantis (QA) is a multi-user virtual environment (MUVE) for school children. QA is one of the most well known examples of how the videogame features that foster extended engagement and learning in commercial games present enormous potential for fostering inquiry-oriented learning in educational contexts. Developed by Sasha Barab at Indiana University, QA employs a virtual reality multi-user platform and a narrative scripting engine like those in commercial immersive videogames. Questers move their avatars through a three-dimensional space, interacting with other players via text-based "chat," and with non-player characters (NPCs) via structured dialogues (Figure 8.1). The scripts for each NPC allow for dynamic responses based on player choices, creating variation in the player experiences. As players make

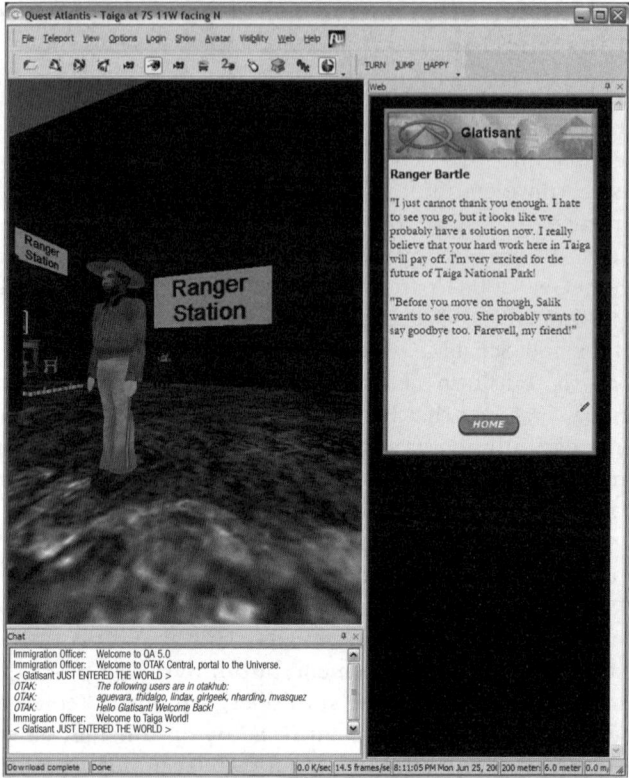

Figure 8.1 The Quest Atlantis Environment and the NPC Ranger Bartle.

progress towards their unfolding goals, NPC dialogues reflect the individual's progress through the narrative, giving players new information that reflects the system's awareness of the player's ongoing activity. QA is one of the most well-developed immersive educational games, with dozens of curricula "worlds" and thousands of users worldwide.[1]

1 In the interest of space, this description of QA and Taiga will be brief and focused. Interested readers are directed to the other referenced papers detailing the several "worked examples" (Gee, 2010) that are currently being developed These networked multimedia artifacts are being developed as part of the MacArthur Foundation's Digital Media and Learning. As of press time, a site called *Working Examples* (http://working.dev.deeplocal.com) includes one project for the videogaming principles presented in this chapter (*Designing for Participation in Educational Videogames*, Project 34), as well as the application of these same principles to e-learning contexts (*Designing for Participation, Understanding, and Achievement in eLearning*, Project 41), and to secondary language arts (*Fan Fiction*, Project 32). Another site called *Worked Examples* (http://workedexamples.org) includes a detailed description of the Taiga environment in Quest Atlantis and a more detailed explication of the principles in this chapter to e-learning.

In QA, it is the various written "quests" that students complete that structure much of the students' engagement (Figure 8.2). Players interact with NPCs and gather other information to draft responses that are typically 25 – 100 words long. These responses are submitted electronically in-game to the ranger NPC and then reviewed and either accepted or returned, typically with written feedback. Significantly, the teacher inhabits the role of the ranger in the underlying narrative and reviews the Quest submissions from that perspective. Meanwhile, the teacher simultaneously participates in the broader curriculum from the classroom teacher's role as well. This is perhaps one of the most salient and educationally-relevant aspects of Quest Atlantis. At the center of the QA studies we report in this chapter were the insights from our prior studies, which we used to enhance the quality of the discourse in and around these quests.

Taiga was the first comprehensive world built in QA. The virtual world is a park located along a river, populated by loggers, tourists, an indigenous farming community, a fishing resort, and the park administration. As detailed in Barab, Sadler, Heiselt, Hickey and Zuiker (2007a), Taiga was designed to engage students in complex socio-scientific inquiry (Sadler 2004) while also

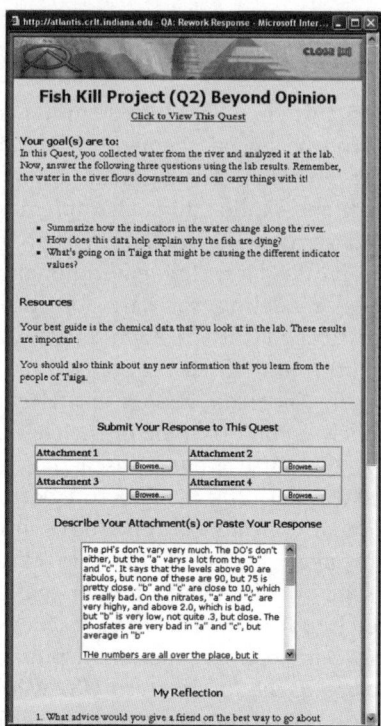

Figure 8.2 Quest 2 Beyond Opinion.

helping them learn ecological science concepts like erosion, eutrophication, and hypothesis testing. The curriculum opens with a detailed letter from Bartle, the park ranger, inviting students to serve as field investigators to help him figure out why the fish population in the river is declining. Students then complete a series of missions, with each mission culminating with the submission of a quest.

This first quest in Taiga asks students to develop an initial hypothesis about the cause(s) of the fish decline, based on the information they gathered interviewing various stakeholders. After submitting their hypotheses, students collect and analyse water samples. They evaluate their hypotheses and speculate on alternative causes of the problem in Quest 2 (shown in Figure 8.2). In order to warrant their hypotheses about the cause(s) of the fish decline, students must use their understanding of (1) various water quality *indicators* such as pH and dissolved oxygen, (2) various *processes* like erosion and eutrophication, and (3) the dynamic *relationship* between indicators and processes in the simulated watershed. Subsequent quests contextualize this scientific inquiry and content within a core socio-scientific inquiry challenge. "Winning" the game entails getting to the final quest, where players learn that the park can only be saved by getting each of the parties taking responsibility for their contribution to the larger problem.

Collaborative Assessment Studies of Taiga

The studies described in this chapter resulted from a collaboration that was initiated in 2005. With the encouragement of the US National Science Foundation, the Quest Atlantis development team brought in another team of researchers with the explicit task of implementing the multi-level model of formative and summative assessment that had emerged in prior studies of multimedia inquiry learning environments. These include the *GenScope* computer-based modeling software for introductory inheritance (Hickey, Kindfield, Horwitz and Christie 2003; Hickey, Zuiker, Taasobshirazi, Schafer and Michael 2006) and three programs from the *Classroom of the Future* (e.g., Taasobshirazi, Anderson, Zuiker and Hickey 2006). Our initial refinements to that model respond to some of the challenges we encountered in fostering productive discourse around discursive formative assessments (Anderson, Zuiker and Hickey 2007). The collaboration reported in this chapter consisted of annual cycles of design studies involving two teachers, who implemented each new version of Taiga in close collaboration with the assessment team. One of the teachers taught one class of academically-gifted fourth graders each year while the other teacher taught four classes of sixth graders each year. Both teachers taught in public schools which were typical of university towns in the Midwestern US. While some diversity was provided by the international community associated with the university and a homeless family shelter, the majority of the students were Anglo – American native English speakers who came from homes where academic success was highly valued.

Participatory approaches to formative and summative assessment

Thanks to influential considerations and reviews, including Frederiksen and Collins (1989), Sadler (1989), Black and Wiliam (1998), and the US National Research Council (Atkin, Black and Coffey 2001), the formative (i.e. educative) potential of assessment is now widely appreciated. What is less well appreciated is that assessment practices are formative only when they provide educationally useful information *and* this information is actually used to advance learning and instruction. Unfortunately, much of the potentially useful information from assessment goes unused or is used in ways that undermine learning and educational improvement. This is typically exemplified in terms of the ways that external achievement tests undermine the formative intent of classroom assessments (Black and Wiliam 1998).

Our embrace of a situative theoretical perspective and participatory views of learning also extends concerns about external achievement tests to classroom assessment. As suggested above, many assume that the isolated and impoverished representations in achievement tests undermine teachers' efforts to foster a deeper conceptual understanding of science and inquiry. We extend this concern to ostensibly formative classroom assessments, which we believe can similarly undermine participation in the communal practices of inquiry. This is because situative views of learning focus primarily on communal participation in social practices, while treating individual cognition and individual behavior as secondary activities. Thus the phenomena of students solving inquiry-oriented performance assessments and answering science achievement test items are *both* secondary artifacts of the primary phenomenon of participating in social discourse concerning inquiry. As such, we assume that the design of inquiry curricula, and the enactment of those curricula in classrooms, needs to be protected from the distortions that occur when the use of scientific knowledge to participate in scientific inquiry is presented as a formal (i.e. complete) individual representation. Of course, this assumption contradicts a good deal of belief and practice in formative assessment. This assumption is reiterated and elaborated in the concluding section of this chapter as our first assessment meta-principle.

Design-based educational research

In key ways, design-based research is consistent with the "use-inspired basic research" that Stokes (1997) used to characterise the Pasteurs' groundbreaking efforts. Research in the so-called "Pasteur's Quadrant" seeks the fundamental understanding needed to solve practical human problems. It is contrasted with the search for a fundamental understanding of natural phenomena regardless of usefulness (e.g., Bohr's pursuit of atomic structure) or with applied research without regard for scientific advance (e.g., Edison's development of consumer products). Proponents of design-based educational research assume that embedding research in the activities of practical reform should yield theoretical principles that are more useful for improving education than those developed in well-controlled experimental studies or in naturalistic observations of practice. As initially articulated by Collins (1992) and Brown (1992), this view is exemplified in the efforts of the Cognition and Technology Group at Vanderbilt (e.g. CTGV 1990) and many other collaborations and collections (e.g. Bell, Hoadley and Linn 2004; Design-Based Research Collective, DBRC 2003; Kelly 2003) have further clarified design-based methods and provide crucial insights for framing and conducting this study.

A central notion in design-based research is that the design of learning environments and the development of theories are "intertwined," and occur within "continuous cycles of design, enactment, analysis, and redesign" (DBRC 2003: 10). In this regard, this study used design-based methods to explore the unique potential of situative theory for supporting engagement in "feedback conversations", and using formative assessment to deliver broad learning outcomes. As such, the study is not a formal test pitting newer situative practices against existing practices. Rather, the study examines the plausibility of the practical solutions and associated "intermediate-level" theories that emerged when using situative perspectives to address a stubborn and widely-acknowledged educational problem. Rather than controlling for factors that might impact upon the generalizability of our findings, we aim to provide sufficient contextual framing so that others concerned with inquiry-oriented instruction in games (and beyond) can decide if these principles are relevant to them. This prepares them to further advance and refine these design principles themselves, and share those new insights with others.

We embrace the framing of design-based research methods outlined by Bell, Hoadley and Linn (2004) and used in the *Design Principles Database* (Kali 2006).[2] These efforts have added value to the design research community by helping to organise and communicate research insights as follows:

- *Features* are any artifact or technology used to advance learning in a specific learning context (such as the formative feedback we added in 2008);
- *design principles* connect several specific features (e.g. that the formative potential of the questing activity needs to be protected from the potentially summative function of that same activity);
- *meta-principles* capture abstract ideas represented by a set of principles

2 www.edu-design-principles.org

(e.g. that the formative potential of all assessments need to be protected from the summative functions of that same assessment).

This chapter describes just a few of the various assessment features that we designed and refined. These features are actually quite specific to the instructional context and lose meaning when presented outside of that context. What travels more readily are the design principles that are behind these features. The bulk of this chapter is devoted to describing five of the most important assessment design principles that emerged in the collaboration between the Taiga assessment and design teams. We present the design principles that emerged across the annual implementations, and illustrate them with a few of the features used to enact them. We also present evidence of increased learning outcomes across years as general evidence of the usefulness of these principles. We conclude our chapter with three meta-principles that emerged in the broader scholarly context of our work, including insights gained as we tried to apply the design principles from this work to other research projects in other domains and contexts.

Learning outcomes and dependent measures

Our efforts were ultimately organised around four *levels* of assessment. Each level is increasingly removed from the enactment of the curriculum, uses increasingly decontextualised and abstract representations of inquiry knowledge, and is oriented toward an increasingly broader curricular scope.

At the *immediate* level, the enactments of the inquiry routines in QA were treated as *event-oriented* outcomes. These outcomes are fleeting and highly contextualised; they are more about the way in which a particular game feature was enacted, rather than how it was designed. For example, we describe below how the first round of results prompted the design team to refine the scripted dialogue between the children playing the game and the NPCs that inhabit it to include more of the targeted scientific formalisms. Once these changes were made, event-oriented observations by the assessment team ensured that those players were actually engaging with those formalisms in those dialogues. These observations provide useful evidence for shaping them in situ (e.g. making suggestions to the teacher) and refining the activities over the longer term (e.g. further refining the dialogue scripts). Our interventions (i.e. feedback on the enactment of the activity) occurred at a fleeting timescale (Lemke, 2000) and our observations were very bound to the design and enactment of those routines. As such they are not particularly meaningful to readers, and will only be discussed as specifically relevant to more generalizable observations. The important point here is that the activity at the *immediate* level was continually shaped by the subsequent activity at the *close* level. This means that we continually looked at the dialogues that players would engage in as they interacted with the NPCs and each other, making sure that it would prepare them to participate more successfully at the close level, when they were preparing and submitting their written reports as part of each quest.

At the *close* level, the content of student quest submissions was treated as *activity-oriented* outcomes. Central to our assessment design efforts was the way that we conceptualised the process of submitting, reviewing, and revising the quests as informal assessments of the immediate-level activities. Framing the quests this way emphasised the need to align the formative functions of those activities with the corresponding quest. In the underlying model, close-level assessments are deemed "activity-oriented" because they are very closely associated with a specific set of activities. They provide evidence whose most salient evidential value concerns the enactment of those activities. This defines a formative feedback timescale for the learner that ranges from hours to days. Hence, the quality of quest submissions, the coherence of the discourse between the student and teacher/ranger in discussing these submissions, students' use of feedback in revising them, and improvement from initial to final submission were at the center of our efforts to enhance close-level engagement.

At the *proximal* level, students completed an open-ended performance assessment which included problems targeting scientific concepts and forms of inquiry covered in the curriculum, but in somewhat different contexts. Such *curriculum-oriented* assessments provide evidence that is very sensitive to the way the entire curriculum is designed and enacted. Such evidence is useful for showing valued learning gains and improving the curriculum. In the very first implementation, students completed extended essays regarding socio-scientific inquiry in other environmental contexts. While these were quite sensitive to the curriculum (because the students had no idea how to even begin on the pretest) they were very time consuming to score, and the scores were not reliable from one scorer to the next. The "Lee River" performance assessment that was used in most of these studies involved another fictional watershed with a different collection of stakeholders who had similar (but not identical) effects on the ecosystem. For example, both Taiga and Lee River involve stakeholders with different land use practices who are arranged along a river. The stakeholders from both scenarios impact their ecosystems by doing things that cause erosion and eutrophication – however, erosion is caused by loggers in Taiga and by construction in Lee River. To capture a range of understanding at the pretest and the posttest, the items covered a broad range of difficulty. Thus one item merely asked students to identify the group in the diagram whose activities added lots of nutrients to the water (i.e. the family farm). Subsequent items became increasingly difficult, asking what the groups who added nutrient runoff could do to reduce their impact, and then asking how those solutions might cause other problems. Embedded in these problems were more specific features that revealed whether students could apply the key Taiga concepts involving water quality indicators and processes and their interactions.

Finally, at the *distal* level, students responded to an achievement test consisting of released test items aligned to targeted content standards, but independent of the curriculum. Scores on such a test are deemed *standards-oriented* outcomes. Because these items are randomly selected from pools of items aligned to the targeted standards, the test included concepts and skills that were not directly addressed by the particular curriculum (as do other externally-developed achievement tests). This makes it possible to predict gains on other externally-developed achievement tests targeting those same standards, and provides valid evidence for comparing versions of the same curricula or entirely different curricula targeting those standards. In practice, pools of 10–15 released multiple-choice items from state achievement tests were created by selecting items (from various websites) that were aligned to the targeted content standards, without regard to their relevance to the Taiga curriculum. Items were drawn at random from the pools for the various tests, which were recreated several times to rule out compromise.

Research cycles, design principles and results

Following is a description of the four annual design research cycles undertaken, and the design principles that emerged. A number of quasi-experimental comparisons were embedded in the design studies. These included informal between-quest/within-class comparison used to compare different way of designing specific features that are not reported here. This also included several more formal between-class/within-teacher comparisons used to examine more comprehensive aspects of the assessment design. Two of these between-class comparisons are included below.

Baseline, communal engagement and formalism (2005 and 2006)

The initial focus in 2005 was engaging questers in personally meaningful ways with an important socio-scientific dilemma, which could only be solved using scientific concepts and information in the game space. Barab et al. (2007a) characterised this as an effort to *narratise the discipline* and described the nascent design theory in terms of considering the *use value* of the various scientific formalisms. This first version was implemented in 2005 by the fourth-grade teacher in one classroom of gifted students. As shown in the first two columns in Figure 8.1, Proximal gains on the socio-scientific inquiry essays described above were large (about 1.6 SD), but gains in achievement were small (0.35 SD) and did not reach statistical significance. The first annual round of refinements was concerned with the aforementioned refinements to the scripted dialogues to include more of the targeted scientific concepts. Barab et al. (2008) characterise this work as an effort to *disciplinise the narrative,* and characterise the nascent game design theory that emerged as *conceptual play.* Taiga was revised accordingly and implemented in 2006,

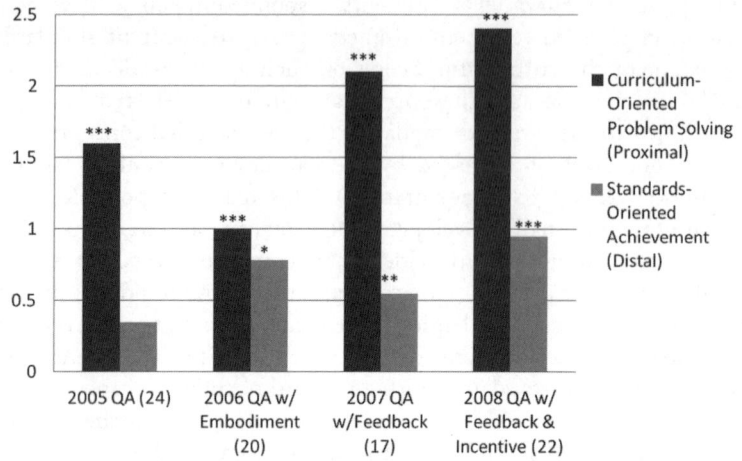

Figure 8.3 Learning Gains in Fourth Grade Classes Across Years (in SD).

by the fourth-grade teacher in one class, and a new performance assessment similar to the Lee River was used. As shown in the next two columns in Figure 8.3, the gains in proximal understanding and distal achievement were both larger and statistically significant. In 2006, this revised version of Taiga was also implemented by the sixth-grade teacher in two of his classes; his other two classes used a custom-made conventional text-based curriculum targeting the same content and standards. Prior achievement was used to assign the classes to ensure the two groups were comparable.[3] As shown in Figure 8.4, gains on both measures in the two sixth-grade QA classrooms were statistically significant, and both were larger than in the comparison classrooms (Barab et al. 2007b). To our knowledge, this was some of the first evidence of increased achievement on external measures from an educational MUVE.

The insights responsible for the improvements from 2005–2006 emerged in isolation from the performance assessment and achievement testing, whose abstracted representations of scientific inquiry and content were irrelevant at best. This is because they represented knowledge of inquiry and science as concepts and skills that individuals could "have." The situative instructional theory that drove this first round of refinements (Barab and Roth 2006) reframed those skills and concepts as "formalisms." These formalisms include both conventional academic content (e.g. *dissolved*

---

3 This study is Study 1 in Hickey, Ingram-Goble and Jameson (2009), and is described in more detail and with additional evidence in a dissertation by Anna Arici (2008).

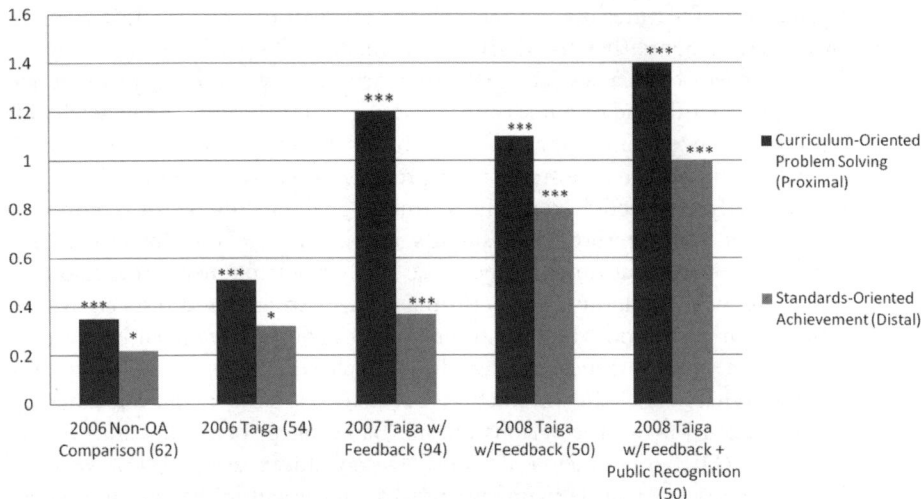

Figure 8.4 Learning Gains in SIxth Grade Classes Across Years (in SD).

oxygen, erosion) as well as experience in working at the intersection of human challenges and fundamental science (i.e. *socio-scientific inquiry*). Framing them as formalisms made it easier to carry out refinements that helped all of the participants "enlist" (i.e. use) those formalisms in shared meaning-making. Put differently, all of the initial revisions were aimed at fostering situated communal engagement in the underlying scientific formalisms within the game narrative. As elaborated elsewhere (Barab et al. 2007b), this design work was carried out using evidence from classroom conversations and analyses of quest submissions, essentially aiming to ensure that the students, teachers, *and* non-player characters enlisted the relevant scientific formalisms usefully and appropriately in shared discourse. Thus, our first assessment design principle eschews any individual characterisations of learning or understanding:

Assessment Design Principle #1: First support communal engagement in relevant domain knowledge practices

In key ways, this principle is a pre-requisite for all of the assessment efforts that follow. In other words, before inquiry-oriented innovators worry about assessing any individually-oriented conceptualizations of learning (i.e. constructing schema, building and reinforcing associations, etc.) or engagement (i.e. self-regulation, learning goals, etc.), efforts to foster inquiry learning should focus on helping all of the participants to better enlist the underlying domain formalisms.

Examples of features used to enact this assessment design principle were the various refinements that the design team made to Taiga. These were largely if the conventional assessment design work that was taking place at the same time. While the resources and insistence of our funding agency (the US National Science Foundation) afforded rigorous assessment of understanding and achievement from the start of our project, in retrospect those efforts may have actually distracted from the primary goal of supporting communal engagement. While those assessments are invaluable for illustrating the usefulness of the assessment model we are presenting here, the resources that went into developing the performance assessments and (especially) the achievement tests from the start of our project might have been better used at that time to continue refining the scripted dialogues used during the game activities, and the interaction between the student/players and the teacher/ranger during the various quests. Based on prior applications of this framework (Hickey, Zuiker et al. 2006; Taasoobshirazi et al. 2006), we knew that it is nearly impossible to impact distal achievement in the first implementation of any specific inquiry-oriented science curricula. We had learned that measuring achievement gains in the initial implementation is discouraging and places innovators in the awkward position of having to "explain away" the unflattering initial findings. As elaborated next, this is not to say that the *process* of selecting standards and conceptualizing assessments did not help us think about the design of Taiga and the embedded close-level assessments.

Another factor contributing to the lack of achievement impact in the first study was that Taiga's designers had identified *ten* different state content standards that *might* be impacted by the curriculum. In addition to creating a very challenging context for measuring gains on an achievement test, these created an exceeding high challenge for creating an external test, which typically needs at least five items per targeted standard to capture the full range of knowledge across students and across the pretest and posttest. Starting in 2006, the list of targeted standards was trimmed to just the four that we were confident we would ultimately be able to impact. This leads to our second assessment design principle:

Assessment Design Principle #2: Focus on a relatively small number of standards or academic goals.

In retrospect, this advice is consistent with that of leading assessment experts like Popham (e.g. 2007). But this advice is routinely violated by inquiry-oriented instructional innovators, who are naturally inclined to list all of the educational standards that might be impacted, in order to further justify the usefulness of their efforts.

Provide Feedback that is Useful and Used (2007)

In the 2006 study, the feedback that the sixth-grade students received was provided by the research team (because this feature of the curricular environment was still quite novel). Our subsequent refinements focused on the second quest. Quest 2 was crucial because it was where each player reported their hypothesis for the declining fish population to the teacher/ranger. Examination of the feedback for Quest 2 showed that it was not terribly substantive and mostly just encouragement. Particularly worrisome was that formal scoring of the Quest 2 submissions by the research team showed that many students failed to enlist many of the targeted formalisms, and that the subset of scores that were resubmitted did not improve in this regard. Thus, while the QA students still gained more proximal understanding and distal achievement than similar students in a well taught text curriculum covering the same topics, the learning that occurred when students drafted, submitted, and revised quests was still quite modest.

As assessment researchers who were concerned with formative feedback, the Quest submission and refinement process was an obvious target for improving learning via improved feedback. It was at this point in the trajectory of the project that we began reframing the quests as close-level informal classroom assessments as described above. The nature of the quests made them well-suited for improving learning via improved formative feedback. This leads to our third assessment design principle:

> **Assessment Design Principle #3:** Reframe the creation of artifacts or projects as close-level assessment and provide useful feedback

From our perspective, nearly every inquiry-oriented instructional innovation has some sort of activity akin to the quest, where students produce some sort of an artifact or report. We enacted this principle in the 2007 implementation using two assessment features added to the crucial Quest 2. The first was a detailed feedback rubric for scoring quests for use by the teacher/ranger which provided explicit criteria and examples for *beginning*, *developing*, *proficient*, and *expert* submissions. The rubric included scripted formative feedback that could be cut and pasted (and customised as needed) when returning the submission to the student. The teacher agreed to only accept initial submissions that were judged *expert* (as only a few initial submissions were). The second source of formative feedback implemented in 2007 was a 30–screen feedback routine (described in more detail in Hickey, Ingram-Goble and Jameson 2009). The feedback that the teacher/ranger gave to students whose Quest 2 submission was rejected encouraged them to revisit the lab technician before resubmitting. Players had previously met the lab technician in the process of getting their various water samples analysed. The access conditions were set so that players who clicked on that character *and* had submitted Quest 2 were

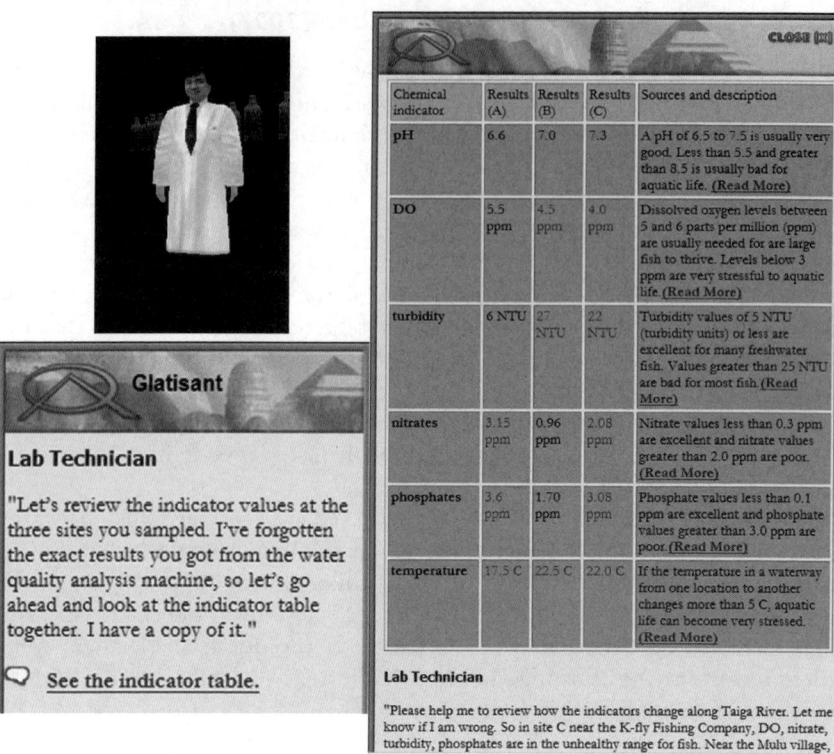

Glatisant

Lab Technician

"Let's review the indicator values at the three sites you sampled. I've forgotten the exact results you got from the water quality analysis machine, so let's go ahead and look at the indicator table together. I have a copy of it."

⬚ **See the indicator table.**

CLOSE [x]

Chemical indicator	Results (A)	Results (B)	Results (C)	Sources and description
pH	6.6	7.0	7.3	A pH of 6.5 to 7.5 is usually very good. Less than 5.5 and greater than 8.5 is usually bad for aquatic life. (Read More)
DO	5.5 ppm	4.5 ppm	4.0 ppm	Dissolved oxygen levels between 5 and 6 parts per million (ppm) are usually needed for are large fish to thrive. Levels below 3 ppm are very stressful to aquatic life.(Read More)
turbidity	6 NTU	27 NTU	22 NTU	Turbidity values of 5 NTU (turbidity units) or less are excellent for many freshwater fish. Values greater than 25 NTU are bad for most fish.(Read More)
nitrates	3.15 ppm	0.96 ppm	2.08 ppm	Nitrate values less than 0.3 ppm are excellent and nitrate values greater than 2.0 ppm are poor. (Read More)
phosphates	3.6 ppm	1.70 ppm	3.08 ppm	Phosphate values less than 0.1 ppm are excellent and phosphate values greater than 3.0 ppm are poor.(Read More)
temperature	17.5 C	22.5 C	22.0 C	If the temperature in a waterway from one location to another changes more than 5 C, aquatic life can become very stressed. (Read More)

Lab Technician

"Please help me to review how the indicators change along Taiga River. Let me know if I am wrong. So in site C near the K-fly Fishing Company, DO, nitrate, turbidity, phosphates are in the unhealthy range for fish. Near the Mulu village,

Figure 8.5 Lab Technician and Technical Dialogue in Formative Feedback Routine.

routed to the three sets of screens providing detailed explanations of water quality indicators, processes, and interactions (Figure 8.5).

These new feedback routines and other refinements to Taiga were first implemented by the fourth-grade teacher, and the new Lee River performance assessment was used. As shown in Figure 8.3, the feedback (and other ongoing refinements and improved alignment with the proximal assessment) resulted in larger proximal gains in the fourth-grade classroom; reflecting the vagaries associated with such small populations, the magnitude of the distal gains actually decreased while their statistical significance increased. In 2007, the sixth-grade teacher implemented this version of Taiga in all four of his classes. As shown in Figure 8.4, the gains in proximal problem solving were much larger than in 2006, but gains in distal achievement were only slightly larger. Analysis of the initial and final quest submissions was quite encouraging. All of the initial and final quests were scored by two researchers, who assigned one or two points for each of seven critical elements. The coding was highly reliable (over 90%). Scores on the quality of the Quest 2 submission increased by 2.4 SD from the initial submission to the final submission. However, our observations during the implementation revealed quite a range of engagement with the formative feedback among the 80 (of 110) students required to resubmit Quest 2. Analysis of QA log files (detailed in Hickey, Ingram-Goble and Jameson 2009, Study 2) revealed strong positive correlations between accessing feedback pages and gains in understanding and achievement. Specifically, we found that students who accessed more feedback pages made larger gains in understanding and dramatically larger gains in achievement. This finding led us to a more specific assessment design principle that is useful for enacting the previous design principle:

> **Assessment Design Principle #4:** Refinements to close-level learning via improved formative feedback can be evaluated by examining their impact on individual understanding via the proximal assessment, and on aggregated achievement via the distal tests.

This principle contradicts a good deal of assessment practice carried out by inquiry-oriented innovators. Consistent with prevailing formative assessment practices, they are likely to use proximal-level individual assessments to assess the learning of individual students and provide them with formative feedback and perhaps additional instruction. We suggest using proximal-level assessments to evaluate and refine the close-level activity and ensure all students take away an adequate level of understanding from that activity. As elaborated in the second meta-principle below, this alignment across assessment levels makes it possible to evaluate and refine the formative value of assessment practices at one level using the summative evidence from the next level. Because these formalisms were "transformed" in their representation in these other measures, they provide useful evidence confirming the formative value of the new design features, even within this relatively weak correlational design.

Motivating use of feedback (2008)

While the refinements to close-level feedback in 2007 certainly helped, there was still plenty of room for improvement. Just 20 of the 80 students who resubmitted their quest submission viewed all 30 of the formative feedback screens. Most of the students viewed some of the screens, while 20 never even visited the technician as instructed. Furthermore, while the 2 SD gain from initial to final Quest 2 submission was certainly promising, it still only represented an average improvement from three points to six points on a scale of 14 possible points. In response, the 2008 implementations tested out a common strategy for motivating engagement and learning in commercial videogames. As detailed in Hickey, Filsecker and Kwon (2010), the fourth-grade classroom and two of the four sixth-grade classrooms employed a *public recognition* condition that offered extrinsic incentives designed to foster friendly competition between students. While this strategy is central to most commercial videogames, it remains controversial in education. This is because of the hundreds of studies showing that incentives undermine intrinsic motivation and subsequent free-choice engagement when the incentives are no longer offered (Lepper and Cordova 1992). Incentives were already part of the fabric of Quest Atlantis. In an effort to break new ground on this crucial question, the 2008 implementation made the existing incentives even more salient for one group of students (via more public recognition of success), while replacing the incentives with more intrinsic sources of motivation for the other group of students.

In all five of the classrooms in 2008, detailed scoring and feedback rubrics were created for all five quests, which the teacher then used to rate each submission to each quest as evidence that the player was *wise, expert, knowledgeable,* or *developing.* In the fourth-grade classroom and two of the (matched) sixth-grade classes, students were also invited to publically display this status by positioning a paper version of their avatar on a physical "leader board" in their classroom (Figure 8.6), and attaching a corresponding "merit badge" to their virtual avatar (Figures 8.7 and 8.8).[4] We referred to these classes as the "public recognition" classes. Students in all of the sixth-grade classes also completed self-report surveys of their intrinsic motivation and

Figure 8.6 Board Used to Display Public Recognition of Proficiency.

4 The design and results of this study are elaborated in Hickey, Filsecker and Kwon (2010).

Figure 8.7 Badges for Player Avatars Displaying *Knowledge, Expertise,* or *Wisdom.*

situational interest while completing Quest 2, and their personal interest in solving three relevant types of scientific problems before and after completing Taiga.

As shown in Figure 8.3, the public recognition condition led to further improvement in gains in understanding and achievement in the fourth-grade classroom. As shown in Figure 8.4, students in the two sixth-grade classrooms with the public recognition condition showed larger gains in understanding than the students in the non-public recognition condition ($p < .02$ in group x time interaction in repeated measures ANOVA) and achievement ($p < = .07$). The public recognition students also reported slightly *higher* intrinsic motivation towards the activity, and slightly improved interest in solving such scientific problems. These results argue against Lepper and Cordova's (1992) "over-justification effect", whereby incentive supplants the intrinsic motivation associated with pleasurable activity, leading to disengagement in the absence of the incentive.

The system we used for logging page views in 2007 was not available to us in 2008, so we were not able to examine the impact of incentives on the number of feedback pages accessed by students. We turned instead to a source of evidence that was actually more informative relative to the concerns that skeptics and critics are likely to raise about the use of incentives. This was provided by a detailed scoring of the final submission for Quest 2. As reported in Hickey, Filsecker and Kwon (2010), the text of a representative sample of Quest submissions were coded for evidence that each of eleven potentially relevant formalisms had been (a) enlisted at all, and (b) enlisted appropriately in this context. Results revealed not only that the public recognition condition was associated with a greater number of formalisms used, but also with more appropriate use of those formalisms. This argues strongly against our biggest concern with incentives – namely, that they would lead students to write anything to get the reward and recognition, without regard to whether what they were writing was correct. This leads to our fifth assessment design principle

Figure 8.8 Players' Avatars Wearing Badges Showing Wisdom and Knowledge.

Assessment Design Principle #5: Motivate students to use feedback, but make sure you don't undermine engagement, intrinsically-motivated learning, or personal interest in the domain.

This design principle, and the specific features used to enact it here seem particularly relevant to inquiry-oriented videogames. But it touches on broader issues about the various strategies that are used in motivation inquiry learning directly (such as incentives, points, etc.) and indirectly (i.e. grades or marks associated with school-based inquiry). This principle touches on a parallel program of research exploring situated theories of motivation introduced in Hickey (2003) and elaborated in Hickey and Schaffer (2006), which has yielded additional design principles that are more directly concerned with issues of incentives.

Assessment meta-principles

While our assessment approach was illustrated and validated in studies of an immersive educational videogame, the design principles presented here are directly relevant to most other inquiry-oriented contexts; we have found in other projects outside science education that their value extends well beyond inquiry-oriented instruction. Translating the design principles across projects and communicating those principles to a broader audience requires us to characterise them more abstractly and generally. Additionally, reading relevant research articles and interacting with those authors and other colleagues further helped us appreciate the more generalizable aspects of our insights. These insights are captured in three meta-principles that we hope will be broadly relevant to nearly any classroom learning context.

Our first meta-principle reiterates our strong embrace of situative theories of knowledge and a participatory view of learning. This embrace leads us to qualify some widely held assumptions about assessment that reflect more conventional cognitive and socio-cognitive assumptions (e.g. Wiliam 2007; Mislevy 2008). In particular, the situative focus on shared social activity raises concerns that the formal representation of scientific inquiry and the scientific concepts in assessments and tests can undermine participation in the shared discourse that we believe is crucial for developing that very understanding:

> *First Assessment Design Meta-Principle: Just as the impoverished representations of scientific inquiry on external tests undermine schools' focus on deeper conceptual understanding of inquiry, the formal representation of that knowledge on classroom assessments can undermine shared participation in discourse about inquiry that is necessary if students are to develop that conceptual understanding.*

This principle was enacted in the way we focused our efforts away from the formal representations of inquiry on classroom assessments or external tests. Rather, our design principles emphasised the need for very informal discursive feedback in the more communal context of the curricular activities that made up the immersive videogame. This contrasts with many approaches to formative assessment which would have brought our proximal performance assessment much more directly into the design and enactment of the curriculum. As elaborated next, using a different type of problem on the performance assessment, and isolating that representation from the design and enactment of the curriculum, established a clear "distance" between the close-level questing activity and the proximal-level performance assessment. This, in turn, enhanced the validity of the scores from the performance assessments as evidence of the impact of close-level activity on student understanding.

The second meta-principle from this body of work concerns the complex relationship between the deep conceptual understanding of inquiry represented by our performance assessment, and the narrowed representations of that knowledge on external standardised test items. While we reluctantly submit to the reality that our work takes the very practical stance that innovations such as these will be unwelcome in schools without evidence of achievement impact, two seemingly nuanced observations lead us to qualify the relationship between performance assessments and achievement tests. Our first observation builds on the concerns about construct-irrelevant variance that Messick (1994) raised in response to the first major wave of assessment reforms. This concern has to do with the impact of design-based refinements like ours on the validity of the scores on our performance assessment. We certainly were not teaching students to solve the actual problems that made up the performance assessment. But our efforts to align the curriculum to that assessment limit the conclusions that can be drawn from increased scores. This is because an unknown (and mostly unknowable) portion of improvement comes from familiarising students with the *types* of problems on the tests. As such, an additional measure further removed from the curriculum and any refinements is necessary if we are to make claims about improvements over time. Perhaps more significantly, some other non-compromised measure is needed to make any claims in comparison studies using some other curriculum that had not been so aligned (as our 2006 study did). One solution might be to have an additional performance assessment, perhaps solving different inquiry problems in a different context. However, this is difficult to interpret, and requires a lot of additional assessment time. Situative views of assessment reframe the problem in a way that offers a promising solution: standardised measures are simply *more peculiar* representations of inquiry discourse than the performance assessment. This means that our efforts to increase understanding on the performance assessment should yield an "echo" of increased achievement on externally-developed test items, as long as those items are aligned to the same standards. Thus:

> **Second Assessment Design Meta-Principle.** *Refinements to classroom discourse that serve to increase deep conceptual understanding according to a performance assessment should indirectly but consistently increase scores on standardised test items targeting the same educational standards.*

Our efforts to put both of these principles in place embraced a situative view of learning that let us characterise the proficiencies targeted by a particular curriculum *and* represented in externally developed standards as formalisms. The notion of formalisms reframes proficiencies as "boundary objects" (Bowker and Starr 1999) that can inhabit multiple activity systems, enabling communication and collaboration across those systems. When a proficiency is characterised as a formalism it "answers to different sets of audiences and pursues different sets of tasks" (Star and Griesemer 1989:388). This is important because objects and methods mean different things at different levels in our assessment model. As such we had to reconcile those meanings in order to align activity across the levels. As Moss, Girard and Haniford (2006: 146) pointed out:

> ...a boundary object is a particular kind of cultural tool that not only crosses boundaries of activity systems, such as a mandated assessment, but is also plastic enough to meet the local needs while maintaining a common identity across sites... A mandated assessment would function as a boundary object when actors in the local context are able to cooperate in providing necessary information to outsiders while maintaining a productive level of authority and agency over their own practice.

Our framework essentially stretches this characterization of "mandated assessment" across the embedded quests, the performance assessment, and the external tests. The manner in which these formalisms are aligned across the levels in our model is embodied in our third meta-principle:

Third Assessment Design Meta-Principle: *Maximise engagement and learning by inviting students to enlist key formalisms across three or more increasingly formal assessment contexts.*

Across several projects, we have taken to using the more colloquial notion of *relevant big ideas* (RBIs) as a way of conveying what we mean here. By calling them RBIs (to be enlisted or used in knowledgeable activity or discourse), we keep the discourse and activity around the process from defaulting to the more familiar notion of "concepts" or "schema" (to be constructed, internalised, and transferred). Needless to say, many of our assessment colleagues find our resistance to individualised characterisations of knowledge confusing (or worse). Several protracted rounds of review and revision have taught us to avoid the more fundamental arguments about whether concepts or schema actually get "internalised." Rather, we embrace Wertsch's (1998: 48) notion of internalization as "closely bound up with particular phenomenon and examples, and thus a term that takes on variety of interpretations." While we certainly interpret success across each level of learning outcomes in terms of enlisting socially defined formalisms, we acknowledge that this challenges the tacit assumptions of many observers. Rather than attempting to overturn those assumptions, we instead focus our efforts on a more pragmatic resistance to allowing those assumptions to reduce inquiry-oriented discourse within learning environments like QA by simply instructing individual students about the facts and concepts of scientific inquiry.

Conclusions and concerns

We concluded that this round of refinements to Taiga resulted in substantial improvements to the underlying multi-level assessment model. In particular, our focus on aligning the design and enactment of activity at the immediate and close level with the proximal level performance assessment overcame many of the challenges we encountered in prior studies in which we tried to foster shared discourse more directly from classroom performance assessments. We have found these insights to be useful in other projects. We hope that others will take up these principles, extend them, and share them with others.

As will be articulated in subsequent papers, work still remained to be done after the 2008 implementation. A major concern that emerged in the 2008 implementation was the sheer volume of Quest submissions and resubmissions. This was manageable for the fourth-grade teacher, who had a single class with fewer students. Notably, she was able to maintain the fiction across the entire curriculum that she was *not* the ranger. While all students quickly recognise that the ranger NPC is sometimes inhabited by a human, the fourth-grade teacher never reviewed quests where the students could see her; during the curriculum, most students assumed it was one of the researchers associated with the QA. However, in the sixth-grade classes, it was impossible for the teacher to review quests away from the computer lab. As such, students quickly figured out that it was the teacher. This led them both to drop the ranger/apprentice projective stances (Gee 2008) and to embrace more conventional teacher/student roles. Additionally, we began seeing more resubmissions that were not substantially improved, and more students asking for more explicit feedback (i.e. "is *this* what you want?"). Our initial analysis did not reveal any differences across the incentive conditions, suggesting that this was not the result of the incentives. Put quite bluntly, it seemed possible that our focus on the quests as close-level assessments may have actually undermined the narrative in the game and made the entire affair feel a lot more like traditional school. As such, the assessment team began searching for ways of maintaining the large gains in understanding and achievement that we had attained, while preserving more of the game-like feel, increasing student agency over the questing process.

Acknowledgements

Special thanks to Sasha Barab for his leadership as the director of the Quest Atlantis project and the lead developer of the Taiga world and curriculum, and Jim Gee for his support of this research since 2007 via the MacArthur Foundation's *21ˢᵗ Century Assessment Project*. Thanks also to Beth Piekarsky and Jacob Summers for continuing participation in the implementation and refinement of Taiga, and for the students in their classrooms for participating in these studies. Anna Arici, Jo Gilbertson, and Bronwyn Stuckey also contributed to the initial curricular design. Adam Ingram-Goble, Ellen Jameson, Steven Zuiker, Eun Ju Kwon, and Anna Arici were instrumental in the assessment design, curricular revision, implementation support, and analysis in this study and the broader program of inquiry. This research was supported by the National Science Foundation Grant REC-0092831 to Indiana University and the MacArthur Foundation. The views expressed here do not necessarily represent the views of the National Science Foundation, the MacArthur Foundation, or Indiana University.

References

Anderson, J. R. (1996) *The Architecture of Cognition*, Mahwah, N. J: Lawrence Erlbaum Associates.

Anderson, K. T., Zuiker, S. and Hickey, D. T. (2007) 'Classroom discourse as a tool to enhance formative assessment and practice in science', *International Journal of Science Education*, 1721–44.

Atkin, J. M., Black, P. and Coffey, J. (2001) *Classroom Assessment and the National Science Education Standards*, Washington, D.C.: National Academy Press.

Arici, A. B. (2008) *Meeting kids at their own game: A comparison of learning and engagement in traditional and 3D MUVE educational gaming contexts*, Unpublished Dissertation, Indiana University.

Barab, S. A. and Roth, W. M. (2006) 'Curriculum-based ecosystems: Supporting knowing from an ecological perspective', *Educational Researcher*, 35 (5): 3–13.

Barab, S., Sadler, T., Heiselt, C., Hickey, D. and Zuiker, S. (2007a) 'Relating narrative, inquiry, and inscriptions: A framework for socioscientific inquiry', *Journal of Science Education and Technology*, 16: 59–82.

Barab, S., Warren, S. and Ingram-Goble, A. (2008) 'Conceptual play spaces', in R. Ferdig (ed) *Handbook of Research on Effective Electronic Gaming in Education*, Hershey, Pennsylvania: IGI Global publications.

Barab, S, Zuiker, S., Warren, S, Hickey, D., Ingram-Goble, A., Kwon, E., Kouper, I. and Herring, S. (2007b) 'Situationally embodied curriculum: Relating formalisms and contexts', *Science Education*, 91: 750–82.

Barrow, L. H. (2006). 'A brief history of inquiry; From Dewey to standards', *Journal of Science Teacher Education*, 17 (3): 265–278.

Bell, P., Hoadley, C. M. and Linn, M. C. (2004) 'Design-based research in education', in M. C. Linn, E. A. Davis and P. Bell (eds) *Internet Environments for Science Education*, Mahwah, N J: Lawrence Erlbaum Associates.

Black, P. and Wiliam, D. (1998) *Inside the Black Box: raising standards through classroom assessment*, London: School of Education, King's College.

Bowker, G. C. and Star, S. L. (1999) *Sorting Things Out*, Cambridge, MA: MIT Press.

Brown, A. L. (1992) 'Design experiments: Theoretical and methodological challenges in creating complex interventions in classroom settings', *Journal of the Learning Sciences*, 2 (2): 141–78.

Cobb, P., Confrey, J., diSessa, A., Lehrer, R. and Schauble, L. (2003) 'Design experiments in educational research', *Educational Researcher*, 32 (1): 9–13.

Collins, A. (1992) 'Towards a design science of education', in E. Scanlon and T. O'Shea (eds) *New directions in educational technology,* New York: Springer-Verlag.

CTGV, C. (1990) 'Technology Group at Vanderbilt; Anchored instruction and its relationship to situated cognition', *Educational Researcher,* 19 (6): 2–10.

Design-Based Research Collective (2003) 'Design-based research: An emerging paradigm for educational inquiry', *Educational Researcher,* 32 (1): 5–8.

Edelson, D. C., Gordin, D. N. and Pea, R. D. (1999) 'Addressing the challenges of inquiry-based learning through technology and curriculum design', *Journal of the Learning Sciences,* 8 (3): 391–450.

Frederiksen, J. R. and Collins, A. (1989) 'A systems approach to educational testing', *Educational Researcher,* 18 (9): 27–32

Furtak, E. M. (2006) 'The problem with answers; An exploration of guided scientific inquiry teaching', *Science Education,* 90 (3): 453–67.

Gee, J. P. (2004) *Situated Language and Learning: a critique of traditional schooling,* London: Routledge.

Gee, J. P. (2008) 'Video games and embodiment', *Games and Culture,* 3 (3–4): 253–63.

Gee, J. P. (2010) *New digital media and learning as an emerging area and "worked examples" as one way forward.* Cambridge, MA: MIT Press.

Greeno, J. G. (1998) 'The situativity of knowing, learning, and research', *American Psychologist,* 53 (1): 5–26.

Greeno, J. G., Collins, A. M. and Resnick, L. B. (1996) 'Cognition and learning', in D. Berliner and R. Calfee (eds) *Handbook of Educational Psychology,* New York: MacMillian.

Hickey, D. T. (2003) 'Engaged participation versus marginal nonparticipation: A stridently sociocultural approach to achievement motivation', *The Elementary School Journal,* 103 (4): 401–29.

Hickey, D. T. and Anderson, K. (2007) 'Situative approaches to assessment for resolving problems in educational testing and transforming communities of educational practice', in P. Moss (ed) *Evidence and Decision Making; The 103rd NSSE yearbook,* National Society for the Study of Education: University of Chicago Press.

Hickey, D. T., Filsecker, M. and Kwon, E. J. 'Participatory examination of incentives and competition on engagement and learning in educational video games', paper presented at the *Annual Meeting of the American Educational Research Association,* Denver, May 2010.

Hickey, D. T., Ingram-Goble, A. A. and Jameson, E. M. (2009) 'Designing assessments and assessing designs in virtual educational environments', *Journal of Science Education and Technology,* 18 (2): 187–208.

Hickey, D. T., Kindfield, A. C. H., Horwitz, P. and Christie, M. A. (2003) 'Integrating curriculum, instruction, assessment, and evaluation in a technology-supported genetics environment', *American Educational Research Journal,* 40 (2): 495–538.

Hickey, D. T. and Schafer, N. J. (2006) 'Design-based, participation-centered approaches to classroom management', in C. Evertson and C. Weinstien (eds) *Handbook for Classroom Management: research, practice, and contemporary issues,* New York: Merill-Prentice Hall.

Hickey, D. T., Zuiker, S. J., Taasobshirazi, G., and Schafer, N. J. and Michael, M. A. (2006) 'Three is the magic number: A design-based framework for balancing formative and summative functions of assessment', *Studies in Educational Evaluation,* 32: 180–201.

Kali, Y. (2006) 'Collaborative knowledge building using the Design Principles Database', *International Journal of Computer-Supported Collaborative Learning,* 1 (2): 187–201.

Kelly, A. E. (ed) (2003) 'Theme issue: The role of design in educational research', *Educational Researcher,* 32 (1).

Kirschner, P. A., Sweller, J. and Clark, R. E. (2006) 'Why minimal guidance during instruction does not work: An analysis of the failure of constructivist, discovery, problem-based, experiential, and inquiry-based teaching', *Educational psychologist*, 41 (2): 75–86.

Klahr, D. and Nigam, M. (2004) 'The equivalence of learning paths in early science instruction. Effects of direct instruction and discovery learning', *Psychological Science*, 15 (10): 661–67.

Lemke, J. L. (2000) 'Across the scales of time: artifacts, activities, and meanings in ecosocial systems', *Mind, Culture, and Activity*, 7 (4): 273–90.

Lepper, M. R. and Cordova, D. I. (1992) 'A desire to be taught: Instructional consequences of intrinsic motivation', *Motivation and emotion*, 16 (3): 187–208.

Linn, M. C., Clark, D. and Slotta, J. D. (2003) 'WISE design for knowledge integration', *Science Education*, 87 (4): 517–38.

Magnusson, S. J. and Palincsar, A. S. (1995) 'The learning environment as a site of science education reform', *Theory into practice*, 34 (1): 43–50.

Messick, S. (1994) 'The interplay of evidence and consequences in the validation of performance assessments', *Educational Researcher*, 23 (2): 13–23.

Mislevy, R. J. (2008) 'How cognitive science challenges the educational measurement tradition', *Measurement: Interdisciplinary Research and Perspective*, 6 (1): 124.

Moss, P. A., Girard, B. J. and Haniford, L. C. (2006) 'Validity in educational assessment', *Review of Research in Education*, 30 (1): 109–62.

Olson, S. and Loucks-Horsley, S. (2000) 'Inquiry and the National Science Education Standards: A guide for teaching and learning', *Washington, D.C: National Research Council*.

Orpwood, G. (2001) 'The role of assessment in science curriculum reform', *Assessment in Education: Principles, Policy and Practice*, 8 (2): 135–51.

Popham, W. J. (2007). *Classroom Assessment: what teachers need to know* (5th edition). Boston: Pearson.

Piaget, J. and Brown, T. (1985) *The Equilibration of Cognitive Structures: the central problem of intellectual development*, Chicago: University of Chicago Press.

Roth, W. M. (1996). 'Teacher questioning in an open-inquiry learning environment: Interactions of context, content, and student responses,' *Journal of Research in Science Teaching*, 33 (7): 709–736.

Ruiz-Primo, M. A., Shavelson, R. J., Hamilton, L. and Klein, S. (2002) 'On the evaluation of systemic science education reform: Searching for instructional sensitivity', *Journal of Research in Science Teaching*, 39 (5): 369–93.

Sadler, D. R. (1989) 'Formative assessment and the design of instructional systems', *Instructional Science*, 18 (2): 119–44.

Sadler, T. D. (2004) 'Informal reasoning regarding socioscientific issues: A critical review of research', *Journal of Research in Science Teaching*, 41 (5): 513–36.

Sadler, T. D., Amirshokoohi, A., Kazempour, M. and Allspaw, K. M. (2006) 'Socioscience and ethics in science classrooms: Teacher perspectives and strategies', *Journal of Research in Science Teaching*, 43 (4): 353–76.

Skinner, B. F. (1953) *Science and Human Behavior,* New York: Macmillan.

Smith, T. M., Desimone, L. M., Zeidner, T. L., Dunn, A. C., Bhatt, M. and Rumyantseva, N. L. (2007) 'Inquiry-oriented instruction in science: who teaches that way?', *Educational Evaluation and Policy Analysis*, 29 (3): 169–99.

Star, S. L. and Griesemer, J. R. (1989) 'Institutional ecology, 'translations' and boundary objects: Amateurs and professionals in Berkeley's Museum of Vertebrate Zoology', 1907–39, *Social studies of science*, 19 (3): 387–420.

Stokes, D. E. (1997). *Pasteur's Quadrant: basic science and technological innovation*. Washington, D.C: Brookings Institution Press.

Taasobshirazi, G., Anderson, K. A., Zuiker, S. J. and Hickey, D. T. (2006) 'Enhancing inquiry, understanding, and achievement in an astronomy multimedia astronomy learning environment', *Journal of Science Education and Technology*, 15: 383–95.

Tamir, P. (1983) 'Inquiry and the Science Teacher', *Science Education*, 67 (5): 657–72.

Tobias, S. and Duffy, T. D. (eds) (2009) *Constructivist Theory Applied to Instruction: success or failure?*, Abingdon: Routledge.

Tobin, K., Tippen, D. and Gallard, A. J. (1994) 'Research in instructional strategies for teaching science', in D. Gabel (ed), *Handbook of Research on Science Teaching and Learning*, New York: Macmillan.

Wenger, E. (1999) *Communities of Practice: learning, meaning, and identity*, Cambridge, MA: Cambridge University Press.

Wertsch, J. V. (1998) *Mind as Action*, New York: Oxford University Press.

Wiliam, D. (2007) 'Keeping learning on track: Classroom assessment and the regulation of learning', in Lester, F. (ed), *Second Handbook of Research on Mathematics Teaching and learning*, Greenwich, CT: Information Age Publishing.

Chapter 9

Orchestration of assessment: assessing emerging learning objects

Barbara Wasson, Vibeke Vold and Ton de Jong

Introduction

Orchestration of assessment in inquiry learning environments requires careful design of mechanisms for both formative and summative assessment. Summative assessment, or assessment *of* learning, occurs at a defined point in time and is generally used to measure learning outcomes (Shute 2009) and reports those outcomes to different stakeholders (e.g. students, parents, teachers, and administrators). Formative assessment, or assessment *for* learning, refers to assessment that is specifically intended to generate feedback on performance to improve and accelerate learning (Sadler 1989; Black and Wiliam 1998; Shute 2007; Stiggins 2002). In this chapter, we address the orchestration of assessment in learning by design environments where the creation of artifacts is both a vehicle for, and a result of, learning. We present a number of assessment mechanisms and illustrate how these can be supported in a learning design environment. In particular, using the SCY (Science Created by You) project as an example, we illustrate how we intertwine assessment mechanisms with the learning process, and facilitate these mechanisms with features of the learning environment and with assessment tools.

It is currently commonly understood that learning for understanding in science requires an active cognitive approach (e.g. Bransford, Brown, and Cocking 1999; Jonassen 1991; Mayer 2002; von Glaserfeld 1987). Dewey stressed the importance of "doing" science, mathematics, and history to gain an understanding of these domains (Dewey 1916). "Doing" means that learners abstract, discover and prove. One of the prominent ways to engage learners in those active processes is to involve them in design activities (Puntambekar and Kolodner 2005). Learning by creating is one of the basic ideas behind *constructionism*: "... knowledge construction takes place when learners are engaged in building objects" (Kafai and Resnick 1996). The rationale behind learning by design is that abstract knowledge needs to be translated into concrete objects and this process helps to reflect on the knowledge acquired. By "working" with their knowledge, students are involved in knowledge transformation processes, and adapt and extend their understanding. Often design is inherently a collaborative process that leads to meaning negotiation and thus, again, to reflection on one's own knowledge (Zahn, Pea, Hesse and Rosen 2010). Learning by design also has a motivational aspect since the objects that are designed often have some kind of real world function. The kind of objects that are constructed vary widely and can be computer models (de Jong and van Joolingen, 2007; Hestenes 1987; Pata and Sarapuu 2006), physical objects and artifacts (Crismond 2001; Mehalik, Doppelt, and Schuun 2008), drawings (Hmelo, Holton, and Kolodner 2000), concept maps (Novak 1990), games (Kafai 1996), computer programs (Mayer and Fay 1987), podcasts (Lee, McLoughlin, and Chan 2008), videos (Zahn et al. 2010), or even instruction (Vreman-de Olde and de Jong 2006).

The SCY project produces learning environments that are based on this pedagogical approach of learning by design. In SCY learning environments, learners create artifacts (that we have labelled "Emerging Learning Objects" (ELOs; see Hoppe et al. 2005) in the context of a real life challenging assignment that in itself also finds its completion in making a final encompassing ELO. ELOs include (System Dynamics) models, concept maps, artifacts, data sets, hypotheses, tables, summaries, reports, plans, and lists of learning goals. One of the SCY learning environments, for example, uses the assignment of creating a CO_2-friendly house where learners create a design of such a house as a final product. On their way to this final product, they generate many kinds of other ELOs, such a data sets from a house simulation, a concept map of the greenhouse effect, and sets of experimental questions and hypotheses.

The artifacts that learners produce (both the final one, and the ones produced on the road) are vehicles for gaining an understanding of general science skills, social and presentations skills, and, in the first place, science concepts underlying the design of the artifact (see e.g. Mehalik et al. 2008). For the creation of ELOs, learners have to gather and process information, design and conduct experiments, make interpretations and abstractions, and communicate their conclusions; in other words, they have to engage in processes of active learning. In addition to being the driving force for students' active learning, ELOs play a central role in student collaboration, in gathering information for adaptation of the SCY learning environment, and in assessment (de Jong et al. 2010).

In this chapter, we first further explain the learning process in SCY, focusing on the role of ELOs in this process and reviewing relevant research on peer and self-assessment, before focusing on the formative assessment mechanisms, which are materialised in the form of peer feedback (students giving feedback on each other's ELOs), a self-reflection process (as they add ELOs to an ePortfolio), and the summative mechanisms used (as they reflect on the design learning process) as they create a portfolio to be submitted for summative assessment. We then illustrate how we implement these mechanisms in SCY environments by presenting two SCY assessment tools that facilitate these mechanisms.

Learning with SCY

The SCY learning experience begins with students being presented with a challenge, such as *Create a Healthy Pizza*, *Determine a DNA profile*, *Create a video of water quality*, or *Design a CO_2-friendly house* (for an overview, see de Jong et al., submitted). This challenge is the main assignment in a SCY Mission (as a SCY concrete learning environment is called). In the "*CO_2-friendly*" house mission, for example, the focus is on designing a house that takes into account its impact on the environment, and the reduction of CO_2 emissions in particular (see Figure 9.1 for the general assignment for the CO_2-friendly house mission).

What is the challenge?

Your job is to design a CO_2-friendly house. So you have to think of all kinds of measures and applications, that will reduce the CO_2-emissions of your house. But, although the reduction of CO_2-emissions is the central issue, your house has to provide room and a reasonable level of comfort for a family of four members (two parents and two children). At the end of this project, you have to present your CO_2-friendly house to the rest of the group. Throughout this project, you have to complete a number of assignments. The Mission Map (at the bottom-right corner of your screen) will guide you through the project.

You will be working on your house design in a small group of students (your design group). Before you can actually start to design your house, you have to become an expert. Each member of a design group will be assigned a specific expert role. You are either (1) a thermal expert, (2) an energy expert, or (3) a domestic expert. Especially in the first half of the mission, you will collaborate with classmates with the same expert role. The main task of this expert group is to find information and to do real and virtual experiments. You will present your expert findings in a concept-map.

Figure 9.1 CO_2 Friendly House Mission Challenge.

From the learner's perspective, a SCY mission comprises a series of "Learning Activity Spaces (LASs)" through which they navigate via a "Mission Map". Figure 9.2 shows the Mission Map that gives learners an overview of the LASs in the CO_2–friendly house mission. By hovering over a pictogram, a description of the main ELO for that LAS and a list of concrete ELOs created by the learner in that LAS appears (see the description of a concept map to be developed in Figure 9.2). During a SCY mission, learners move from LAS to LAS, create ELOs along the way and finally create the main assignment ELO as an end product. In each LAS, one or two ELOs are central and are the main output of the LAS.

Upon entering a LAS for the first time, the LAS is decked with a curtain (not shown) that gives an overview of the activities to be carried out in the LAS and lists the learning goals that the activities address. Closing the curtain reveals one or more ELOs, including the main ELO of the LAS that

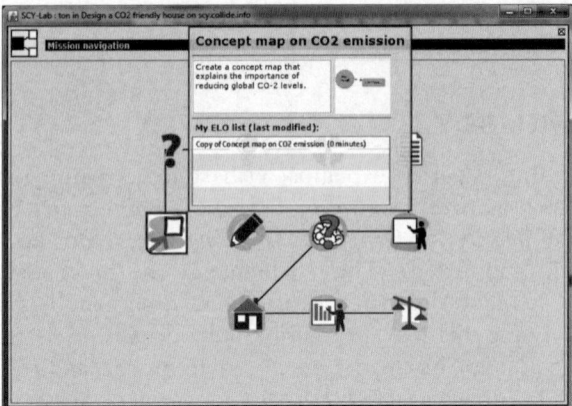

Figure 9.2 Mission Map for the CO_2 Friendly House Mission.

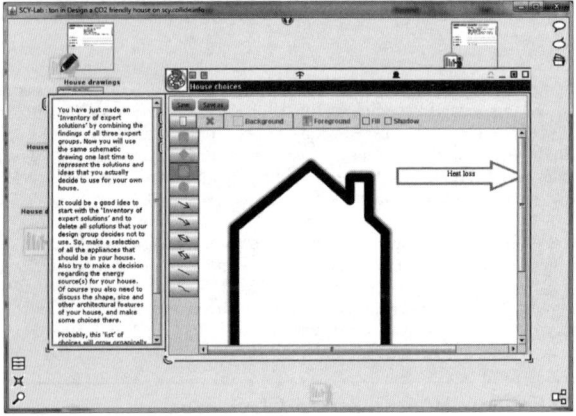

Figure 9.3 Concept Map LAS in the CO_2 Friendly House.

should be completed before moving on to another LAS (this ELO is located in the top right of the LAS window under the open ELO, see Figure 9.3).

When learners open an ELO, a tool is launched that can be used to edit the ELO (e.g. a concept mapping tool to create a concept map, a simulation to create a data set, etc.). The ELO being created is surrounded by a number of drawers, a kind of side window that can be opened from the ELO tool, each for a different function. The top drawer contains a description of the task that needs to be carried out to create the ELO, the second drawer presents background information (so-called "resources") that students need to create the ELO, the third drawer is for asking for feedback on the ELO, and the fourth drawer is for social tagging of the ELO. If the learner invites other learners to collaborate on the ELO, a fifth drawer (on the right side of the ELO and only visible when collaboration is invoked) becomes available to facilitate chatting with co-learners about this specific ELO. Figure 9.3 shows an ELO with the first drawer open. In this example the SCYMapper tool is being used to produce a concept map of an overview of Energy in, out and use in their house design. In this case, a pre-defined template in the concept map scaffolds the activity.

Another feature of SCY is that all ELOs are saved in a database. Students can search this database to find their own ELOs, but also ELOs from other students, possibly triggering collaboration through reuse, or reflection by comparing the ELO to their own or viewing the social tags associated with the ELO (fourth drawer on left), and maybe adding a social tag of their own. Finally, SCY provides a number of assessment mechanisms to support both formative and summative assessment. The remainder of the chapter addresses assessment in SCY.

Peer and self-assessment

As learner-designed objects are central in learning by design, they should also be central in assessment. Ronen and Langley (2004) point to the benefits of peer assessment when students are afforded the opportunity to learn from artifacts created by their peers, and Falchikov (2003) shows how peer assessment assists students to create higher quality artifacts. As such, this type of assessment needs to be embedded within the learning process. As we have shown, in SCY the ELOs are central to the learning process, and we embed both peer feedback (a form of peer assessment) on ELOs and student's assessment of their own learning (as they add ELOs to an eportfolio) in the learning process by providing tools whose use is integrated into the workflow of the learning student. While peer and self-assessment are the subject of much research, we review only the most relevant research before presenting our approach.

Contemporary views see assessment as being an integrated part of the learning process as a designed tool to maximise students' learning (Swan, Shen, and Hiltz 2006), where students actively participate in all aspects of assessment (Dysthe 2004). One popular approach is peer assessment. Peer assessment can be described generally as a process whereby students evaluate, or are evaluated by, their peers (van Zundert, Sluijsmans, and van Merriënboer 2010). This evaluation has been further described as "an educational arrangement where students judge a peer's performance quantitatively and/or qualitatively and which stimulates students to reflect, discuss and collaborate" (Strijbos and Sluijsmans 2010). Peer assessment enables students to take charge of their learning, and become active learners who could take responsibility for, and manage, their own learning (Black, Harrison, Lee, Marshall and Wiliam 2002; Boud 1995; Dochy et al. 1999; Topping 2003; Yang et al. 2006). Research findings also indicate that many students became more aware of their own learning and the learning of others around them, through the implementation of a peer or self-assessment method. Several researchers have argued in the favour of *formative* peer assessment since it was found to enhance learning (Gale et al. 2002; Sluijsmans, Brand-Gruwel, van Meeriënboer 2002) and to promote cooperation among students (Boud 1995). For instance, when students are involved in giving and receiving feedback, referred to as *peer feedback*, they develop meta-cognitive awareness (Falchikov 1995). In self-assessment, students are encouraged to take deliberate thought and reflection over what and how they are learning, and in this way develop meta-cognitive skills, or what has been referred to as *self-regulating capacity* (Carneiro 2006). Reflection on created objects and the receiving and reacting upon external feedback are two of the learning processes that comprise self-regulation (Nicol and MacFarlane-Dick 2006). Furthermore, van Aalst and Chan (2007) argue that in order to promote learning that involves conceptual learning at a deep level, both the content and the inquiry process must be reflected upon.

Feedback, from a formative perspective, from a teacher, expert, peer, or even as self-assessment, is given during the learning process and aims at impacting the learning process as it unravels. Several comprehensive meta-reviews of research on feedback have concluded that feedback greatly impacts the quality of student performance and effectively promotes student learning across disciplinary areas, types of outcomes, and levels (Black and Wiliam 1998; Hattie and Timperley 2007; Shute 2008). Feedback, as an integral part of the students' learning process, has the potential to make the process more productive (Dysthe, Lillejord, Wasson, and Vines 2009).

There is a plethora of research on peer assessment, and much of the literature argues for using peer assessment to support learning, while others are cautious and identify weaknesses with peer assessment (e.g. students need to be trained in peer assessment, Sluijsmans et al. 2002). Some students do not take peer assessment seriously unless they receive a reward (Brown et al. 1997); peers appear sometimes to produce ratings based on friendship, or to give extremely low scores to others in order to keep their own achievement at a relatively high level (Lin, Liu and Yuan 2001). Furthermore, some research findings are contradictory. For example, some researchers argue that peer assessment deviates considerably from teacher assessment (Topping 2003; Magin and Helmore 2001), while others would argue that this does not matter. Frost and Turner (2005) explain that peer feedback (formative peer assessment) is valuable because feedback is given in "student-speak" rather than "teacher-speak" or "science-speak", and students may be more willing to accept feedback from peers. It has also been emphasised that the accuracy of the peer feedback may not be that crucial. In fact, Gielen et al. (2009) report that "while peer judgements or advice may be only partially correct, full incorrect, or misleading this consequence of variety of accuracy in peer feedback might just be a benefit" (*cf* Topping 1998).

Assessment Mechanisms in SCY

In an empirical study of students engaged in the CO_2 Friendly House Mission (Kluge et al. 2010) we observed students spontaneously asking for and giving feedback on each other's ELOs. We were inspired by the ease with which the students interacted and engaged in feedback dialogues. In particular, we observed (from Wasson and Vold, forthcoming):

- students were looking at each others' products (ELOs);
- students took initiative by asking each other questions (e.g. why did you make a round house?);
- students naturally engaged in feedback dialogues with both their peers and their teacher;
- students obtained useful information from examining other students' ELOs that they used to further develop their own skills (e.g. how to calculate the area of a round house) and improve their own ELOs;
- students seemed to be motivated by playing with other student's simulations;
- students need support to communicate with each other, and give each other feedback;
- student discussions showed evidence of both general and specific skills.

These observations, together with an analysis of how students work on a SCY Mission and the literature on formative peer feedback and self-reflection, resulted in the identification of a number of assessment mechanisms to support peer feedback and self reflection, including:

- Asking for feedback on one's own ELO;
- Receiving feedback on one's own ELO;
- Giving feedback on a peer's ELO;
- Reflecting over one's own ELO with respect to learning goals;
- Reflection over one's own ELO with respect to its creation;
- Reflecting over one's participation in a Mission;
- Receiving feedback on one's reflections.

In order to facilitate these mechanisms in SCY, SCYFeedback, SCYePortfolio, and SCYAssessment, three tools have been developed. For SCYFeedback, the tool supporting formative peer feedback, we designed a tool that supports spontaneous interaction and is tightly integrated in SCY-Lab, the SCY learning environment. To support self-refection and summative assessment. we have developed the SCYePortfolio tool where students need to reflect over not only the individual ELOs they add to the portfolio, but also over the inquiry/design learning process and their own participation in the learning process. In order to provide summative assessment, we developed the SCYAssessment tool, which supports teachers in providing summative assessment of a student's participation in a Mission by evaluating their eport-folio; this tool is beyond the scope of this chapter and will not be presented here.

SCYFeedback and SCYePortfolio

SCYFeedback is a peer assessment tool with which students can easily ask for and provide feedback on ELOs as they are being developed in a Mission. Inspired by Web 2.0 tools where students use 21st Century skills (Jenkins et al. 2006) to interact, collaborate and negotiate, we have developed a lightweight, playful tool that supports spontaneous interaction (see Wasson and Vold, forthcoming). Asking for feedback on an ELO involves asking a question or giving a comment on your own or your group's ELO, and providing feedback requires selecting an ELO on which to give feedback. The mechanism of asking for feedback is integrated seamlessly into the ELO tool via the feedback drawer. While working on an ELO in SCY-Lab, a student can open the feedback drawer (third hook on the left side of the ELO tool, see Figure 9.4), ask a question related to the ELO, and submit it for feedback. SCYFeedback supports the mechanisms for giving and receiving feedback by providing functionality that enables students to:

- Receive feedback on their own ELO;
- Browse an ELO gallery of ELOs submitted for feedback;
- Provide feedback on any ELO in the ELO gallery.

In order to inform the students as to whether there are new ELOs waiting for feedback, and to let a particular student know that their own ELO has received feedback, two feedback icons, "get feedback" and "give feedback", have been placed in the top right hand corner of the SCY learning environment (referred to as SCY-Lab). When the student's ELO has received feedback, the "get feedback" icon lights up, giving the student notice that someone has given feedback on one of his or her ELOs. Similarly, when there are new ELOs awaiting feedback, the "give feedback" icon lights up. These mechanisms are similar to those that today's students are used to from Web 2.0 social media such as Facebook.

Students activate the SCYFeedback tool by clicking on either the "give feedback" or "get feedback" icon; both open the tool, but to different views. When opening SCYFeedback via the "give feedback" icon, the student is presented with an ELO Gallery of the most recently posted ELOs (i.e. those that are awaiting feedback), see Figure 9.5. The student selects an ELO for which to give feedback by clicking on the ELO thumbnail. It is also possible to filter the ELO gallery to show only ELOs that fall within an ELO category (e.g. House data) by clicking on the ELO category name (over the

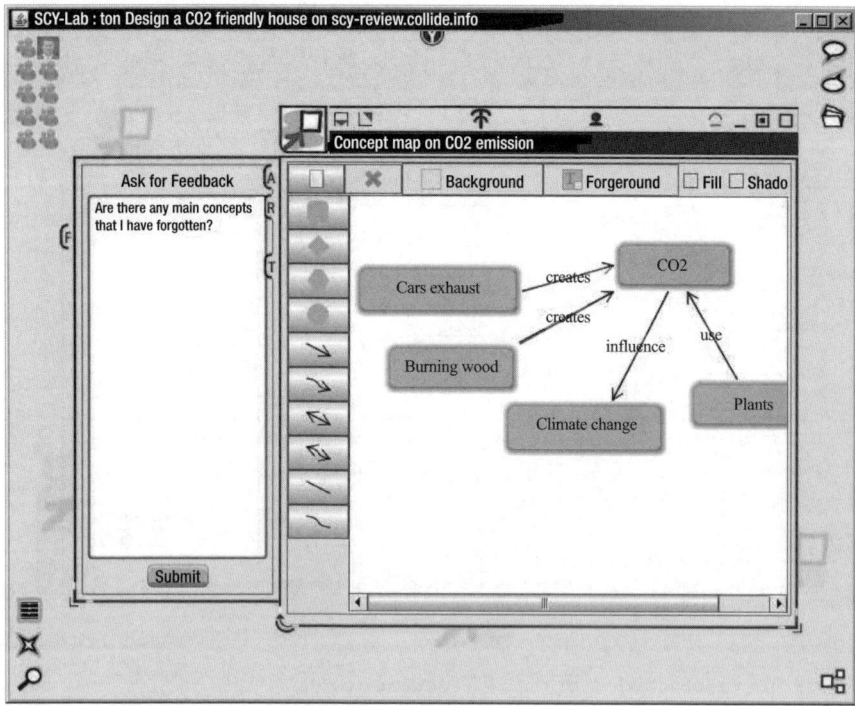

Figure 9.4 Asking for feedback on an ELO.

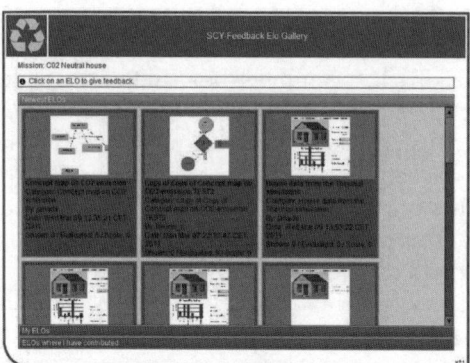

Figure 9.5 ELO Gallery in the SCYFeedback tool.

ELO thumbnail). This view also gives easy navigation to an overview of the student's own ELOs by clicking on the *MY ELOs* accordion panel, or to a view of the ELOs to which the student has contributed feedback by clicking on the *ELOs where I have contributed* accordion panel.

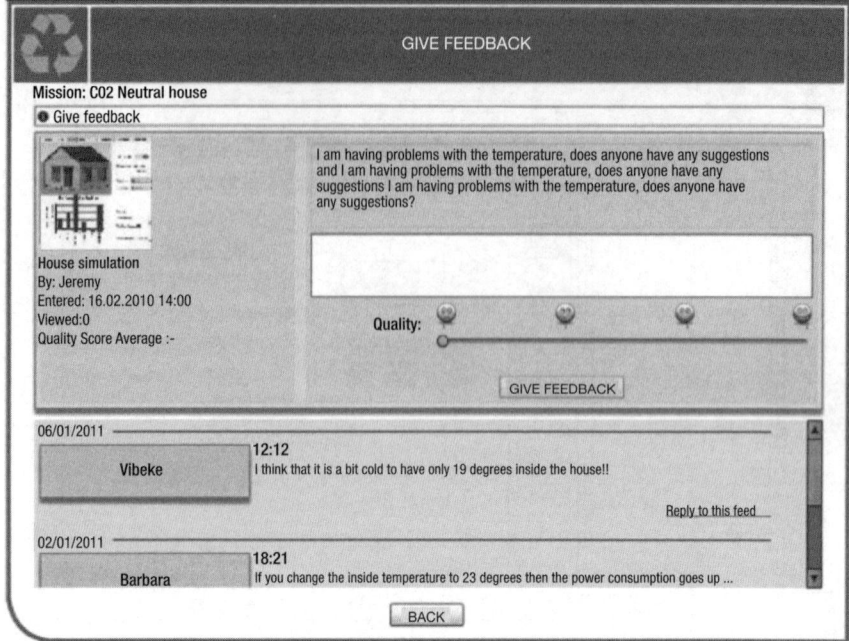

Figure 9.6 Feedback view of the SCYFeedback tool.

Figure 9.6 shows the ELO Feedback screen, where students can give feedback on a peer's ELO, or receive feedback on their own ELO. Information about the ELO is visible in the top left of the screen; the comment/question on which to give feedback, a comment box, and rating scale in the top right. By clicking on the "give feedback" button, the student's comments are added to the threaded discussion that can be seen under the ELO and feedback area. It is also possible to reply to a feedback by clicking the *Reply to this feedback* link. If a student has been informed that they have received feedback on one of their ELOs, the student clicks on the "get feedback" icon in SCY-Lab and SCYFeedback opens to this view with the student's ELO visible.

SCYePortfolio is an eportfolio tool with which students add ELOs to a working portfolio and build Mission portfolios (i.e. a collection of obligatory ELOs) to submit to their teacher for summative assessment. A structured reflection form, which a student must fill out before the ELO can be added to their working portfolio, facilitates the assessment mechanism of reflection on their own ELO with respect to learning goals, and with respect to its creation. The reflection on one's participation in a Mission mechanism requires the student to select ELOs from their working portfolio to include in their Mission portfolio, followed by filling out a structured reflection on various aspects of their participation in the Mission as a whole (e.g. collaboration), before submitting their Mission portfolio for summative assessment. The mechanism for receiving summative assessment of their Mission portfolio is supported by providing a feedback view in the tool. SCYePortfolio supports these mechanisms for reflection by providing functionality that enables students to:

- Add ELOs to their working ePortfolio;
- Build a Mission portfolio (e.g., CO_2 Friendly House portfolio);
- Submit a Mission portfolio for assessment;
- Receive and view the summative assessment of an assessed Mission portfolio.

To add an ELO that they are working on to their eportfolio, the student drags the ELO thumbnail and drops it on the ePortfolio icon, which is situated in the top right of the SCY-Lab window, see Figure 9.4. This results in SCYePortfolio opening to the Add ELO view, see Figure 9.7.

As can be seen in Figure 9.7, when adding an ELO to their eportfolio a student must give a description of the ELO, identify the specific and general learning goals the ELO addresses, and answer some specific reflection questions authored by the teacher[1]. The reflection on the ELO with respect to its learning goal mechanism scaffolds the learner by providing cognitive prompts that list the general and specific learning goals associated with the Mission. The reflection on the ELO with respect to its creation mechanism is implemented with sentence starters (e.g. "The most important thing about CO_2 friendly houses this . . .") or a question (e.g. "How helpful was building a concept map in identifying the main concepts related to reducing global CO_2 levels?").

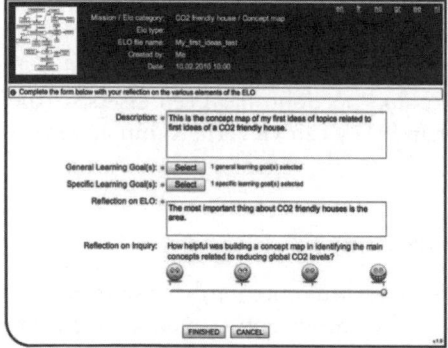

Figure 9.7 Reflection on ELO view in SCYePortfolio.

1 SCYAuthor, the SCY authoring tool, is used by teachers to specify which ELOs must be included in the Mission portfolio, to specify the reflection questions and format (e.g. textbox or slide bar) to be associated with each ELO, and with the entire reflection questions and format for the student's participation in the Mission.

Once all the obligatory ELOs have been added to their working portfolio, students can build a Mission portfolio that will be submitted to the teacher. The student builds a Mission portfolio by selecting the ELOs to be included, and then reflecting on different aspects of the Mission, such as inquiry, collaboration, or their own effort (these have also been authored by the teacher before the beginning of the Mission). Figure 9.8 shows the reflection screen where students reflect over the learning process in the Mission. In this version, students are asked to reflect on the Mission, on Collaboration, on Inquiry, and on their Effort, and again various cognitive prompts are provided, such as sentence starters, questions, and the ability to browse through the included ELOs and their reflections (moving the cursor over an ELO icon opens a pop-up frame that summarises the reflections the student made on that ELO). Once this Mission reflection is complete, the student can submit the Mission portfolio to their teacher for summative assessment.

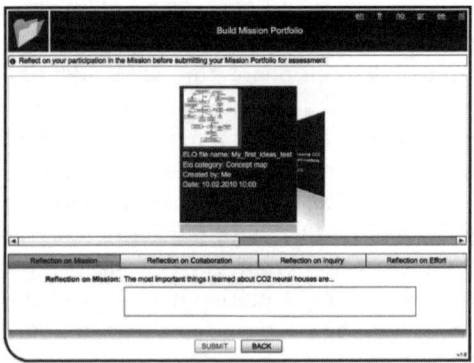

Figure 9.8 Reflection on Mission view in SCYePortfolio.

Once the teacher has assessed the Mission portfolio, the student receives notice that their Mission portfolio has been assessed (the ePortfolio icon in SCY-Lab lights up) and they can view the summative assessment (not shown here).

Concluding Comments

In this chapter, we have attempted to demonstrate how orchestration of assessment in learning by design environments can be composed through the implementation of assessment mechanisms in the learning environment and in specially designed tools. Drawing on learning by design literature that shows the centrality of designed artifacts in the learning process, and peer and self-assessment literature that addresses feedback on such artifacts, both by peers and by self-reflection, we have identified a number of assessment mechanisms that underlie both formative and summative assessment.

We have used the SCY project to illustrate our approach. In SCY, the tools and corresponding features of SCY-Lab are the vehicles through which the assessment mechanisms are realised. Taking on a SCY Mission, the students go through a process of constructing, testing, giving and receiving feedback, and reflecting upon theoretical and working models (ELOs) relevant for creating a CO_2 friendly house (for example). Thus, the students acquire science knowledge and skills that enable them to engage in a final design activity where the output is a CO_2 friendly house design. As in learning by design environments, these ELO's play a central role in students' active learning, their collaboration, their reflection, and also in the summative assessment of students' performance. We have introduced features of SCY-Lab and the SCYFeedback and SCYePortfolio tools that implement these mechanisms.

We view the SCY assessment tools as tools *for* learning, and we have attempted to integrate their use into the learning workflow of the SCY students on a Mission. Our design of the SCY ePortfolio encourages reflective practice and self-evaluation (Stefani et al. 2007), self-reflective skills (Mcalpine 2005), and reflective learning (Barrett 2005) that can be used for assessment purposes. For example, providing a feedback drawer on the ELO tool enables the student, without too much disruption, to ask for feedback. Similarly, dragging an ELO thumbnail over the ePortfolio icon in SCY-Lab instigates a reflection process where the student is scaffolded in their reflection over the ELO they have created. Providing a checklist of learning goals in the reflection view of the SCYePortoflio tool is a cognitive prompt that enables the student to focus on the role of creating the ELO, and not on trying to remember the learning goals. This is in line with van Aalst and Chan's (2007) recommendation that the students' own assessment must be aligned to the learning goal. Likewise, it is thought that providing sentence starters and reflection questions on the content or process of creating the ELO prompts a reflection and will have the student quickly focus on the role of the ELO in the Mission. The structured reflection in which the student engages extends the learning process beyond the Mission and engages the student in meta-cognitive processes meant to deepen the learning experience and develop higher-order thinking skills. We also think that reflecting on the ELO as they add it to the ePortfolio may trigger a realisation that the ELO could be improved. During an upcoming field trial we will watch to see if this occurs. In order to provide more reflection on the learning process that can be used during summative evaluation by the teacher, we have provided reflection prompts related to various aspects of the learning process and participation in the Mission, namely on inquiry, on collaboration, and on one's own effort. This is in line with van Aalst and Chan's (2007) recommendation, and with one of Nicol and MacFanlane-Dick's (2006) principles that good feedback practice facilitates the development of self-assessment (reflection) in learning.

SCYFeedback, on the other hand, is also a tool *for* learning where we attempt to engage students as participants and givers of peer feedback by drawing on the new media skills that students are developing by participation in social environments. The design of SCYFeedback has been inspired both by literature, participatory environments, and our empirical study of a SCY Mission field trial, summarised in Wasson and Vold (forthcoming) as:

- the recognition that many people (students included) take part in participatory worlds that offer interaction among the participants around a common interest;
- an increasing view of learning as a participative activity (Kollar and Fischer 2009);
- SCY's focus on emerging learning objects which reinforces research on how peer assessment introduces the students to the perspective that the focus of instruction is not only on the end product(s), but also on the process, and highlights the value of collaboration (e.g. social interactions, trust in others; Noonan and Duncan 2005);
- the recognition that peer assessment can motivate students to engage in the learning process (Sluijsmans 2002);
- research that indicates that formal instructional intervention requiring students to reflect on feedback from peers does not significantly increase learning gains (Gielen et al., 2010);
- peer assessment assists students to create higher quality artifacts (Falchikov 2003);
- students are more willing to accept feedback given in "student-speak" (Frost and Turner 2005);
- empirical observations of a SCY Mission, in which students looked at each other's ELOs, spontaneously asked and responded to each other's questions, and in some cases used this feedback to improve their own ELO;
- an interest in trying "something new, lightweight, and motivating" designed to take advantage of new media skills within the field of peer assessment.

We are hoping that the seamlessness with which students can ask for feedback, and that we draw on to provide aspects of an active participatory environment (see http://digit.no) and features that they are familiar with from web 2.0 applications, will create a motivating and easy to use feedback tool that facilitates easy, lightweight interaction between peers, where we will see evidence of the interactions we observed in our empirical study (for examples, see Wasson and Vold, forthcoming). The SCYFeedback ELO gallery, which facilities browsing of ELOs created by peers, not only provides the opportunity for students to look at each others ELOs and give feedback, but also possibly to give them new ideas for their own ELOs. The threaded discussion format is familiar and encourages collaborative discussion of an ELO.

Orchestration of assessment in design learning environments is a challenge. We will be empirically testing our approach in the next months and evaluating how well our features and tools support the identified assessment mechanisms. Furthermore, we will be looking for evidence that our students actively participate in asking for and giving feedback, receiving feedback that they use to improve their ELOs, and that they are able to reflect on the artifacts they have created, and on their participation in the learning processes that have guided their creation. Only then can we argue that our approach to orchestration of assessment has been successful.

Acknowledgements

This study was conducted in the context of Science Created by You (SCY) which is funded by the European Community under the Information and Communication Technologies (ICT) theme of the 7th Framework Programme for RandD (Grant agreement 212814). This document does not represent the opinion of the European Community, and the European Community is not responsible for any use that might be made of its content. The authors would like to thank the WP3 members, Jeremy Toussaint for implementation of the SCY tools, and Henrik von Schlanbusch and Kaido Hallik for the integration of these tools into SYC-Lab.

References

Barrett, H. and Carney, J. (2005) *Conflicting Paradigms and Competing Purposes in Electronic Portfolio Development*. Online. Available at: http://electronicportfolios.com/portfolios/LEAJournal-BarrettCarney.pdf (accessed June 2010).

Barrett, H. (2007) 'Researching electronic portfolios and learner engagement: The REFLECT initiative', *Journal of Adolescent and Adult Literacy*, 50 (6): 436–449.

Black, P., Harrison, C., Lee, C., Marshall, B. and Wiliam, D. (2002) *Working Inside the Black Box: assessment for learning in the classroom*. London: Kings College.

Black, P. and Wiliam, D. (1998) 'Assessment and classroom learning', *Assessment in Education: Principles, Policy, and Practice*, 5 (1): 7–74.

Black, P. and Wiliam, D. (2005) 'The formative purpose: Assessment must first promote learning', in M. Wilson (ed) *Towards Coherence Between Classroom Assessment and Accountability*, Chicago, IL: University of Chicago Press.

Boud, D. (1995) *Enhancing Learning Through Self-Assessment*. London: Kogan Page.

Bransford, J. D., Brown, A. L., and Cocking, R. R. (1999) (eds) *How People Learn: brain, mind, experience, and school*, Washington, D.C: National Academy Press.

Brown, G., Bull, J. and Pendlebury, M. (1997) *Assessing Students' Learning in Higher Education*, London: Routledge.

Carneiro, R. (2006) 'Motivating School Teachers to Learn: Can ICT Add Value?', *European Journal of Education*, 41 (3–4): 415–435.

Crismond, D. (2001) 'Learning and using science ideas when doing investigate-and-redesign tasks: A study of naive, novice, and expert designers doing constrained and scaffolded design work', Journal *of Research in Science Teaching*, 38: 791–820.

de Jong, T. and van Joolingen, W. R. (2007) 'Model-facilitated learning', in J. M. Spector, M. D. Merrill, J. J. G. van Merriënboer, and M. P. Driscoll (eds) *Handbook of Research on Educational Communication and Technology*, 3rd edn, Mahwah, NJ: Lawrence Erlbaum.

de Jong, T., van Joolingen, W. R., Giemza, A., Girault, I., Hoppe, U., Kindermann, J., et al. (2010) 'Learning by creating and exchanging objects: The SCY experience, *British Journal of Educational Technology*, 41: 909–921.

de Jong, T., Weinberger, A., van Joolingen, W. T., Ludvigsen, S., Ney, M., Girault, I., et al. (submitted). Designing complex and open learning environments based on scenarios.

Dewey, J. (1916) *Democracy and Education: an introduction to the philosophy of education,* New York: MacMillan.

Dochy, F., Segers, M. and Sluijsmans, D. (1999) 'The use of self-, peer-, and co-assessment in higher education; A review', Studies *in Higher Education*, 24: 331–350.

Dysthe, O. (2004) 'The challenges of assessment in a new learning culture'. Paper given at NERA/NFPF Conference in Reykjavik, Iceland March 11–13. Online. Available at: www.uib.no/iuh/ansatte/dysthe/nera-nfpd_32.pdf (accessed June 2010)

Dysthe, O., Lillejord, S., Wasson, B. and Vines, A. (2009) 'Productive e-feedback in higher education: Two models and some critical issues', in S. Ludvigsen and Saljo. R. (eds) *Learning Across Sites*, Oxon: Routledge.

Falchikov, N. (1995) 'Peer feedback marking: Developing peer assessment', Innovations *in Education and Training International*, 32: 175–187.

Falchikov, N. (2003) 'Involving students in assessment', Psychology *Learning and Teaching*, 3:102–108.

Frost, J. and Turner, T. (eds) (2005) *Learning to Teach Science in the Secondary School*, Second Edition. London: Routledge.

Gale, K., Martin, K. and McQueen, G. (2002) 'Triadic Assessment', *Assessment and Evaluation in Higher Education* 27 (6): 557–67.

Gielen, S., Peeters, E., Dochy, F., Onghena, P. and Struyven, K. (2010) 'Improving the effectiveness of peer feedback for learning', *Learning and Instruction*, 20 (4): 304–315.

Hattie, J. and Timperley, H. (2007) 'The power of feedback', *Review of Educational research*, 77 (1): 81–112.

Hestenes, D. (1987). 'Towards a modelling theory of physics instruction', *American Journal of Physics,* 55: 440–454.

Hmelo, C. E., Holton, D. L. and Kolodner, J. L. (2000) 'Designing to learn about complex systems', *Journal of the Learning Sciences,* 9: 247–298.

Hoppe, H. U., Pinkwart, N., Oelinger, M., Zeini, S., Verdejo, F., Barros, B., et al. (2005) 'Building bridges within learning communities through ontologies and "thematic objects"', in *Proceedings of the 2005 Conference on Computer Support for Collaborative Learning*, Mahwah, NJ: Lawrence Erlbaum Associates.

Jenkins, H., Clinton, K., Purushotma, R., Robison, A. J. and Weigel, M. (2006) *Confronting the Challenges of Participatory Culture: media education of the 21st Century.* Chicago, The MacArthur Foundation.

Jonassen, D. H. (1991) 'Objectivism versus constructivism; Do we need a new philosophical paradigm?', *Educational Technology: research and development,* 39: 5–14.

Kafai, Y. B. (1996) 'Learning design by making games: Children's development of design strategies in the creation of a complex computational artifact', in Y. B. Kafai and M. Resnick (eds) *Constructionism in Practice: designing, thinking, and learning in a digital world*, Mawhaw, NJ: Lawrence Erlbaum Associates.

Kluge, A., Furberg, A. L., Ludvigsen, S., Dolonen, J. A., Norenes, S. O., Vold, V., et al. (2011)

'SCY first formative evaluation report. European Commission IST-212814, *SCY Research Report DIX*. 2.

Kollar, I. and Fischer, F. (2010) 'Commentary: peer assessment as collaborative learning: a cognitive perspective', *Learning and Instruction*, 20 (4): 344–348.

Lee, M. J. W., McLoughlin, C. and Chan, A. (2008) 'Talk the talk: Learner-generated podcasts as catalysts for knowledge creation', *British Journal of Educational Technology*, 39: 501–521.

Lin, S. S . J., Liu, E. Z. F. and Yuan, S. M. (2001) 'Web-based peer assessment: feedback for students with various thinking-styles', *Journal of Computer Assisted Learning*, 17: 420–432.

McAlpine, M. (2005) 'E-Portfolios and Digital Identity: some issues for discussion', *E-Learning*, 2 (4).

Magin, D. and Helmore, P. (2001) 'Peer and teacher assessments of oral presentation skills: how reliable are they?', *Studies in Higher Education*, 26: 287–298.

Mayer, R. E. (2002) 'Rote versus meaningful learning', *Theory into Practice*, 41: 226–232.

Mayer, R. E. and Fay, A. L. (1987) 'A chain of cognitive changes with learning to program in logo', *Journal of Educational Psychology*, 79: 269–279.

Mehalik, M. M., Doppelt, Y. and Schuun, C. D. (2008) 'Middle-school science through design-based learning versus scripted inquiry: Better overall science concept learning and equity gap reduction. *Journal of Engineering Education*', 97: 71–85.

Nicol, D. J. and MacFarlane-Dick, D. (2006) 'Formative assessment and self-regulated learning: A model and seven principles of good feedback practice', *Studies in Higher Education*, 31 (2):199–218.

Noonan, B. and Duncan, C. R. (2005) 'Peer and self-assessment in high schools. Practical Assessment, Research and Evaluation', 10 (17).

Novak, J. D. (1990) 'Concept mapping: A useful tool for science education', *Journal of Research in Science Teaching*, 27: 937–949.

Orsmond, P., Merry, S. and Reiling, K. (1996) 'The importance of marking criteria in the use of peer assessment. *Assessment and Evaluation in Higher Education*', 21 (3): 239–250.

Pata, K. and Sarapuu, T. (2006) 'A comparison of reasoning processes in a collaborative modelling environment: Learning about genetics problems using virtual chat', *International Journal of Science Education*, 28: 1341–1368.

Puntambekar, S. and Kolodner, J. L. (2005) 'Toward implementing distributed scaffolding: Helping students learn science from design', *Journal of Research in Science Teaching*, 42: 185–217.

Ravet, S. (2005) 'ePortfolio for a learning society, eLearning Conference, Brussels, May 19–20, 2005.

Ronen, M. and Langley, D. (2004) 'Scaffolding complex tasks by open online submission: Emerging patterns and profiles', *Journal of Asynchronous Learning Networks*, 8: 39–61.

Sadler, R. (1989) 'Formative assessment and the design of instructional systems', *Instructional Science*, 18: 119–144.

Sadler, D. R. (1998) 'Formative assessment: Revising the territory', *Assessment in Education*, 5: 77–84.

Shute, V. J. (2007) 'Focus on formative feedback', *Review of Educational Research*, 78: 153–189.

Shute, V. J. (2009) 'Simply Assessment', *International Journal of Learning and Media*, 1 (2): 1–11.

Sluijsmans, D. (2002) 'Establishing learning effects with integrated peer assessment tasks', The Higher Education Academy. Online. Available at: http://www.heacademy.ac.uk/resources/detail/resource_database/id437_establishing_learning_effects (accessed June 2010).

Sluijsmans, D. M. A., Brand-Gruwel, S. and van Merriënboer, J. J. G. (2002) 'Peer assessment training in teacher education: Effects on performance and perceptions', *Assessment and Evaluation in Higher Education*, 27: 443–454.

Stefani, L., Mason, R. and Pegler, C. (2007) *The Educational Potential of e-Portfolios; Supporting development and reflective learning.* London and New York: Routledge and Taylor and Francis Group.

Stiggins, R. J. (2002) 'Assessment crisis: The absence of assessment FOR learning', *Phi Delta Kappan*, 83 (10): 758–765.

Strijbos, J. W. and Sluijsmans, D. (2010) 'Unravelling peer assessment: Methodological, functional, and conceptual developments', *Learning and Instruction*, 20 (4): 35–53.

Swan, K., Shen, J. and Hiltz, S. R. (2006) 'Assessment and Collaboration in Online Learning. *Journal of Asynchronous Learning Networks*', 10 (1): 45–62.

Topping, K. (1998) 'Peer assessment between students in colleges and universities. *Review of Educational Research*, 68: 249–276.

Topping, K. (2003) 'Self and peer assessment in school and university: Reliability, validity and utility', in M. Segers, F. Dochy and E. Cascallar (eds) *Optimizing New Modes of Assessment: in search of qualities and standards.* Dordrecht/Boston/London: Kluwer Academic Publishers.

Van Aalst, J. and Chan, C. K. K. (2007) 'Student-Directed Assessment of Knowledge Building Using Electronic Portfolios', *Journal of the Learning Sciences*, 16 (2): 175–200.

Van Zundert, M., Sluijsmans, D. M. A. and Van Meeriënboer, J. J. G. (2010) 'Effective peer assessment processes: research findings and future directions', *Learning and Instruction,* 20 (4): 270–279.

von Glaserfeld, E. (1987) 'Learning as a constructive activity', in C. Janvier (ed) *Problems in the Representation in the Teaching and Learning of Mathematics*, 3–17. Hillsdale, NJ: Lawrence Erlbaum.

Vreman-de Olde, C., and de Jong, T. (2006) 'Scaffolding the design of assignments for a computer simulation', *Journal of Computer Assisted Learning,* 22: 63–74.

Wasson, B. and Vold, V. (forthcoming) 'Leveraging New Media Skills in a Peer Feedback Tool', *Journal of Internet in Higher Education.*

Yang, M., Badger, R. and Yu, Z. (2006) 'A comparative study of peer and teacher feedback in a Chinese EFL writing class', *Journal of Second Language Writing*, 15:179–200.

Zahn, C., Pea, R., Hesse, F. W. and Rosen, J. (2010) 'Comparing simple and advanced video tools as supports for complex collaborative design processes', *Journal of the Learning Sciences,* 19: 403–440.

Chapter 10

Inquiry learning in semi-formal contexts

Ann Jones, Canan Blake and Marilena Petrou

Introduction

Most research studies concerned with inquiry learning have focused on understanding classroom-based inquiries that are contextualised within specific curricular frameworks. There is, thus, a pressing need for work which resources our understanding of the process of inquiry learning in less formal contexts, such as after-school clubs. Over the last few years, educational policy makers in the UK have been very concerned with a personalisation agenda (see Chapter 1), although this is defined and understood in many different ways. One aspect of the personalisation agenda is the possibility of learner choice, and this element of choice is reflected in the idea of personal inquiries.

In this chapter, the focus is on personal inquiries that students themselves develop in the semi-formal context of an after-school club, supported by their teachers and researchers, and resourced by a technology toolkit: nQuire. In the Personal Inquiry project (PI), discussed in this chapter, we interpret personal inquiry as giving learners opportunities to design inquiries that are meaningful to them. So, the emphasis is on supporting learners to investigate issues that affect their lives and relate directly to their interests and curiosities. The discussion of bridging informal and formal contexts in the literature (e.g. Hofstein and Rosenfeld 1996) often refers to finding ways of harnessing the positive (often affective) aspects of semi-formal learning and applying this to more formal settings. In the PI project, bridging involved tracking and supporting students' science inquiries across different contexts – from school, out to field trips, and back into the school and home.

Other chapters have considered orchestrating inquiry learning within a range of contexts including the classroom and the field, and how a combination of teachers and technology can set up and guide inquiry learning activities. Chapter 2 discussed how such orchestration involved bridging the everyday-familiar and the scientific world, and how the nQuire toolkit supported students in re-visualising everyday things as the objects of scientific inquiry. In this chapter, we focus on how personalised inquiry learning can be supported and guided across a semi-formal context (an after-school club) and an informal context (home). In a home context, where the teacher is absent, much of the guidance for the inquiry needs to move to the technology itself – here, it is the nQuire toolkit developed by the Personal Inquiry (PI) project.

The case study explores the processes of inquiry learning in a Geography after-school club, which ran for 11 weeks. We will consider the nature of personalised inquiries within this semi-formal context; how they were resourced and supported at home without teacher support; the implications for engagement and attitudes towards sustainability; and the challenges of running and supporting inquiries in this context. The after-school club setting discussed here provided a) an opportunity to carry out inquiries that would not have been possible within the formal school curriculum, and b) for the choice of inquiry to be decided by the students themselves, an important part of personal inquiry. A key advantage of this approach is that it can lead to high engagement.

We consider the importance of semi-formal inquiry science learning and how informal and non-formal learning is discussed and defined within the literature. There follows a brief review of related work on technology-supported informal and non-formal learning in different settings, including science clubs and centres, and field trips. We discuss how the nQuire toolkit, developed by the PI project, supported the inquiry in its different stages and contexts, the students' engagement and attitudes and what they learnt about the inquiry process.

Inquiry learning in science outside schools

Why it matters

Our contemporary world provides us with challenging problems and competing sources of evidence, some of which, like climate change, will have a particular impact on future generations. So inquiry skills, including being able to engage in critical activities (e.g. assessing and collecting evidence) in order to reason about and make sense of the complex world around us are particularly important. School Science curricula emphasise exactly such inquiry skills. For example, the US National Science Education Standards developed by the National Research Council (1996) states that:

> Students at all grade levels ... should have the opportunity to use scientific inquiry and develop the ability to think and act in ways associated with inquiry, including asking questions, planning and conducting investigations, using appropriate tools and techniques to gather data, thinking critically and logically about relationships between evidence

and explanations, constructing and analysing alternative explanations, and communicating scientific arguments.

(National Science Educational Standards, 1996. p105)

Unfortunately, voluntary participation in Science in most Western countries has been declining over a number of years (e.g. Ainley, Kos and Nicholas 2008). Negative attitudes towards Science (Osborne and Collins 2000) may be one of the factors resulting in many students' disengagement with Science in schools. However, there are increasing opportunities for learning Science outside the formal schooling system, offered by, for example, science clubs, centres, field trips and museums. There is some evidence that such activities can support affective aspects of learning (see Eshach 2007), and can positively influence students' attitudes towards science learning and their engagement. In the US, interest in Out-of-School-Time settings (OST) STEM programmes in Science, Technology, Enginnering and Mathematics has grown considerably recently, and the need to assess and document such programmes has been recognised and discussed. Thus it is important to understand the processes of learning and teaching in contexts such as after-school clubs (Bevan et al. 2010)

Challenges of defining out-of-school learning

So what is semi-formal learning, and how does it relate to informal and formal learning? There has been extensive debate about the nature of informal learning (e.g. Dierking 1991; Livingstone 1999; Burbules 2006; Eshach 2007), and suggested definitions have changed and developed and have also focused on different aspects. One view is of a kind of continuum of learning with formal learning at one end and informal at the other. In our review, we include informal learning as there are some important aspects that are shared with semi-formal learning contexts. For example, Vavoula's typology of informal learning (Vavoula 2004) emphasises the *control* of learning, both of the learning process (i.e. the tools and methods used) and of the learning goals (i.e. whether with the teacher or the learner). This is particularly important in considering personal inquiry, as one way for an inquiry to be personally meaningful is for the inquirer to decide on the goals of the inquiry.

Like Vavoula's typology, Livingstone's definition of informal learning precludes direct teacher support: 'all forms of intentional or tacit learning in which we engage either individually or collectively without direct reliance on a teacher or externally organised curriculum' (Livingstone 2006). We suggest that after-school clubs sit between informal and formal learning, and fit Eshach's description of non-formal learning quite well:

Non-formal learning occurs in a planned but highly adaptable manner in institutions, organizations, and situations beyond the spheres of formal or informal education. It shares the characteristic of being mediated with formal education, but the motivation for learning may be wholly intrinsic to the learner.

(Eshach 2007 p. 173)

However, Eshach's review of formal, informal and non-formal science learning, which adopts this definition, assumes that it occurs *outside* school, for example in museums, science centres or field trips. This was not the case for the after-school club, as it took place in the school, although its activities also extended to the home. We should note though that as Eshach (2007) and others (e.g. Dierking 1991) have argued, sharp distinctions between different types of learning are problematic, especially when based on settings or structure. For example, although the after-school club in our case study has most of the non-formal characteristics outlined by Eshach, some school rules relating to formal learning, such as wearing uniform and ways of addressing teachers, apply. So, as the after-school club setting differs from the non-school settings referred to above and the club activities are based on the National Curriculum, we use the term *semi-formal* to refer to the types of learning in the after-school club, reflecting its hybrid nature, with aspects of both formal and informal learning.

Public engagement and affect

There is increasing evidence that large numbers of people choose to partic-ipate in non-formal learning activities, for example by attending museums and science centres (National Research Council 2009). What is striking is that these learners have a positive view of these non-formal environments for science learning and carry out these activities in their leisure time (e.g. Ivanova 2003 and Briseno-Garzon, Anderson, and Anderson 2007). A range of evaluation studies show that 'out-of-school programs can have positive effects on participants' attitudes toward science, grades, test scores, gradu-ation rates, and specific science knowledge and skills' (National Research Council 2009). This is particularly significant in science where, as we have noted, many children opt to stop studying science at school once they are able to do so. Two important related features of non-formal learning as viewed by Eshach (2007) are the voluntary nature of the activity, and that the motivation is 'typically intrinsic'. In a similar vein, Stocklmayer, Leonie and Gilbert (2010) include the following affective factors in their summary of factors found to encourage informal science learning: providing for free choice; being internally driven and challenging; and being entertaining, interesting and enjoyable. They relate these factors to engagement, motivation and appeal to the learner.

Affective benefits may also be linked with after-school clubs, according to Chapman and Smith (2007), whose list of reasons for running such clubs include: developing problem solving and thinking skills; bridging the gap between classroom science and the real world; links between schools and industry; providing activities for Gifted and Talented (GAT) children; developing confidence and communication skills; and motivating students. They emphasise the importance of children having a role in deciding on the activities, and the possibilities of working with real scientists. Both these factors featured in the after-school club case study discussed here.

Evidence for high engagement in science-related after-school programmes is also provided in the review by Stocklmayer et al. (2010) (op. cit.), in which they note that some enhanced engagement in Science in semi-formal programmes is also linked to inquiry approaches (e.g. Laursen et al. 2007). Other interventions and activities involved professional scientists and also report affective benefits (e.g. Rennie and Howitt 2009). Similar arguments are made by Banks et al. (2007), and echoed in conclusions drawn by Bell and his colleagues in reviewing 'Learning Science in Informal Environments' (National Research Council 2009, p. 1). They suggest that in environments such as after-school clubs, learners can engage in science interest and inquiry and reflect on their experiences through verbal and other interactions. Often, these non-formal or semi-formal learning opportunities facilitate individuals' interest and motivation to learn more about phenomena they encounter in their daily lives, i.e. personal inquiry learning. So, in summary, there is evidence of semi-formal and informal science learning being associated with high motivation and engagement, positive attitudes and the acquisition of relevant skills. In the case study, we draw on the National Science foundation's (NSF) framework for assessing learning outcomes of informal learning focusing on three dimensions of the framework: 'engagement', 'attitudes' and 'skills'.

Bridging in- and out-of-school science learning with technologies

The portability of mobile devices means that they can easily be carried around for use in field settings, for example, and so have been used to support location-based environmental learning (Chen, Kao and Jang-Ping 2003; Chen, Kao and Sheu 2004; Uzunboylu, Cavus and Ercag 2009). However, such research has tended to focus on supporting particular inquiries or investigations (e.g. Chen and colleagues' work on developing technologies to support bird watching and watching butterflies). Although these two contexts are different, both are concerned with identifying species. So the challenge of supporting a *range* of investigations remains, and indeed Frohberg, Goth and Schwabe (2009) discuss the challenge of combining both location-based learning and flexible support for learning. We believe that the development of the nQuire toolkit in the PI project is a helpful step in addressing this challenge as it can be used to support inquiries across a range of settings.

In the literature, the idea of bridging learning in and out of schools, or informal and formal education more generally, is widely interpreted. It is often concerned with connecting out-of-school interests and in-school work, in order to harness the affective and cognitive benefits that we have already noted for out-of-school trips (e.g. Hofstein and Rosenfeld 1996), or to make or strengthen connections between practice in the two settings (Cook, Pachler and Bradley 2008). Technologies are often viewed as playing an important role. For example, Rosenfeld (2004) suggests that technologies 'might act as "bridges", to help transport educational tools and resources in both directions, between different communities of practice' (i.e. those involved in formal or informal learning). Mobile technologies can also play a bridging role by supporting an investigation that is distributed between two or more different contexts, as in Chen et. als birdwatching study (Chen et al. 2003). In the Personal Inquiry project, versions of the nQuire toolkit can support inquiries that move between contexts, typically starting in a formal context (the classroom), and moving to less formal contexts (a school fieldtrip, or the student's home) before returning to the classroom. As a web-based tool, accessible in a variety of locations and on a range of networked devices, the nQuire software itself is the main resource for bridging between contexts – and an example of this is given in the case study below.

Case Study: Sustainability Squad

The three year Personal Inquiry (PI) project, funded by the Technology Enhanced Learning Program was jointly conducted between the University of Nottingham and The Open University, and focused on supporting students' learning of evidence-based inquiry (Collins et al. 2008) across formal and informal settings.

The 'Sustainability Squad' after-school club was run by three geography teachers who had taken part in other PI trials. It focused on addressing issues related to food sustainability and, in particular, on encouraging students to carry out personal evidenced-based inquiries. The theme of sustainability, which related to one of the curriculum topics, was chosen by the teachers who aimed to encourage students to plan an evidence-based inquiry to be carried out at home. The focus of each session varied, and was decided on in discussions between the researchers and the teachers. Students worked independently in small groups of their choice and selected a food product to investigate for their inquiries. They decided they were interested in food rotting and so designed inquiries into the storage and decomposition of food, including investigations into packaging. Alongside their inquiries, students conducted their own research of other stages of the food production cycle in relation to the product of their choice, e.g. internet research on carbon footprints.

Sustainability Investigator

nQuire can be customised to reflect the specific requirements of each inquiry and, to support the inquiries in the Sustainability Club, we worked with teachers to develop the Sustainability Investigator (SI), an instantiation of nQuire. The students could access the SI via web-enabled Asus Eee PC netbooks in any location with an internet connection, or it could be used in standalone mode if necessary. They were loaned data-gathering equipment: cameras, Flip video cameras and sensors provided by Sciencescope[1], enabling the measurement of light, humidity and temperature data relevant to food composition.

The design of the SI was informed by the development of a personal inquiry framework integrating phases of the inquiry learning cycle described in Chapter 1. The SI represented the inquiry process in five phases, each of which contained a number of activities. The SI supported pupils through these phases by a menu bar that appeared on the left of each webpage.

- Phase 1 – Focus: this links to two main activities types. It supports hypothesis generation and the entry of findings from web searches;
- Phase 2 – Methods: links to activities in which students can design their own measures by defining variables and how they are described;
- Phase 3 – Data collection: links to an 'add data' activity and enables students to enter and record multiple data readings during their inquiry. Here, the SI also provided the opportunity to students to upload photos, text or video data.
- Phase 4 – Results: displays a table of the data that the students have recorded, and enables students to select and display data in bar charts;
- Phase 5 – Conclusion: links to an 'answer' activity including text boxes where students can reflect on whether their initial hypothesis is supported by the data collected. In addition, this links to a 'reflect on our investigation' activity where students consider and discuss what went well or not with their investigation.

Research design

The teachers invited 40 students (aged 12 – 14) to join the club who they thought were particularly interested in geography, and a further 10 students asked to join the club of their own volition. The club was held immediately after school for an hour one day per week, over a period of 11 weeks. Students were also encouraged and supported to work at home on their investigations

---

1 Sciencescope provides educational data logging and sensing products (see http://www.sciencescope.co.uk/index.html)

in between the sessions at school and over half term. Attendance was voluntary and the number of students each week shifted between 8 and 30, with around 12 students attending almost all club sessions, so both the club membership and number of children in the groups differed from time to time. This was not ideal for planning and conducting investigations, but we discussed how best to deal with this and decided that new attendees should join existing groups. When one group lost all its members except one, she then joined another group. The two focal groups selected for closer study were the two groups that attended almost all sessions and completed their inquiries. When they all attended, one group (all boys) had 5 members and the second (all girls) had seven members.

The focus of this study was to support students' own inquiries in order to develop scientific inquiry skills across the contexts of the after-school club and home. One of the requirements that informed the design of the nQuire toolkit was continuity, i.e. to support inquiries across different settings, moving from school to home and back to the school again for discussing and sharing results (see Sharples et al. 2011) The SI (the instantiation of nQuire used for the Sustainability Squad) provided them with a semi-structured online environment that they could personalise and use through the different phases of inquiry in both the school and at home.

The two focal groups conducted two inquiries: into bananas (girls' group) and cheese (boys' group), investigating the time it took for different kinds of bananas or cheese to rot in different storage conditions. The banana group compared organic packaged, organic unpackaged, value packaged and value unpackaged bananas all kept in one house, and the cheese group compared blue cheese and cheddar cheese stored in a box, in the open air and in the fridge in three different houses. The investigations started in the after-school club, where the students decided on the focus of their inquiry, the measures they would need etc. The inquiry then moved into the students' homes and the sequence of club–home–club–home continued throughout the life of the club, with students carrying on with their own inquiries in-between the weekly club sessions.

Researchers providing technical support attended the club in the school, video recording the work of two focal or case study groups, and taking field notes. One challenge for both supporting the club and collecting data was that much of the teachers' planning of the sessions was just-in-time, in line with their view that the club should differ from usual classroom work, and should be largely run by the students. In this context, therefore, we did not consider carrying out pre- and post-intervention tests of students' understanding. However, we did probe their understanding of both the inquiry process and of the domain (sustainability) in interviews, and indications were also evident in transcripts of children's dialogue in the after-school club sessions taken from the video and from the students' presentations. We also interviewed the teachers and the children's parents.

So in summary our data set includes audio, video, notes and transcriptions of:

- two focal groups during the club sessions;
- participatory design meetings held with teachers;
- post-intervention interviews with two teachers and with students in the two focal groups;
- post-intervention telephone interviews with 11 parents;
- students' work, including SI input with a record of edits.

Data analysis

Qualitative methods were used to analyse the data. We adopted a deductive approach in our analysis and drew on the NSF evaluation framework for informal science education (NSF 2008) to code data into themes. The framework includes five *impact categories* to help plan, assess and evaluate projects: knowledge, engagement, behaviour, attitudes and skills. Here, we draw upon data that probe three of these categories: engagement, attitudes and skills. *Engagement* refers to learners' engagement and interest in science, *attitudes* focuses on changes on worldviews or views about science, while *skills* refers to students' understanding of scientific content and knowledge. The other two categories were not relevant to our context and analysis as the *behaviour* category relates to projects in settings such as museums that aim to change visitors' behaviour in the long term and we did not assess changes in childrens' knowledge. In the next section we report the results of our analysis of engagement, attitudes and skills. All the quotations are from the interviews with students, parents and teachers.

Findings: engagement, attitude and skills

The maximum number that attended the club was 30. After a few weeks, there was a core of 12 students – three groups – including the two focal groups. One group stopped early because they had finished their inquiry. These young people had busy after-school lives, and discussions with them and their teachers revealed that the club meeting times clashed with other events that they wanted to attend, including school play rehearsals which many of them were enthusiastic about. It would have been difficult for them to prioritise the after-school club over the play. We therefore view the attendance of the 12 core students as a positive indicator of engagement, as they chose to attend, week after week and, in between the timetabled after-school sessions, worked on their inquiries at home.

Students in the two focal groups expressed interest, excitement and motivation to learn about issues related to food sustainability, and all the students were positive about their experience of working in a semi-formal context where they had more control and choice. For example, one said:

> I joined the club 'cause I am interested in sustainability and ... I wanted to find out and learn new things and the fact that we could choose what sort of sustainability project we did was really good.

Another student commented:

> it was fun in the aspect that we could really do what we wanted.

This suggests that, as indicated in the literature, relevance and choice were very important in this semi-formal activity.

Parents also agreed that personal interest and enthusiasm kept their children engaged in the club activities. One said:

> I was asking him whether or not he was enjoying the classes ... and he was really keen, and he was interested. And he really enjoyed the whole project... he was definitely enthusiastic about the whole club and everything... If it would have been on again he would have quite happily gone back to it.

Overall, both parents and students regarded club activities as a setting in which the students had the opportunity to experience interest and motivation to learn.

The second aspect investigated was students' attitudes. Our data suggest that students' involvement in the club activities influenced their views about sustainability and increased their empathy on issues related to food production and packaging. Students in the focal groups talked about being 'more sustainable', e.g. 'it is important to try to be sustainable and try kind of in a way not be greedy'; 'Think before you buy'; 'Get free range eggs. Buy these bananas that aren't in packaging'

Here, the children are using the term sustainable in a rather different way from the way it has been used in their inquiry projects, where they investigated whether the type of food product (e.g. organic or fair trade) and its packaging had an impact on how well it kept. Their notion of being more sustainable and 'not greedy' seems to be more concerned with how consumers can lessen the environmental impact of their shopping by buying unpackaged goods (bananas) and 'thinking' before buying. They are also perhaps concerned about animal welfare ('free range eggs').

One of the parents commented about changes in the students' thinking about purchasing:

> ... it made him think about whether or not we need things in packaging, and how long things last...

There was also an example of small changes in a student's behaviour that then influenced one of her parents. Pamela's mother has been explaining that Pamela's behaviour has changed since she has been involved in the project, and that she now takes bags from home instead of accepting bags in shops for her shopping – and then comments that she found herself also refusing a bag:

A: Ur, but if we go to any other shops, urm, we now, Pamela wanted to take any bags we had at home ...

A: Urm, and also if we go anywhere, and Pamela ever buys anything. ... If they say do you want a bag, she always says no...

A: So that's one thing I can tell you. And today we went shopping, in Clintons, and they asked if we wanted a bag, and I said no

Evidence about students' skills improving comes from interviews with them, their teachers and their parents, from their discussions and also from their presentations. In talking about what they thought they had learnt about scientific inquiry one student noted the importance of detailed planning and manipulating variables:

It is really important that you plan every little thing 'cause you have to think about how every variable is going to affect your investigation because if you get some really weird results and you don't know why...

The parents also commented that through their experience students learnt to plan and carry out scientific inquiries. 'I should think probably recording results is probably the most important side that she had to ensure she did properly.' Elaborating further she said:

You know she will have been probably set science homework, and given conditions within which to operate, and it sounds like (here) you didn't give them nearly any conditions, urm, so, yeah I suppose she'll have learnt how to set up a fair experiment, or a fair test.

What she is referring to, in saying 'you didn't give them nearly any conditions', is that the students themselves were responsible for planning their inquiry, including deciding which variables to control and measure. This is very different to their usual class-based work.

Evidence of students' understanding of how to plan a scientific inquiry was also present in their discussions around their presentations. During the last two sessions and at home, each group prepared a presentation to the other group (based on their SI entries) and the teachers asked them to design a poster that they then used to discuss their inquiries. The focus of this discussion was on reflecting on the inquiry, and making suggestion about how each group's inquiries could have been improved. For example, the group studying cheese realised that their decision to rot cheese in three different houses made their investigation unfair since temperature was not controlled and could have affected their results.

Researcher: OK and what about doing it in three different houses ... Do you think that that had any effect on your experiment?

Student: That one cheese was hotter than the other ...

Researcher: That one room was hotter than the other. Do you think that that could have affected it?

Student: 'cause at one house the heating could be on and in the other not.

Student: It would make it rot faster.

This intrusion of their real world into their efforts to be scientific and control their investigations was apparent at various times, and was one of the challenges of working in this way. For example, in deciding about distributing their inquiry work, the boys' group decided that each of them should buy one of the cheeses. When they were asked about any problems in designing the investigation Jason commented on the difficulty of buying equivalent products:

> I think it was basically trying to get them all at the same time, for the same and the same amount that was probably the hardest bit, 'cause one of us could have just bought all of it.

How the Sustainability Investigator supported the inquiries

The students used the SI to support them in defining and carrying out their inquiries across the contexts of the after-school club and home. We draw here upon examples from the two focal groups' inquiries.

During the first sessions, students entered their predictions into the appropriate free-text box in the SI (see Figure 10.1) and started to think about how to conduct their inquiries. The SI prompted students to make predictions which they shared with each other and which they were able to revisit and change. During the planning stage, an expert from our partner company Sciencescope visited the club for consultation on available equipment and on the feasibility of the students' plans. This session (week 4) was critical as it was through their discussion with each other and the expert that the students came to realise the importance of having a clearly defined plan and controlling conditions in their experiment, and they also started to realise the constraints on what they could do.

Most of the groups modified their planned inquiries as a result of their discussion with the expert. His visit prompted them to rethink and to refine their investigation plans. For example, one focal group changed their focus from decomposing beef to cheddar and blue cheese. The other focal group changed from decomposing chicken to peaches and eventually bananas. In addition, the students started thinking more deeply about fair testing, controlling variables and the feasibility of their initial plans. They also started viewing temperature and moisture as important variables that might affect rotting. One student, commenting on the 'expert's' visit, said: 'he helped us think about things that we haven't thought about before'. Practical considerations were also important in these inquiries, as the students were responsible for sourcing and obtaining the food that they used in their inquiries. Whereas with classroom inquiries, teachers would ensure that the resources were available, here it was the students' responsibility. While health and safety issues were one reason for one group changing the subject of their investigation to cheese rotting as opposed to beef, the other group were unable to buy peaches at the local supermarket and so decided to change to bananas

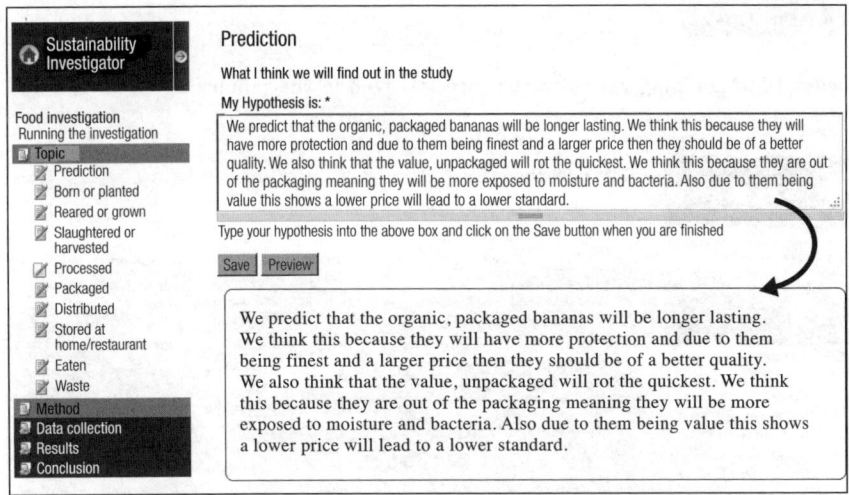

Figure 10.1 Entering a prediction into the Sustainability Investigator.

After having planned realistic and achievable inquiries, the students spent some time thinking about where they could safely carry out their inquiries and how to measure the variables involved in their investigations. They led the process of choosing the variables and measures with some support from the teachers and researchers. The SI provided students with the opportunity to specify the variables they wanted and this was then configured by the researchers in response to requests by the students and supported by their teachers, using the authoring tools in the software.

The variables were then represented in the SI as shown in Figure 10.2, which illustrates the variables created by the group who was rotting bananas.

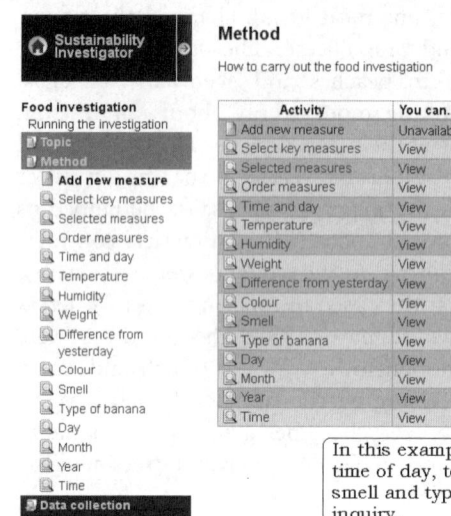

Figure 10.2 Defining variables that are involved in the inquiry.

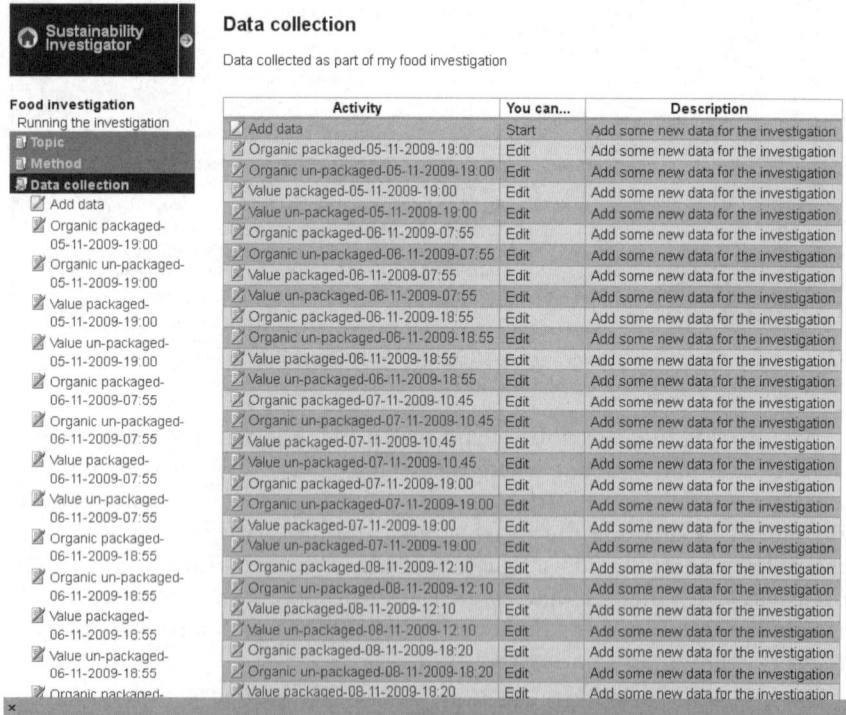

Figure 10.3 Recording data in the Sustainability Investigator.

Table 10.1 Section of Helen's data-recording on the bananas

Type	Day	Month	Yr	time	Temp	Colour	Smell	Difference
Organic packaged	06	11	2009	18:55	16.8	Yellow / Black patches	04	A bananas skin has torn and its leaking
Organic un-packaged	06	11	2009	18:55	16.8	Yellow / Black patches	04	Nothing really
Value packaged	06	11	2009	18:55	16.8	Yellow/ quite black	05	More black and squishy
Value un-packaged	06	11	2009	18:55	16.8	Yellow/ quite black	03	More black and squishy
Organic packaged	07	11	2009	10.45	16.8	Yellow / quite black	05	There are some that are really black

Table 10.2 Section of Helen's data-recording on the bananas

Type	Day	Month	Yr	time	Temp	Colour	Smell	Difference
Value un-packaged	13	11	2009	07:45	16.8	Really Black	07	Same as yesterday
Organic packaged	13	11	2009	19:30	16.8	Yellow / Very black	06	Same as yesterday
Organic un-packaged	13	11	2009	19:30	16.8	Really Black	07	Smells more
Value packaged	13	11	2009	19:30	16.8	Mostly black now	06	Same as yesterday
Value un-packaged	13	11	2009	19:30	16.8	Really Black	07	Same as yesterday

The group selected and collected data concerning the type of banana, time, temperature, weight, colour, smell and difference as their variables. The SI captured the variables that they had chosen whilst working together in the club at school. One student, Helen, kept the bananas in her house and monitored the changes as they decomposed. At home, Helen could add all her observations by going to the data collection phase in the SI. The SI shows 69 entries made over 9 days, starting in the evening with an entry for each of the four types of banana, and then for the following 8 days, four entries were made each morning and evening. Figure 10.3 shows the data collection screen, and Tables 10.1 and 10.2 show some of her observations, put into a table.

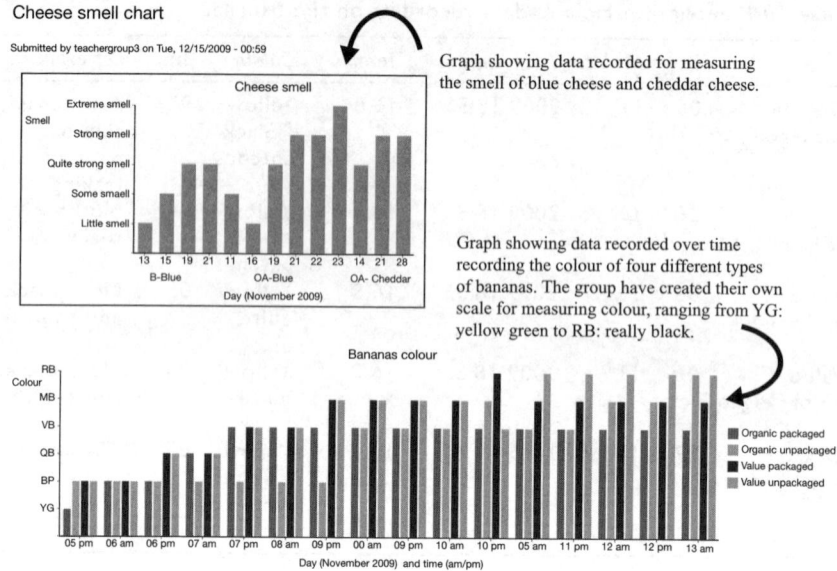

Figure 10.4 Representing data using the Sustainability Investigator.

The SI was able to support Helen's data entry at home. Entries shown in Table 10.1 include detailed descriptions such as "A bananas skin has torn and it's leaking" in the difference column, with the entries in the colour column showing little variation, whereas the colours have changed in the later entries shown in Table 10.2 .

However, the data tables also suggest some difficulties arising from the measures that the group used. For example, they chose to measure 'difference' (from yesterday), but it is not clear when 'yesterday' is (i.e. the baseline), and it is possible that data was not recorded in the SI from the very beginning.

With data collection complete, the students used the SI to create graphical representations of their data. Figure 10.4 shows examples of graphs that were created by the two focal groups in our study.

Here there are suggestions that the children may have made some errors in recording and presenting their data as the cheese chart, for example, shows the smell decreasing after its peak. However, it seems that the boys have combined their cheeses in this chart. The girls' chart for the bananas also does not give the colour codes, although some are apparent when we look at Table 10.2 and can see, for example, that MB is Mostly Black. Some aspects of the chart are odd – e.g. the banana moving from really black one day to moderately black the next. However, these bananas were in bunches and so it would have been difficult to describe their overall rotting when there were differences within the bunch.

So by representing the students' inquiry planning and supporting their data recording, the SI supported effective learning in a semi-formal setting, and was able to resource continuity between home and school. In addition, it supported them in starting to think of themselves as science learners in their own homes in the absence of teacher guidance. The SI provided students with the opportunity to engage in the process of scientific reasoning, by supporting them in manipulating, testing, exploring, observing and making sense of issues relating to sustainability in their natural and physical world. Not surprisingly, these young people also probably made some errors in recording their data – however, as we saw earlier, in doing so they learnt about the importance of detailed planning and controlling variables.

So using the SI supported the students in planning and carrying out investigations in their own homes, outside the context of the classroom and the constraints of the formal curriculum. One of the teachers commented that:

> the resources and technology gave the students the support they needed yet allowed them to remain independent in their work. Without the appropriate technology, the students would not have been able to continue with the experiments at home.

The SI was also able to support the slightly different inquiries into cheese and bananas where the children measured different variables.

Challenges

Personalisation

In the PI project, developing inquiry activities that learners found personally engaging was challenging. Some early inquiries were perceived as 'too personal' for some children, and some inquiries (e.g. Collins et al. 2008) were constrained in how much choice (personalisation) was possible by curriculum requirements. The after-school club context allowed us to investigate the process of conducting personal scientific inquiries in a semi-formal setting – and to see how well the SI could support this process. Over successive inquiries that we co-constructed and conducted with this school, the degree of choice was increased where possible, but it was only in the after-school club that the students could choose their own inquiries. As we noted in the literature review, this element of choice, giving control over the inquiry, is an important motivational factor (e.g. Keller 1987). The evidence from the after-school club is that the students who completed their enquiries were indeed engaged.

However, even in this semi-formal context, it was not possible to allow the students unfettered choice. Although the groups were initially enthusiastic about rotting meat and we discussed how we might support this (e.g. keeping meat in rat proof containers!), we concluded that health and safety precluded such inquiries. As an 'outsider', one role played by our science expert was to gently direct the students away from rotting meat. This resulted in one group deciding not to continue after they had been very enthusiastic about the idea! However, the group that moved to rotting cheese was excited by the smelliness of the cheese. Other practical but very important constraints included finding research questions/inquiries that could be supported by the available instruments, that could be carried out within the time available and that were suitable for conducting at home. So whilst the SI was successful in supporting these inquiries chosen by the learners themselves, the choice of personal inquiry will always be constrained by factors such as timescale, practicality, health and safety and the young learners' level of skills.

The semi-formal context

The very lack of formality – and nature of the sessions that allowed the students the freedom to develop their own inquiries – also had disadvantages. For example, the students were volunteers and were already motivated by the idea of the club, so this type of club might not benefit hard to reach students. Another disadvantage is that the fluctuating attendance affected both the continuity of the inquiries and the consistency of group membership. However, the SI was able to support the continuity by keeping track of what students had done and reminding them (and informing new group members) where they were in the inquiry process.

Other challenges of this semi-formal setting emerged during the early planning sessions. The teachers were keen that the after-school club should be fun and should not closely resemble the way that the students worked in school. This differentiating between normal 'classtime' work and after-school club activities meant that they (like us) wanted the club activities to be student-led. They felt that teacher input should be minimal – it was up to the children to decide how they proceeded. So whilst the teachers strongly led the first two sessions, they increasingly took a back-seat role. In practice, whilst the students were enthusiastic, planning inquiries that were realistic and achievable in the time period was challenging. The time that the teachers had available lessened as the term progressed and other curriculum activities had to take priority. Their planning was more limited and often on a weekly basis rather than having an overall plan for the term's work – and objectives were less clear than they had been in curriculum-based inquiries.

Technology

For the children, the technology itself, as well as the activities, was appealing. They brought in their netbooks every week, as requested, but they were also distracted by them. At times they played games and visited favourite websites during the club sessions, and the teachers had to ask them to close their netbooks. Whilst the size and mobility of the netbooks supported their use across the school–home context, there were problems at times with connecting to the wireless network in both locations. (The netbooks were initially configured to auto-boot to the school configuration). The research team was able to help them at school but not directly at home. Whilst some students connected successfully in the end, some students did not manage this and others adapted to their home conditions (e.g. using wired connections when wireless connections could not be established).

To summarise, choice of inquiry was an important factor in the students' engagement. The students' inquiries were distributed between the after-school club, where the groups came together to plan their inquiries and to discuss, share and reflect on their findings, and the students' homes where the children collected and recorded their data. The SI was able to resource this to-ing and fro-ing where the process was distributed between different contexts, and between groups and individuals. However, we also noted a number of challenges and trade-offs around the choice of inquiry, the semi-formal nature of the context and the technology itself.

Conclusion

In our brief review earlier, it was noted that most technologies developed to support science investigations support a particular study or application, such as birdwatching (Chen, et al. 2003). Working with the after-school club confirmed that nQuire was not only able to support inquiries in a semi-formal context, when there was no teacher support (when the students worked at home), but also that it could support a limited range of different personal inquiries. These inquiries were distributed between work at school and at home. As nQuire is web-based, and in our trials implemented on small netbooks, students were able to carry it around with them, referring to it in whichever context they were in. In this way, it provided a support for: the process of the inquiry; student choice; a representation of a jointly negotiated, personalised version of inquiry; defining the inquiry; providing a shared focus; and for bridging the contexts of school and home. In addition, it resources cognitive engagement in data interpretation and representation, and stores individuals' contributions to group activities so that group members can be kept up to date. Thus it enabled students to make connections between, and to build on, the information they had gathered in physical and virtual contexts.

Given the increasing rise and importance of science inquiry learning in a range of less formal settings, it is important to understand more about both how students learn in such settings and about how such learning can be supported by technology, yet these contexts have had less attention to date. We hope that the study into inquiry learning described here is one step in increasing our understanding of such settings.

References

Ainley, J., Kos, J. and Nicholas, M. (2008) 'Participation in Science, Mathematics and Technology' in *Australian Education, ACER Research Monograph No 63*, Australian Council for Educational Research. Available at: http://www.dest.gov.au/NR/rdonlyres/46D7FF05–BB9D-4731–A21B-792F2D2E0D8F/24467/ParticipationSMTFINALResMon63Report.pdf (accessed 22 November 2010)

Banks, J. A., Au, K. H., Ball, A. F., Bell, P., Gordon, E. W., Gutiérrez, K., Heath, S. B., et al. (2007) *Learning In and Out of School in Diverse Environments: lifelong, life-wide, life-deep.* Seattle: Center for Multicultural Education, University of Washington.

Bevan, B, Michalchik, V., Bhanot, R., Rauch, N. Remold, J., Semper, R. and Shields, P. M. (2010) Report of conference on: 'Out-of-School Time STEM: Building Experience, Building Bridges: Trends, Questions, and Findings from the Field, Exploratorium, San Francisco. Available at: http://cils.exploratorium.edu/resource_shared/downloads/4378/STEM_OST_Conf_Report.pdf, Accessed 5 October 2011

Briseno-Garzon, A., Anderson, D. and Anderson, A. (2007) 'Adult learning experiences from an aquarium visit: the role of social interaction in family groups', *Curator, 50* (3), 299–318.

Burbules, C. (2006) 'Self-educating communities: collaboration and learning through the internet', in Z. Bekerman, N. C. Burbules, and D. Silberman-Keller, (eds) (2006) *Learning in Places: the informal education reader*, New York: Peter Lang.

Chapman, S and Smith, A (2007) *School Science Review*, December 2007, 89 (327)

Chen, Y., Kao, T. and Sheu, J. (2003) 'A mobile learning system for scaffolding bird watching learning', *Journal of Computer Assisted Learning*, 19 (3): 347–359

Chen, Y., Kao, T., Yu, G. and Sheu, J. (2004) 'A mobile butterfly-watching learning system for supporting independent learning', in: *Proceedings of the 2nd IEEE International Workshop on Wireless and Mobile Technologies in Education.* JungLi, Taiwan: IEEE Computer Society, 11–18.

Collins, T., Gaved, M., Mulholland, P., Kerawalla., C., Twiner, A., Scanlon, E., Jones, A., Littleton, K., Conole, G. and Tosunoglu, C. (2008) 'Supporting location-based inquiry learning across school, field and home contexts'. Paper presented at MLearn, Telford.

Cook, J., Pachler, N. and Bradley, C. (2008) 'Bridging the gap? Mobile phones at the interface between informal and formal learning', *Journal of the Research Center for Educational technology*, 13 (1): 3–18.

Dierking, L. D. (1991) 'Learning theories and learning style. An overview'. *Journal of Museum Education*, 16(x): 4–6.

Eshach, H. (2007) 'Bridging In-school and Out-of-school Learning: Formal, Non-Formal, and Informal Education'. *Journal of Science Education and Technology*, 16(2): 171–190.

Frohberg, D., Goth, C. and Schwabe, G (2009) 'Mobile Learning projects – a critical analysis of the state of the art', *Journal of Computer Assisted Learning*, 25: 307–331.

Hofstein, A. and Rosenfeld, S. (1996) 'Bridging the gap between formal and informal science learning', *Studies in Science Education*, 28: 87–112.

Ivanova, E. (2003) 'Changes in collective memory: The schematic narrative template of victimhood in Kharkiv museums', *Journal of Museum Education, 2 8* (1): 17–22.

Keller, J. M. (1987) 'Strategies for stimulating the motivation to learn', *Performance and Instruction*, 26 (8): 1–7.

Laursen, S., Liston, C., Thiry, H. and Graf, J. (2007) 'What good is a scientist in the classroom? Participant outcomes and program design features for a short-duration science out reach intervention in K-12 classrooms', *CBE-Life Sciences Education*, 6 (1): 49–64.

Livingstone, D. (1999) 'Exploring the Icebergs of Adult Learning: Findings of the first

Canadian Survey of Informal Learning Practices', *Canadian Journal for the Study of Adult Education*, 13 (2): 49–72.

Livingstone, D. (2006) 'Informal Learning: conceptual distinctions and preliminary findings', in Z. Bekerman, N. C. Burbules and D. Silberman-Keller (eds) (2006) *Learning in Places: the informal education reader*. New York: Peter Lang.

National Research Council. (1996) *National Science Education Standards*. National Committee on Science Education Standards and Assessment, Washington, D.C: National Academy Press.

National Research Council (2009) 'Learning Science in Informal Environments: People, Places, and Pursuits'. Committee on Learning Science in Informal Environments, in P. Bell, B. Lewenstein, A. Shouse and M. Feder (eds) *Board on Science Education, Center for Education. Division of Behavioral and Social Sciences and Education*, Washington, D.C: The National Academies Press.

National Science Foundation (2008) *Framework for Evaluating Impacts of Informal Science Education Projects*. Available at: http://caise.insci.org/resources/Eval_Framework.pdf (accessed July 2010).

Osborne, J. F. and Collins, S. (2000) *Pupils' and Parents' Views of the School Science Curriculum*, London: King's College London

Rennie, L. J., and Howitt, C. (2009) *Science has changed my life!: Evaluation of the Scientists in Schools Project (A report prepared for CSIRO.)* Canberra, Australia: Department of Education, Employment and Workplace Relations. Available at: http://www.scientists inschools.edu. au/evaluation.htm (accessed 25 November 2010)

Rosenfeld, S. (2004) 'Waltzing with the Muses: How Might Computer Technology Help Bridge the Gap between Formal and Informal Science Learning', in S. Sotiriou (ed) *Proceedings of the International Symposium on Advanced Technologies in Education*, Kefalonia, Greece, 4–6 July.

Sharples, M., Collins, T., Feißt,M., Gaved, M., Mulholland P., Paxton, M and Wright, M. A (2011) '"Laboratory of Knowledge-Making" for Personal Inquiry Learning', in *Proceedings of the Artificial Intelligence in Education (AIED) 2011 Conference*, Auckland, New Zealand, 28 June- 1 July, pp.312–319.

Stocklmayer, S. M., Leonie, S. J. and Gilbert, J. K. (2010) 'The role of the formal and informal sectors in the provision of effective science education', *Studies in Science Education*, 46 (1):1–44.

Uzunboylu, H., Cavus, N., and Ercag, E. (2009) 'Using mobile learning to increase environmental awareness', *Computers and Education,* 52 (2): 381–389.

Vavoula, G. (2004) 'KLeOS: *A Knowledge and Learning Organisation System in Support of Lifelong Learning*. Unpublished Thesis (PhD), University of Birmingham.

Index